The European Left: Italy, France, and Spain

Edited by
William E. Griffith
Massachusetts Institute of
Technology

LexingtonBooks
D.C. Heath and Company
Lexington, Massachusetts
Toronto

Library of Congress Cataloging in Publication Data

Main entry under title:

The European Left: Italy, France, and Spain.

1. Communism—Italy—Addresses, essays, lectures. 2. Socialism in Italy—Addresses, essays, lectures. 3. Communism—France—Addresses, essays, lectures. 4. Socialism in France—Addresses, essays, lectures. 5. Communism—Spain—Addresses, essays, lectures. 6. Socialism in Spain—Addresses, essays, lectures. I. Griffith, William E.
HX238.5.E88   335.43'094   79–7711
ISBN 0–669–03199–2

Second printing, December 1980

Published simultaneously in Canada

Printed in the United States of America

International Standard Book Number: 0–669–03199–2

Library of Congress Catalog Card Number: 79–7711

Contents

Preface

This volume is the result of a conference on the left in Latin Europe which was held at the Bologna Center of the School for Advanced International Studies, The Johns Hopkins University, on September 14–16, 1978. The conference was sponsored jointly by the Center for International Studies of the Massachusetts Institute of Technology, the Center for European Studies of Harvard University, the Bundesinstitut für ostwissenschaftliche Studien in Cologne, and the Istituto Affari Internazionale in Rome. It was made possible by generous grants to the Center for International Studies, MIT, by the German Marshall Fund and to the Bundesinstitut by the Volkswagen-stiftung. The conference was designed to bring together American and European specialists and political figures interested in and active in the Latin left in addition to the authors of the papers. It was the result of a small planning meeting held at the Center for International Studies, MIT, in March 1977, also made possible by the German Marshall Fund, in which the participants were Donald Blackmer, Suzanne Berger, and myself (MIT), Stanley Hoffman and Peter Lange (Harvard University), Robert Legvold (then Tufts University, now Council on Foreign Relations), Joan Urban (Catholic University), Ronald Tiersky (Amherst College), Pierre Hassner (Fondation nationale des sciences politiques, Paris), and Heinz Timmermann (Bundesinstitut, Cologne). Aside from the writers of this book, who presented papers at the Bologna conference, its other participants were Pierre Hassner (Paris), Kevin Devlin (RFE Munich), Stanley Hoffman and Peter Lange (Harvard), Leo Mates (Belgrade), Gerard Fuchs (PS, Paris), José María Maravalle (PSOE, Madrid), Giorgio Napolitano and Giuseppe Boffa (PCI, Rome), and Professors Wilfrid Kohl, Patrick McCarthy, and Giancarlo Pasquino of the Johns Hopkins Center. I am most grateful to the German Marshall Fund and its president, Robert Gerald Livingston; to the Volkswagenstiftung; to the Bundesinstitut and particularly its director, Dr. Heinrich Vogel, and Drs. Wolfgang Berner and Heinz Timmermann; and to the Istituto Affari Internazionale and particularly its director, Professor Cesare Merlini, and Dr. Stefano Silvestri for their great help and support in organizing the conference. The conference would not have been successful without the willingness of the Bologna Center and particularly its director, Prof. Wilfred Kohl, to act as its host. Their hospitality, and the ambience of Bologna, were faultless.

I have been greatly helped by discussions with my colleague Suzanne Berger, in editing by my research assistant, John Van Oudenaren, and by my secretary, Suzy Zipkin, who retyped much of the manuscript. I am also grateful to the Earhart Foundation for general research support.

William E. Griffith

1

Introduction: The Left in France, Italy, and Spain

William E. Griffith

Much has been written about "Eurocommunism," less about "Eurosocialism," and even less about the West European left *tout entière*. This book analyzes the left in the three Latin European countries, France, Italy, and Spain, where it is of great political and economic importance.[1]

Particularly in the United States, the expectation, and often the fear, that the West European left, or even the West European Communists, will come to power has recently considerably diminished. It is therefore the more appropriate to study it now as a phenomenon and a policy problem.

One methodological point first of all: I seriously question the use of the current clichés "Eurocommunism" and "Eurosocialism." In the case of the former, the policies of the French Communist party (PCF) are by now in almost all respects markedly different from those of the Italian (PCI) and Spanish (PCE) Communist parties—if not always in theory, as in the case of parliamentarianism, then at least in practice. The French and Spanish Socialist parties are large while the Italian is small. All three are different in theory and practice from the two major governing social democratic parties in Western Europe, the West German Social Democratic party (SPD) and the British Labour party. "Eurocommunism" and "Eurosocialism," as these terms are usually used, therefore conceal reality more than they illuminate it. I shall therefore put "Eurocommunism" in quotation marks and use it to refer almost exclusively to the PCI and the PCE.

Until its defeat in the March 1978 French parliamentary elections, it seemed that the left was on the threshold of power in Latin Europe. The Italian Communists, the Spanish Socialists, and the French Socialists and Communists all seemed to be on the way to forming governments or at least to participating in them to a major degree. I shall begin, therefore, by outlining why the Latin left was rising before I turn to why it has so far not succeeded in taking over, or participating in, power.

First, left-wing parties historically usually gain votes when the economic situation worsens, as it has since the quadrupling of oil prices subsequent the 1973 Middle Eastern war. The result has been stagflation in much of Europe, the more serious in exactly those Latin countries which have no domestic energy resources and where exports have not compensated for increased oil imports, as they have in West Germany. The previous period of affluence, which generally had enfeebled the left, made the contrast, and therefore the gain for the left, even greater. And stagflation breeds political mobilization and discredits parties in power.

1

Second, the Latin right had been long in power. It was tired, often corrupt, discredited by Francoism in Spain, bereft of de Gaulle in France, and harassed by scandal and terrorism in Italy. For most Latin intellectuals, the right wing had also been discredited by its collaboration with the Nazis in World War II. They have thus generally been leftist in sympathy, a trend which intensified in the 1970s.

Third, rapid modernization and the consequent intensification of political and social mobilization favored the left. The Roman Catholic Church in Latin Europe is weaker, less integralist, and thus less of a barrier to the rise of the left. Fourth, the perceived decline of the cold war, resulting from East-West détente, made the Latin non-Communist left less likely to be polarized against the Soviet Union. The Latin Communists also profited from détente, because they were thereby less tarred by association with the warlike Soviet Union and therefore more able to recover a nationalist or seminationalist image. Fifth, affluence produced an intellectual, professional, and service sector of Latin society, many of whom rejected centralized, stratified, bureaucratic, consumerist, affluent West European society in favor of an attempt to return to "community" (*Gemeinschaft*), in the hope of recovering its cohesive, decentralized, egalitarian values. This trend, which surfaced dramatically in the May 1968 Paris demonstrations, combined the Latin heritage of utopian socialism and anarcho-syndicalism with the ecological and antinuclear movements and other aspects of the New Left, the results of the "alienation of affluence." It began and reached its peak *before* the post-1973 stagflation. It left behind it a New Left sensibility, a taste for extreme left-wing radicalism, and the ideology of workers' self-administration, often known by the French term *autogestion. Autogestion* has become one of the principal goals of French socialism today. It combines the heritage of French anarcho-syndicalism, the attraction of this aspect of Yugoslav communism, and the current leftist enthusiasm for decentralization and communitarianism.

The attitude of the Latin working classes toward such issues as *autogestion,* ecology, and "no growth" is complex. The Communist parties have generally opposed them, for most workers regard ecology and "no growth" as fads of the affluent, while the Communist leaders see *autogestion* as a threat to their own control of industry in a left-wing government. Yet for many workers *autogestion* is a way of increasing their own power and lessening that of the capitalists. And for the intellectual, professional, and student strata *autogestion* provides a utopian "third road" between western capitalism and eastern bureaucratic socialism: the last best hope of a new, "pure" socialism.

There are other political reasons for the recent rise of the Latin left. It is primarily working class-based. The Latin left-wing parties, Communists as well as Socialists, have understood that the revolutionary road to power is closed to them for the foreseeable future and that therefore they are unlikely to come to power unless they can attract a significant proportion of the middle-class vote, and that to do so they must move toward reformism. The reasons why they have done so are thus the same ones which drove the pre-1914 German Social Democrats in the same direction. Both of them moved with the same slowness, reluctance, and evolution of practice first and theory later.

Thus primarily domestic compulsions, not foreign policy developments, pushed the Latin left toward reformism. This move was earlier and more rapid in Italy, much more recent in Spain because of the duration of Franco's *caudillismo,* and last of all among the French Socialists, who, exceptionally, moved toward the left, and the French Communists, who moved the most slowly and the least toward the right.

Foreign policy developments also played a significant role in improving the Latin left's electoral image. One of these was their increasing distance from, and criticism of, Soviet and East European policies. Two West European tendencies also favored this trend: the tarnished image of West European unity and the rise of West European nationalism. As Western Europe became stronger, it became more nationalistic, less dependent on and influenced by the United States, and also less attracted to, and less fearful of, the Soviet Union. The massive Soviet nuclear and conventional military buildup in Europe did not reverse this trend, for the signature in the early 1970s of SALT I, the German treaties, and the Conference on Security and Cooperation in Europe (CSCE) final declaration intensified East–West détente in Europe and thus diminished fear of the Soviet Union.

The Soviet Union also declined rapidly as an attractive model of anything except military power. This decline centered among intellectuals, notably in Paris, and its influence spread from there throughout Latin Europe. It reflected the Latin left's disillusionment as Moscow crushed its hopes, which it had once had, of liberalization and reform in the Soviet Union and Eastern Europe. Moscow's crushing of the Hungarian Revolution in 1956 was the first major impetus of this disillusionment. The Soviet invasion of Czechoslovakia in 1968 was the second and more severe one. Brezhnev's increasing domestic repression, in contrast to Khrushchev's erratic and partial tolerance of the "thaw," brought imprisonment, consignment to insane asylums, and exile to Siberia to many Soviet dissidents. Rising anti-Semitism in the Soviet Union plus the 1967 Middle Eastern war revived Zionism there and intensified Soviet repression of it. Then, because western indignation about this repression rose, Moscow allowed enough dissident intellectuals to leave so that their horror stories of the repression, which intensified the greater impact of Solzhenitsyn's *Gulag,* took hold in Western Europe. Moreover, any attractiveness of the Soviet model of technological modernization was destroyed by massive Soviet imports of western and Japanese technology and of U.S. grain. Finally, those Latin Communists who had believed in Soviet-led "proletarian internationalism" lost their faith in it under the blows of the Sino-Soviet split, the Mao-Nixon rapprochement, the Soviet-American agreements, and, most recently, the Vietnamese invasion of Cambodia and the Chinese invasion of Vietnam. By now, for the great majority of the Latin left the Soviet Union is no longer the future they once dreamed of but a repressive, imperialist, backward state whose military power they fear: not a model but an antimodel of socialism.

The Latin left has for some time been returning to the traditional political aims, strategies, and tactics of the traditional national leftist parties and to much of the historic political cultures. This process began the earliest with the PCI, much later with the Spanish Socialist Worker's Party (PSOE), and started late in the PCF, only to be partially reversed at the twenty-third PCF Congress in May 1979. The Italian left is pro-European and so is the Spanish; the French left is somewhat indecisive (PS) or hostile (PCF). The Italian and Spanish left is less anti-American and would like Washington to be less against it; the French left, especially the PCF, is anti-American and anti-West German. Indeed, at a time when Giscard and some of the moderate French center and right have moved toward a partnership with Bonn and rapprochement with Washington, the French left is "Gaullosocialist" and "Gaullocommunist."

Has the Latin left passed the peak of its power? If so, why? Although it has made major gains among the bourgeoisie, they have not been enough for it to grasp power, or even to participate in it. The principal reason, in my view, is that the Latin left has not been reformist enough and therefore has not appealed to enough of the new voters and the non-working-class floating vote to put it in power. The bourgeoisie's understandable fear of a major economic crisis if the left came to power, brought about by capital flight and ending in currency collapse and autarky, remains great. For the Latin countries cannot individually or collectively isolate or insulate themselves from the other Organization for Economic Cooperation and Development (OECD) economies and from the need for U.S., Japanese, and West German economic aid—and none of these three has confidence in the Latin left. Indeed, given the ever-rising economic power of West Germany, neither prosperity nor independence for West Europe can be attained and preserved without its active participation—and this would be at a price that little of the Latin left would like or would even be willing to pay.

Whether the Latin left has passed its peak we do not and cannot know. We can only say, in 1979, that it is still out of power. Moreover, while the Labour party has been replaced by the Conservatives in Great Britain, the SPD is stronger than it was two years ago, while the Christian Democratic Union/Christian Social Union alliance (CDU/CSU) is in a leadership crisis. The French left, sharply split, seems unlikely to gain power for at least a decade to come. In 1979 the Spanish Socialists lost another parliamentary election and later their party leader, Gonzalez, resigned, but only temporarily, when he was defeated at a party congress in his attempt to remove "Marxist" from the party vocabulary. The Italian Communists ceased to support the Christian Democratic government at a time when public opinion polls showed that they would probably lose, not gain, votes in the next election. The elections did in fact result in a 4 percent loss (over the 1976 elections) for the PCI, the first setback it had suffered in a national election since 1948, and one which was larger than had been expected throughout the campaign. The PCI losses, which were particularly heavy in the south and among youth, made it a virtual certainty that the PCI would not enter the government. But even if, which is unlikely, the PSOE were to form a government in Spain and the PCI were to participate in one headed by the Christain Democratic party (DC) in Italy, still France, West Germany, and Great Britain, the three most important West European countries, would be under conservative or social democratic rule. Thus the Latin left is not likely to become a major factor in European or global politics in the near future.

This also seems now to be the general perception in the United States and Western Europe. And this perception is itself an important political reality. When one remembers how much talk there was about "Eurocommunism" in 1977 and early 1978, and how it has almost become an "unissue" since the French left's March 1978 defeat, one can see in retrospect that "Eurocommunism" and "Europe going left" have turned out to be overdrawn "threats" indeed. On the other hand, in addition to the usual dangers of prediction in politics, there is another looming factor which may give the Latin left something of a new lease on life: the intensification of stagflation likely in Europe (and in the USA and Japan) as a result of the Iranian crisis and the probable forthcoming global excess of oil demand over supply.

Having sketched the present situation of the Latin left, let us turn to a more detailed consideration of its drift toward reformism. One must first of all repeat the first qualification which this statement requires: this is far more true in Italy and Spain than in France.

The Latin left has not been weak enough to fall into sectarianism but it has not been strong enough to come to power by either revolutionary and electoral means. Revolution became increasingly unrealistic and by now out of the question. The Latin Communist parties, once the cold war was on in earnest, could not realistically expect to come to power by Soviet help, political, revolutionary, or military. The same cold war threw the Communists out of government in France and Italy and split the Socialists, turning the French Socialists, and some of the Italian Socialists, against them.

The key factor in pushing the Latin left toward reformism was the rising prosperity of Western Europe and its association, in the minds of so many voters, with the Catholic center–right parties. These same parties were also closely associated with anti–Soviet and anti–Communist policies. When opportunity replaced frustration, reformism was born again.

As I have remarked above, the parallels to the growth of reformism in Socialist parties around the turn of the century, notably the German SPD, are striking indeed.

Yet there are great differences among the Latin left in this respect, some going back even to the turn of the century. The historical and ideological traditions of Latin communism, socialism, and social democracy are, like the three Latin countries themselves, different from each other and from those of the northern European left, notably the SPD. Anarchism, anar-cho–syndicalism, different intensities and degrees of pervasiveness of nationalism, and more flexible Marxist ideology (for example, Labriola and Jaurès) made the Latin left susceptible to right and left "deviations" from Kautskyist Marxist orthodoxy.

Let us take Italy as the most useful place to begin, for it is a country where the left began to change first, has changed the most, and where a Communist party has the best chance of sharing power. The traditions of Labriola and Gramsci gave Italian communism a different, less sterile, intellectually more appealing, and politically more moderate ideology than was the case in France or Spain. Its repression under Mussolini and its major role in the *Resistenza* gave it political legitimacy: the PCI is thought by most Italians to be the most left Italian political party, not a group of Russian agents. Italian socialism's split and the flexibility of the PCI made it, uniquely in Western Europe, far more powerful than either Socialist party or both. The smaller majority Socialist party, the PSI, was not social democratic and the Italian Social Democratic party (PDSI), which was, was far smaller still.

As soon as he returned from Moscow in 1944, Togliatti adopted a long-term, gradualist, parliamentary strategy for coming to power. His support of Soviet policy during the cold–war period was calculated but reluctant. As soon as he felt able, beginning briefly in 1956 but clearly after 1959, he turned toward a more autonomist course. After 1968, when it condemned the Soviet invasion of Czechoslovakia, the PCI was primarily identified in Italy with Italian rather than Soviet interests. By the late 1970s it endorsed not only West European unity but NATO as well. Yet it did not intend to sever party relations with Moscow and it continued to support Soviet for-eign policy on almost all but European issues.

Spanish socialism and communism today were forged in the under-ground and exile struggle against Franco. They were therefore by practice as well as by tradition radical, for the radicalizing effect of the Civil War was further intensified by the struggle against Franco thereafter. Indeed, it was the failure of this struggle as long as Franco lived, the moderating impact on Spanish political life of the surviving memories of the Civil War and the intense determination to avoid a repetition of its slaughter, and, finally, the prosperity in which by the late 1970s Spain lived which moved the PSOE and PCE toward reformism. Spain is traditionally a nationalist country and the PCE was still tarred by its abjectly pro–Soviet policies during the Civil War and the long years of exile and underground thereafter. The PSOE, on the other hand, in the mid–1970s had its sclerotic exile leadership replaced by a young, dynamic, and flexible one from within the country. Finally, the skill in maneuvering of King Juan Carlos and his second prime minister, Adolfo Suárez, gave the PSOE and the PCE all the opportunities and all the disincentives necessary to push them toward a more moderate, and for the PCE a more nationalist, course.

The French left, like France itself, is very different. France has always believed itself to be the natural political and cultural center and leader of Europe. It alone has a truly Jacobin left tradition: a revolutionary nationalism of the left. It alone was long dominated by a *Résistance* leader of the nationalist center–right, General de Gaulle. It alone now has a Socialist party (PS) which is stronger than the Communists. The PS combines left socialism and *autogestion,* intellectuals, the service classes, and some workers, and, like the Gaullists and the Communists, is suspicious of the United States. Indeed, one of the many reasons why the unity of the French left has never really occurred is that the PS is so much a creature—the only one in Western Europe—of the intellectual and service strata ("postindustrial" is the fashionable cliché, but I am skeptical of its usefulness), while the PCF is still the party of the encapsulated, alienated, *ouvrièriste* working class. It is not surprising, therefore, that the PCF could not accept the probability of the PS's being stronger than it if the left won, and that it therefore finally preferred to lose rather than to win. By now the PCF is autonomist vis-a-vis the Soviet Union, that is, it neither breaks with Moscow nor obeys its general line. It is also anti–United States, anti–West German, and anti–EEC—that is, "Gaullo-Communist." Finally, in its May 1979 twenty-third Congress, Georges Marchais led it back to a harder-line policy and one less critical of the Soviet Union. The PS, still reeling from the shock of defeat, remains caught in a struggle between Mauroy and Rocard on the one hand and the aging Mitterand on the other.

Had the French left won the March 1978 parliamentary elections, France today would be in economic crisis, Western European unity set back, monetary unity out of the question, and West Germany the most powerful state in Western Europe. But because the left lost, and because the Gaullists are weakened, Giscard's position now seems unchallenged, his relations with Chancellor Helmut Schmidt are closer than ever, the European Monetary System (EMS), which he and Schmidt sponsored, has gone into effect, and, ironically enough, Western Europe, led by Giscard and Schmidt, is taking a more independent attitude toward the United States: exactly what the French left declared that it would do itself! Thus one once again sees the continuity of French politics.

It is difficult for English-speaking readers, unless they are steeped in the culture of Latin Europe, to rate highly enough the role of intellectuals there—one far greater than in the Anglo-Saxon world. And while in the United States and Great Britain the general political stance of most intellectuals is on the left, this is far more so in Latin Europe. Indeed, implementing Gramsci's doctrine of *egemonia,* the PCI has long worked to bring Italian intellectuals to its side, and it has in large part succeeded. In France one of the leading traditions of intellectuals is *pas d'ennemis à gauche.* For this reason, out of the French Jacobin nationalism of which it is a part, and of the leftist tradition of the *Résistance,* post-World War II French intellectuals were overwhelmingly leftist. This prolonged their engagement in and sympathy for the Soviet Union and Eastern Europe and their reluctance to condemn, for example, the Soviet suppression of the Hungarian Revolution.

But what had drawn French intellectuals, Communist, Socialist, and free-floating leftist, to the East was essentially their emotional rejection of bourgeois society in France and of "Americanization," that is, of mass culture, which downgraded the aristocratic, elitist role which French intellectuals have always seen it legitimate for them to play. The Vietnamese and Algerian wars added to this revolution against French colonialism. Thus Ho Chi Minh and Castro, and for a time Mao, other available and attractive idols, replaced Moscow leaders in their pantheon.

In Paris, Rome, and Madrid the double impact of the Soviet suppression of the Prague spring and of the influx of stories, often personally told by émigrés, about Soviet repression finally cured most Latin intellectuals of what Raymond Aron had so correctly—and so long ago—called the "opium of the intellectuals." The publication of Solzhenitsyn's *Gulag Archipelago* was the final blow for many—certainly for those *nouveaux philosophes* who have recently had such a *succès d'estime* in Paris. Today in Paris, and if not today then tomorrow in the other Latin countries of Europe, intellectuals are no longer pro-Soviet and many are increasingly becoming anti-Soviet. This trend reinforces the other reasons why the French, Italian, and Spanish Communists have kept their distance from the Soviet Union. Yet the anti-Americanism and pro-"third worldism" of leftist Latin intellectuals still make it all the easier for these Communist parties to continue to endorse Soviet foreign policies, particularly outside Europe.

Many West European intellectuals have always had a certain fondness for the "two and one-half International"—something which keeps alive their belief in socialism while condemning or at least not endorsing its Soviet realization. Yugoslavia has been one post-1948 *locus classicus* of this attraction, although for many, including Jean-Paul Sartre, Cuba and Vietnam were for a while even more appealing. Yugoslavia has one aspect, *autogestion,* which has become particularly attractive to Latin European intellectuals, students, and some workers. Why?

If communism is identified with Soviet bureaucracy and social democracy with capitalist bureaucracy, if one believes that small is beautiful, and if one retains from Marxism the belief in the virtue, ability, and centrality of the working class, *autogestion* offers, it would seem, the perfect new dream. This is the more so in Latin Europe, where the traditions of anarchism and anarcho-syndicalism, although no longer embodied in significant political movements, still persist. And the rapid rate of industrialization, technological progress, and therefore inevitably greater complexity of society in post-1945 Latin Europe intensified its appeal. *Autogestion*, developed in Paris, has become the most distinctive ideology of the PS. (It is also popular in the PSOE and the PSI.) The Communist parties have been generally hostile to them, as Lenin was and the Soviet Union still is, for *autogestion* would destroy the leading role of the Communist party. However, the PCI and PCE have made some mildly favorable statements on the subject.

Whether one thinks *autogestion* practical or not (but Engels and Marx certainly did not) it is clearly a Sorelian myth in the French Socialist left. In political terms, it is another barrier to reconciliation between the PCF and the PS—although, even without it, there are plenty of other barriers to prevent that.

The rest of the reformist ideology—as opposed to *autogestion*—of the Latin left is in my view transitional, that is, it is unlikely to stay where it is now. Rather, it will probably move more in the direction of social democracy or, less likely, go backward toward Leninism. This has been the course of reformism in the past, and the presumption should therefore be that it will continue to be so. Second, unless there is a major economic crisis in Western Europe, the impetus of affluence toward reformism will also continue. Third, while ideology normally comes after practice, as for example when Bernstein wrote after de facto SPD revisionism had arisen in Imperial Germany, once the ideology does appear it acquires a force of its own. One can see this with Carrillo's *Eurocommunism and the State:* as long as he or people like him remain in control of the PCE, the party is unlikely to reject the ideology in his book, and, particularly, younger cadres are likely to be attracted to it. Finally, while it seems to me unlikely that the Latin Communists will break with the Soviet Union, the continued tension between them and Moscow will probably push at least the PCI and PCE to define more clearly their reformist views.

The ideological and political development of the Socialists (as opposed to social democrats) is more difficult to divine because more inchoate.

Basically, the same reformist trends are at work. The competition with the increasingly reformist Communists intensifies them. The younger leaders and cadre, more flexible than their elders, intensify them. One may of course argue that the contrary is occurring in the PS, and that is still true. Yet its left wing, the Center for Socialist Study and Research (CERES), is itself factionalized, and in the long run, after its defeat, it is likely also to become more subject to reformist pressures.

Another reason why the Latin Socialists are tending toward reformism is the influence on them, within the revitalized Socialist International, of the social democratic parties, notably the SPD. Conversely, because the Latin Communists have become more reformist and the PS more leftist and *autogestionnaire,* there is also another tendency in the opposite direction. Moreover, that the Italian and Spanish leftist parties are pro–EEC, while the PCF is anti–, does not mean that the former are pro–American. On the contrary, they hope that the EEC can become an independent Western Europe, if not equidistant between Moscow and Washington, then at least an equal and not too warm ally of the United States. In any case, Communist-Socialist convergence in Western Europe seems even less likely than their coming to power.

Not only have the Latin Communists not broken with the Soviets but the Soviets have not broken with them. If, as seems likely, this uneasy coexistence continues, we will really have entered a new era of inter–Communist relations: neither allegiance nor expulsion, "neither peace nor war." In this context, the 1976 East Berlin Communist conference, as much as the Soviets have been denying it, was not only a watershed but in fact the most convincing signal of this new era. The recent Indochinese imbroglio is likely, in my view, to lengthen rather than shorten this new phase. Insofar as this new phase stabilizes itself, the great unknown in Soviet–European Communist relations will again become Yugoslavia after Marshal Tito. For in the international Communist world the West European Communists need the Yugoslavs and Romanians as allies against Soviet pressure just as much as the latter need them. The Indochinese imbroglio has had one other effect: it has so divided the West European Communists amoung themselves and vis-à-vis the Yugoslavs and Romanians that any "Eurocommunist unity" has become even more of a myth. Rather, we are faced, and are likely to continue to be faced, with shifting, complex coalitions and varying degrees of coolness vis-à-vis the Soviet Union.

Finally, western, and particularly American policy. I find Prof. Löwenthal's analysis rare in that it throws more light than heat on the controversy. I do not, however, entirely agree with his policy proposals. That the West European governments and the United States would prefer that the Communists not enter western governments seems to me both obvious and in principle desirable. This is true, particularly for the United States, not primarily because they are "Communists"—as indeed, *grosso modo,* they still are—but because of their foreign policies. (That their domestic policies and those of socialists allied with them and dependent on the alliance, would bring economic crisis and therefore hurt the OECD economies altogether is true but also not the primary western policy problem.) It is, rather, that with the exception of the PCI and PCE policies toward Western European unity, and partially toward NATO (but only partially), Communist and some Socialist *foreign* policies are much closer to those of the Soviet Union than to those of the United States and the major West European governments—including the SPD–FDP (Free Democratic party) coalition in Bonn. That these foreign policies reflect the views of their constituencies and are caused by them, not primarily by following the Soviet line per se, is also true, but in the last analysis irrelevant, for western governments must judge the Latin left's foreign policies by their results, not their motives.

Even so, Professor Löwenthal's tactical judgments seem to me to be largely, if not entirely, valid. It would be a blunder, because it would be counterproductive, for Washington or Bonn or other West European governments to declare constantly their determination to prevent the left from coming to power. If it does, they must deal with it. But there is, in my view, and here I differ with Prof. Löwenthal, no convincing argument why they should not on occasion declare them, and several arguments, notably that they have the right and duty to declare their interests, why they should, while also stating that they will accept whatever decision the peoples of the Latin countries decide to take. Even if western governments wanted to be as "hands-off" on this issue as Prof. Löwenthal would have them, I doubt that they could. Certainly Washington cannot and in my opinion should not as well. But western governments should also be aware of and acknowledge changes. For western flexibility, as Prof. Löwenthal concludes, is not only necessary per se on this issue but is the best way to ensure that Moscow loses more on this issue than the West does.

Notes

1. On the European left in general, see Bernard E. Brown, ed., *Eurocommunism and Eurosocialism: The Left Confronts Modernity* (New York: Cyrco Press, Inc., 1979); my chapter, "The Communist and Socialist Parties in Italy, Spain, and France: 'Eurocommunism,' 'Eurosocialism,' and Soviet Policy" in Karl Kaiser and Hans–Peter Schwarz, eds., *America and Western Europe* (Lexington, Mass.: Lexington Books, D.C. Heath and Company, 1978); and Heinz Timmermann, "Die Linke im Vorfeld der Europawahlen," *L'76* 10 (1978). On West European communism, see Rudolf L. Tökés, ed., *Eurocommunism and Détente.* (New York: NYU

Press for the Council on Foreign Relations, 1978); David D. Albright, ed., *Communism and Political Systems in Western Europe* (Boulder, Colo.: Westview, 1979); Wolfgang Leonhard, *Eurokommunismus: Herausforderung für Ost und West* (Munich: C. Bertelsmann, 1978); Annie Kriegel, *Un autre communisme?* (Paris: Hachette, 1977); the chapter by Heinz Timmermann, "Eurokommunismus im Wandel," in Timmermann, ed., *Eurokommunismus* (Frankfurt: Fischer, 1978); and Donald L.M. Blackmer and Sidney Tarrow, eds., *Communism in Italy and France* (Princeton: Princeton Univ. Press, 1975), which includes bibliography. On West European socialism, see Werner J. Feld, *The Foreign Policies of the West European Socialist Parties* (New York: Praeger, 1978) and Frank L. Wilson, *The French Democratic Left 1963–1969* (Stanford: Stanford Univ. Press, 1971). For recent studies on the relations of West European Communist parties with the East, see Richard Löwenthal, "Moscow and the Eurocommunists," *Problems of Communism,* July–August 1978, and my chapter, "The Diplomacy of Eurocommunism," in Tökés, ed., *Eurocommunism and Détente.*

2

The Italian Left, 1944–1978: Patterns of Cooperation, Conflict, and Compromise

Wolfgang Berner

Introduction: Some Remarks on the Present Situation

Any critical survey which proposes to analyze certain aspects of Italian politics must inevitably begin with a short glance at the general state of the Italian nation. Here one should be careful not to give too much weight to those alarmist reports currently abounding in the international press which tend to depict Italy as a doomed country, a fathomless swamp of corruption and mismanagement, fatally poisoned by Communist machinations and red guerrilla terrorism, so irremediably sapped and demoralized that either economic collapse or political catastrophe (or both) seem to be waiting for her just around the corner. Such overly pessimistic accounts do not reflect the real situation, which is considerably less cataclysmic and much more complex.

The picture revealed by a sober assessment of the available economic data and of relevant political and sociopsychological factors is surprisingly balanced, although not devoid of many ambiguities. It is worth noting, for instance, that recent years were marked by steadily rising levels of prosperity, particularly among industrial and service workers in the northern and central regions, along with considerable improvements for most social insurance beneficiaries.[1] Undaunted by somber expert forecasts bewailing the deep-rooted economic recession of the time, Premier Andreotti's seemingly weak government, inaugurated in summer 1976, gradually succeeded in stabilizing the lira, reactivated the country's productive energies, and brought the economy to the verge of a new boom, before it was compelled to resign on January 31, 1979. But while Italy was able, in 1978, to boost exports by 10 percent, and to pile up an impressive $6.4 billion balance of payment surplus, unemployment figures continued to increase: by January 1979 people in search of work totaled 1,632,000, compared with 1,503,000 unemployed twelve months before.[2]

Whatever the political complexion of the next government that will emerge from the long impasse following the general elections held in early June 1979, it will invariably have to face a number of extremely complicated, pressing problems, particularly in the fields of internal security, reorganization of the economy's large public sector, economic assistance programs for the southern regions, reduction of "structural" unemployment (concentrated mainly in the South), antiinflation measures, and reorganization of the entire public education system. Other urgent tasks include modernization of the cumbersome, inefficient, partly corrupt administrative apparatus, stricter application of internal revenue legislation, financial stabilization of regional and local self-governing bodies, and effective enforcement of other important reform laws, not to mention the imperative need to reduce the country's permanent dependence on massive fuel, commodity, and food imports.

All things considered, Italy nevertheless has a fair chance finally to emerge from the profound crisis of her entire institutional system which originated in the late 1960s, if not earlier, and which came to affect all aspects of her political, economic, and cultural structures. Her pace of economic recovery is impressive, with growth rates sometimes double those of other industrialized countries in the West. The target set for 1978 by the administration's three-year recovery program ("Pandolfi Plan"), which envisaged a 2 percent increment of GNP, was topped by a 2.6 percent gain. Moreover, it should be remembered that for 1960–75 Italy's GNP increases amounted to a real per capita growth of roughly 71 percent, while, for example, the Soviet Union's growth did not exceed 68 percent during this period.[3] Great efforts were made to contain the rate of inflation at 13.3 percent in 1978, after it had reached 18.9 percent in 1977.[4] A further reduction to levels under 11 percent is contemplated.

The onslaught of organized violence perpetrated by disaffected elements belonging to very different social and political groups is still rampant. In 1978 the record of political terrorism included twenty-five assassinations (with the Christian Democrats' party chairman Aldo Moro among the victims) and 2,370 additional cases of armed attack or other forms of physical assault. Five hundred thirty-seven incendiary and bomb attacks were directed against party and labor union offices (282), school buildings (125), and police stations (130). In the same period more than 1,000 banks and 800 post offices were raided. Most frequently hit by acts of political terrorism were the cities of Rome (604 cases in 1978), Milan (296), Turin (160), Padua (148), and Bologna (83). Although right-wing violence played a certain role, authorship for eleven times as many acts of political terrorism has been claimed by ultraleftist groups.[5]

Obviously the security and police forces, challenged while themselves undergoing a demanding review and reorganization process, were unable to cope with the sudden upsurge of terrorist operations, which after a slow and fumbling start in 1969 had become a sustained large-scale offensive by 1977. The Red Brigades and other left-wing groups participating in this guerilla campaign have always been eager to stress both their Marxist-

Leninist inspiration and their pretension to act as the Communist party's armed revolutionary vanguard.

But whatever the guerrilla leaders' objectives may have been, the main result turned out to be a very broad feeling of solidarity embracing the vast majority of Italy's "political class," which, first of all, drove the Communists much closer than ever before toward the Christian Democrats in joint condemnation of political violence in general and Red Brigade terrorism in particular. The climax of the Moro tragedy produced an almost comprehensive national consensus, unparalleled in Italy's postwar history. This gruesome experience caused most parties and trade unions, mass media and individual citizens to close ranks and rally in defense of the established order of representative democracy. In the course of the discussion over alternative responses to the challenges of terrorism, the leadership groups of both the Democrazía Cristiana and the Communist party adopted very similar positions, marked by an unequivocal commitment to the principles of the rule of law.

In fact, it should be recognized that the Italian political establishment, in spite of all its evident weaknesses, glaring defects, and striking incongruities, proved to possess much more stamina and coherence than expected. Faced with the emergency situation created by the Moro abduction and the difficult choices which ensued, all the major political parties and their leaderships showed a considerable measure of public-mindedness and a strong sense of joint responsibility for the common cause.

Upon closer examination this consociative spirit had become manifest even earlier, in response to a long sequence of critical situations which began in June 1976, after the general elections, when a new government formula acceptable to the Communists had to be elaborated. It stood the test of the breakdown of Premier Andreotti's six-party government platform in January 1978, as well as that of President Leone's forced resignation six months later on charges of personal enrichment in office. The fact that Leone was replaced, finally, as head of state by the old-guard Socialist, *Resistenza* veteran, and anticlerical free-thinker Sandro Pertini, with an overwhelming majority of roughly 83 percent of the total vote of the Electors' Assembly, seems to indicate an increased chance for solutions dictated primarily by the national interest at the expense of narrower party preferences, even among the Democrazía Cristiana.

Thus, on the whole, there is evidence enough of a renascent public-mindedness combined with democratic solidarity and cooperation across ideological barriers and party distinctions. The Italian institutional system has resisted relatively well both strong internal pressures and disturbing, sometimes disrupting outside influences, for the international environment cannot be ignored altogether. It is easy enough to chalk up a variety of external causes of Italy's recent economic recession, or to prove the determining impact of the Vietnam war on the development of Italy's student and youth rebellion, or even to discover apparent links existing between Italy's native terrorist groups and diverse foreign or transnational terrorist activities.

There are also several other foreign connections to be mentioned, which, independent of party affiliations, continue to arouse considerable anxiety among Italian political leaders. It often happens that these "scares" exert a very marked influence on political attitudes and decisions, particularly within the Italian left.

Thus, both the Communist and the Socialist parties have always been seriously afraid of American political interference or even stronger forms of superpower intervention intended to thwart their attempts to replace DC hegemonic rule by an alternative majority government of the Italian left. Another subject of much concern is the possibility of a major change in Belgrade's foreign policy after Tito's demise. Should Yugoslavia accept some form of closer association with the Warsaw Pact, both the PCI and the PSI leaderships would certainly feel obliged to reexamine the whole range of their own positions regarding NATO, Italy's security interests in the Mediterranean area, and Italian defense commitments in general.

The third cause of permanent apprehension is the prospect of yet another, possibly more serious oil crisis which could bring Italy's economy to a standstill within less than a month. One of the presumable consequences would be a very profound radicalization of the entire Italian left including a broad majority of the labor movement. Such a turn of events could be expected to touch off rather sweeping personnel changes within the various hierarchies. Perhaps only a minority of today's ranking PCI or PSI leaders would be considered sufficiently "proletarian" and aggressive to be reelected to their present party functions.

That the Communist leadership is rather susceptible to criticisms and pressures emanating from the party's intermediate cadres and membership "base" became evident after the May 1978 local elections which—for the first time since 1946—resulted in severe losses for the PCI in most of the contested constituencies, representing roughly one-tenth of the Italian electorate. Subsequent developments revealed that PCI militants tended to interpret this setback primarily as a consequence of their leadership's decision to opt for a policy of "national unity," before joining the government coalition on the very day of the Moro abduction (March 16, 1978). By this move the PCI abandoned, in fact, its customary and profitable opposition role for the sake of a five-party cooperation agreement, equivalent to a pledge for active, sustained parliamentary and extraparliamentary support of Premier Andreotti's *monocolore* DC minority cabinet.

As it happened, the durability of the PCI's policy change was immediately tested when it was called upon to defend, in close company with the

Christian Democrats, two keenly disputed laws—the first on the public funding of political parties, the second on measures for the protection of public order in the face of rising terrorism and common criminality— against abrogation by referendum. Although the antiabolitionists, on June 11, won the contest on both issues, its patchy, and in the case of the subsidization law, even narrow, outcome proved to be a Pyrrhic victory for the Communist party. Quite obviously, substantial segments of the electorate to which the PCI owed the triumphs reaped in 1975 and 1976 had become increasingly critical of the political choices made by the party summit.[6]

Extremely worried by the profound identity crisis festering among the organization's lower echelons, the PCI leadership began to prod their new Christian Democratic allies for a more equitable apportionment of government power, and in particular for direct Communist cabinet participation. Thus the collapse of the five–party coalition preliminary to Premier Andreotti's resignation in January 1979 was a matter of necessity after the DC leadership had categorically rejected the Communists' suggestion to barter a number of cabinet posts in exchange for the PCI's parliamentary support for the administration's economic recovery program (based on the "Pandolfi Plan"). A related factor contributed to predispose most PCI leaders in favor of a tactical retreat: as a Communist party congress had been scheduled for the first quarter of the year (it actually was convened for March 30– April 3, 1979), Secretary-General Berlinguer and his chief aides evidently preferred returning to a stance of "constructive opposition" before they would report to the delegates on the "state of the party," rather than carrying on as coalition partners of the Democrazia Cristiana in a quite uncomfortable, seemingly subservient position.

The precongress debate as well as the assembly's proceedings disclosed, however, that Berlinguer was not at all prepared to jettison his strategy of the "historic compromise." He finally secured almost unanimous approval for the ninety–three "theses"[7] submitted to the congress by the party executive, a programmatic platform which openly commits the PCI to persevere in its drive for a "government of national unity." This stereotype denotes a government formula excluding neither the Communists nor the Christian Democrats, with Socialist participation considered an important additional prerequisite.

In the meantime anticipated general elections had become unavoidable, because strong factions within the DC leadership felt confident that their party, favored by a steady economic upswing, not only could secure sizable gains but also rout the PCI, which was expected to suffer heavy losses comparable to those in the May 1978 local elections. Their mounting assertiveness induced even those DC exponents to yield who would have preferred a negotiated solution of the government crisis (for example, Zaccagnini and Andreotti). President Pertini, too, had to surrender after several unsuccessful attempts to devise new coalition patterns contingent upon Socialist support, the denial of which finally led to the dissolution of Parliament (April 2, 1979).

Each of the three major parties was disillusioned, however, by the results of the elections held on June 3–4: DC voting strength dwindled from 38.7 to 38.3 percent in the Chamber of Deputies (Senate: 38.3 percent); the PCI vote sagged from 34.4 to 30.4 percent (Senate: 31.5 percent); and the PSI obtained only minimal gains, polling 9.8 percent in the Chamber (0.2 percent) and 10.4 percent in the Senate (0.2 percent). Thus, with the PCI's losses small enough to maintain the party above the "magic" 30 percent level, the overall balance of forces remained substantially unchanged. Although a DC–PSI coalition could rely on combined basic majorities of 170 to 145 seats in the Senate and of 324 to 306 seats in the Chamber, prospects for such an alliance under a DC premier are very slim, while the DC will not easily accede to Socialist demands for the premiership. It is probable, therefore, that in due time some kind of cooperation among the three major parties will have to be restored, and that joint efforts to reestablish a "programmatic" five-party coalition—convertible into a more "organic" government coalition if convenient—will find growing support in many quarters including large sections of the DC, PSI, and PCI leadership groups.

Leftist Pluralism—Italian Style

It was Aldo Moro, the late chairman of the DC's National Council, who ventured to predict that the severe electoral defeats suffered by his party in May 1974 (failure of the antidivorce referendum) and in June 1975 (regional and provincial elections) were bound to usher in a "third phase" in the DC's own destiny and in the nation's postwar history.[8] In Moro's judgment the marked swing to the left which became manifest in all social strata after the oil shock experienced in winter 1973–74 was not a purely accidental, transitory change of mood. He rather believed it to express a profound and enduring change in the overall climate. This assessment was confirmed, he felt, by the outcome of the general elections held in June 1976, when the Communists obtained their record score of 34.4 percent of the vote—a figure only 4.3 points below the DC results (38.7 percent). The aggregate share polled by the entire left—Social Democrats (PSDI) included—amounted to 51.3 percent of the total vote in 1975 and to roughly 50 percent in 1976.

The "first phase" of the process Moro had in mind covered the reconstruction years between 1944 and 1947. It was the period of "three-party cooperation" during which the Christian Democrats, led by Alcide De Gasperi, the Socialists (in the PSIUP—Partito Socialista Italiano di Unità Proletaria), led by Pietro Nenni, and the Communists (PCI—Partito Comunista Italiano) and joined forces to solve a number of basic problems, often in coalition with other political parties or movements of lesser importance. The priority tasks were the settling of the "institutional question" (the abolition of the monarchy), the conclusion of a peace treaty, and the introduction of a new republican constitution. All these objectives had been achieved by early 1948. In spite of numerous, clearly defined ideological divergences and repeated quarrels over conceptual matters, the three parties had performed the work to be done, on the whole, with much reasonableness and a high sense of responsibility. Equal credit for this accomplishment could be claimed by the Christian Democratic, the Communist, and the Socialist representatives.

Although PCI and PSIUP participation in government ended in May 1947, their exclusion did not mean the immediate termination of any kind of cooperation among the three parties. On the contrary, it continued within the Constituent Assembly until January 31, 1948. Apparently De Gasperi, who would have preferred to postpone the showdown, had to give way to strong pressures stemming partly from the ranks of his own party, but also from the Vatican and from Washington.[9] Despite mounting tensions during this opening phase of the cold war, the Italian Communists and Socialists accepted their ousting without resistance, although the PCI, in particular, would have been able to mobilize a well-equipped irregular army of an estimated 170,000 guerrilla veterans.[10] Seemingly unmoved, however, the Constituent Assembly had worked on, under the chairmanship of Umberto Terracini, a Communist, without paying much heed to these ominous developments. Approved on December 22, 1947, by a clear 453 to 62 majority bolstered by the solid PCI bloc vote, the new constitution came into effect on January 1, 1948.

But in the meantime, after the founding of the Communist Information Bureau (Cominform) in September 1947, the Kremlin had initiated a large-scale political offensive which soon led to the Communist takeover in Prague (February 1948). A similar design in Finland was foiled at the last moment. A few weeks later, in March 1948, the Soviets wrecked the Interallied Control Council for Germany. These events contributed to generate an extreme polarization of Italy's public opinion, and when parliamentary elections were held on April 18, 1948, the Democrazía Cristiana reaped the greatest triumph of its history (48.48 percent), winning an absolute majority of seats in both houses.

This sweeping victory in the 1948 electoral contest was to become the durable basis for the DC's hegemonic role, the main characteristic of the "second phase" of Italy's postwar politics. While the Democrazía Cristiana had demonstrated considerable power of aggregation with regard to the Communists and Socialists in the preceding period, it now began to develop comparable capabilities of synchronization, and even amalgamation, with the "lay" parties of the upper and lower middle classes (Liberal party [PLI], Republican party [PRI], PSDI) as well as with substantial nonorganized groups of the population holding moderately conservative attitudes and convictions. The DC progressively expanded its power base throughout the state bureaucracy, the government–controlled sectors of the economy, and local and provincial administration, thus finally establishing a deep-rooted, far–flung, closely knit system of domination, patronage, and clientelistic interdependencies. That it should prove at the same time both inefficient and corruption–engendering goes without saying. The alliance struck between the ambitious party manager Amintore Fanfani, who started a thorough drive for the reorganization of the DC in 1954, and the industrial empire–builder Enrico Mattei, the president of the state-owned ENI oil trust, was of symbolic significance.

In spite of all this, the DC's availability for a "leftist" political course never completely evaporated. It continued to be a large popular party with a substantial, although not always politically strong, wage–earner and trade-unionist wing. For a while a group of reformers led by Giuseppe Dossetti tried to combine social activism and pacifist commitment with the utopian struggle for a truly "Catholic society," and succeeded in gaining considerable influence within the party leadership. These "integralist left–wingers" were finally defeated by their more pragmatist and secularist rivals, but many elements of their general program have become integrated into the party's collective consciousness.[11] Similar developments had occurred even earlier in the process of bringing under party control several Catholic mass organizations (Italian Catholic Action [ACI], Italian Catholic Action Youth [GIAC], Italian Catholic Workers Association [ACLI], Italian Catholic University Federation [FUCI], and so on), which for some years had been utilized by clerical traditionalists with the purpose of transforming the Democrazía Cristiana into a crusading movement supporting the Vatican's battle against socialism, liberalism, and modernism.[12]

The DC's ideology perpetuated the three key maxims inherited from party founder De Gasperi. It stuck rather consistently to his concept of a party based as much on Christian values as on democratic convictions and secular orientations. Likewise the DC defended its claim to be the only "authorized" party for all Catholics in Italy. It was quite logical that as long as it could uphold this claim, the DC would not renounce the principle of "interclassism," which recognizes the existence of diverging class interests but at the same time postulates an active commitment to reconcile such divergencies or antagonisms, both within the party's own ranks and within Italian society.

It should be noted that the DC leaders, even in periods marked by maximum emphasis on the anti–Communist, last-ditch function of their party, never really tried to get the revolutionary left–wing parties outlawed (which by definition included the PSI until the late 1950s). Quite to the contrary, when the Democrazía Cristiana was prodded to "open up to the left" by the Socialists, beginning in 1953, the PSI's overtures were immediately taken up by the DC's labor wing and remained a permanent subject of internal discussions on alternative DC coalition policies. After some years of stalling, indeed, the DC's right wing had to yield, and in spring 1961 the first local governments based on "center–left" coalitions were inaugurated, thus preparing the ground for the subsequent transition from "centrism" to a new "center–left" course with Socialist participation.

This shift to the left was greeted by broad segments of the DC membership and electorate with great hope for a lessening of tension in domestic affairs. But there were many obstacles still to be removed in both camps before the first geniune "center–left" cabinet could be formed in December 1963, a cabinet headed by Moro as premier and Nenni as vice–premier, to which Palmiro Togliatti lent a hand by dropping some encouraging remarks. In reality, the new policy of reform began in a rather unfavorable climate, because it was immediately confronted by a twofold crisis of a very serious nature.

This challenge was first posed by an economic recession which soon developed into a structural crisis encompassing the entire economic system. The second component, however, was a general crisis involving the whole system of traditional moral values as well as social standards and conventions. It must be recalled, in this context, that crucial processes of secularization and emancipation were still to be carried through in Italy, in a country whose people historically had remained scarcely touched by the great European experiences of the Reformation and the Enlightenment.

These crises with which the "center–left" governments had to cope were both delayed sequels to the vast processes of migration, structural rearrangements, and modernization which had been permitted to develop in rather uncontrolled fashion during the years of Italy's "economic miracle" (1951–63). Almost typically, they reached a danger point only with the advent of the economic recession which followed when the pressures of increasing economic difficulties, partly aggravated by the impact of outside influences, became so intense that they suddenly burst into the open with devastating explosiveness, as evidenced by the extraordinary vehemence of the Italian youth revolt and "contestation movement" (1967–72).

While the rebels of the new "young" left pretended to fight primarily for the liberation of the "proletariat" from DC and bourgeois oppression, most of them attacked the PCI leadership, too, denouncing with particular acrimony its obvious unwillingness to make use of the revolutionary potential of their movement for the overthrow of the established system. In a way, it was this vitriolic campaign launched by ultraleftist critics against the PCI which, for the first time, made larger sections of Italy's public opinion realize that the Communist leaders had no intention at all of destroying the existing constitutional order, and were demonstrating, on the contrary, a definite propensity to side with its defenders. From the mid-1960s onward the Communists had shown a growing willingness to cooperate in both houses of Parliament, particularly in their commissions, a trend incessantly and scathingly denounced by the five Communist "Manifesto" rebels who kept their seats in the Chamber of Deputies until 1972.[13]

The fact that Berlinguer explicitly referred to the "Chilean lessons" of the Allende era to justify his initiative when he publicly presented his "historic compromise" plan[14] in the fall of 1973 has led many observers to overestimate the impact of these "exotic" experiences on the PCI secretary-general's motivations. On closer examination the offer for long-term cooperation with DC and PSI, which formed the central idea of the proposed policy, appears to be intimately related to traditional basic patterns of the PCI's strategy of alliances, and quite in keeping with long-standing Communist objectives adapted to the actual Italian situation. Particular attention should be given to five aspects:

1. The proposals openly rejected the "left-wing alternative" formula, by arguing against the desirability of a new majority without DC participation. They emphasized, instead, the PCI's unmistakable preference for a pact of cooperation embracing the three major parties (including the DC), as distinguished from a coalition of the parties of the "classical left" (excluding the DC), which at best would command only a small parliamentary majority.

2. The three-party alliance envisaged by the "historic compromise" strategy is clearly reminiscent of the period of "three-party cooperation" during the reconstruction and normalization phase in 1944–47.

3. The proposals also recall Togliatti's offer of a long-term cooperation pact addressed to the DC leadership as early as July 1944, and later suggestions of a similar nature advanced by him to enlist support by the "organized Catholics"—that is, by the DC—for a program of joint peace initiatives.[15]

4. The entire conception can be traced back to Togliatti's firm conviction that the "problem of relations between the Catholic world and the Communist world" must be considered the "central problem" of Italy's postwar development, as stated by him most clearly at Bergamo in March 1963.

5. Beyond that, the PCI's "historic compromise" strategy can be interpreted as a modernized version of the old "national front strategy" or as a particular Italian variety of the "popular front strategy," depending on whether the DC is classified either as a "bourgeois" conservative party or a "petit-bourgeois" middle-of-the-road reform party in the latter case.

From the standpoint of political strategy, the PCI leadership could have numerous motivations for an attempt to resuscitate the "three-party" government coalitions which had been so successful during the "first phase." As a junior partner within a DC–led cabinet the PCI would find it relatively easy to win full "democratic legitimation" abroad, using the DC's prestige and credit to overcome reservations still existing on the part of Italy's Common Market partners and NATO allies. The psychological effect of an open DC-PCI alliance would also contribute to improving the PCI's image on the domestic scene and would facilitate the removal of the persistent ideological obstacles which have so far precluded the Communists' obtaining support in some sections of the working–class electorate. A long-term cooperation pact offers, in addition, good prospects for a gradual shifting of power toward the PCI which thus, ultimately, might achieve senior partner status within the alliance, if backed by an expanding electorate.

The main objective of the PCI's strategy of alliances consists, as officially stated, in the establishment of a new hegemony of the working people (or the "working class").[16] This hegemony is supposed to be jointly exercised by the "popular forces," variously of Communist, Socialist, and Catholic inspiration. The obvious consequence, as indicated by Communist spokesmen, would be a remarkably "open" ideological and cultural pluralism with a vaguely "leftist" orientation, tied to a concerted government program proposing profound socioeconomic structural reforms. According to the PCI leadership, each of the envisaged reform projects should be supported by a very broad popular consensus, so that the risk of losing political control over this "new historic bloc," due to negative votes in Parliament or in future general elections, would be relatively small.

The desired final outcome would be, of course, the replacement of the former DC hegemony by a new PCI hegemony. With this as the crucial point, it is quite understandable why the "historic compromise" concept is rejected by the PSI leadership even more emphatically than by all other parties concerned. The Socialists, on the contrary, assert it to be their "historic task" to ensure that "democracy by alternation" will be established in Italy, for the first time, as a truly operative system of representative government.[17]

In fact, "democracy by alternation" has never yet been a tradition in Italy. Ever since the essentially liberal bourgeois Risorgimento monarchy was installed, the country's affairs have been controlled by a single dominant political force which tended to remain dominate for very long periods. The Socialist party (PSI), founded in 1892, the Catholic People's party (PPI), established in 1919, and the Communist party of Italy (PCI), which split off from the PSI in 1921, were all antisystem parties determined to demolish the power monopoly held by the liberal–bourgeois upper class. When Mussolini took over in 1922, he needed only four years to set up a dictatorship of his own monopoly party. After the war the Democrazía Cristiana developed a new type of hegemony by which it secured an exclusive claim to the premiership, upheld now for a period of thirty-four years without interruption.

Within the DC left wing, in particular, certain forces (which also included Aldo Moro[18]) are not at all unreceptive to the idea of incorporating the Communists once more into a government coalition as a full-fledged partner for an extended transition period, which thus would inaugurate a new "third phase" of Italian postwar politics. They are less afraid of returning to some form of DC–PCI cooperation than of the prospect of continuing Communist electoral advances. Rigid resistance would only favor the PCI, they feel, while inclusion in the government could undercut or end the attraction which the PCI held so long for all kinds of "rejectors" and maverick elements. Basically this approach reflects the conviction that even the Communists will have to pay tribute, sooner or later, to the effects of the adaptation produced by the sharing of government responsibilities. In other words, they rely on *trasformismo* as a specific Italian historical experience.

This was the course laid down by Moro during the first half of March 1978 (*marxismo egemoniale*). It envisaged a period of reform–oriented "leftist" policy (as exemplified by the DC and "center-left" governments in 1962–76), this time marked by Communist participation in the coalition and, possibly rather soon, also in the cabinet. The DC leadership sought to increase systematically its own influence over the "classical" left-wing parties by this strategy, while at the same time it intended to encourage the PCI's further integration into the existing democratic, parliamentary system.

The administrative elections held on May 14, 1978, were expected by many observers to provide a first clue to the feasibility of this policy of cooperative competition (*confronto*), as distinct from an alternative strategy of frontal clash (*scontro*). The returns proved to be quite encouraging for the Democrazía Cristiana, which scored considerable gains: 5 percent above the previous local polls and 3.6 percent above the 1976 general election results. Equally significant were the heavy losses suffered by the PCI, amounting to roughly nine percentage points, as compared with the figures for June 1976. At the same time the PSI (4.1) and the smaller center parties were all able to improve their positions in comparison with the parliamentary elections. The results of the contest (involving about one-tenth of the total Italian electorate) could be interpreted as a signal that the seemingly irresistible advance of the Italian Communist party had finally come to a halt, after many years of unrelenting progress.

Sources of Strength of the Communist Party

The PCI, with nearly 1.8 million members,[19] is the largest and by far the best organized of Italy's political parties. The DC claims to have almost as many members (1.7–1.8 million),[20] but its organizational framework is much less developed. The Socialist party (PSI), with 434,000 members (March 1978), holds third place,[21] followed by the Social Democratic Party (PSDI), with a total of 150,000 members (December 1978).[22] At the polls, in early June 1979, the PSDI garnered only 3.8 percent of the vote for the Chamber of Deputies (Senate: 4.2 percent), compared with a PSI score of 9.8 percent (Senate: 104 percent).

The membership of the Liberal party (PLI) exceeds 135,000 (April 1976),[23] while the liberal–leftist Republican party (PRI) has roughly 110,000 members (June 1978).[24] The PLI polled 1.9 percent of the total vote for the Chamber of Deputies in June 1979 (Senate: 2.2 percent); the PRI obtained a share of 3.0 percent (Senate: 3.4 percent).

Italy's Communist Party is a many–faceted organization. As a party based on the active allegiance of its members it is a mass party and a cadre party at the same time. Considering, furthermore, its ideology and the social origins of the majority of its members and base–level functionaries, it continues to be predominantly a workers' and wage–earners' party (these groups account for over 50 percent in both cases).[25] On the other hand, it has succeeded in attracting general electoral support countrywide, and can be said to have become a truly popular party appealing to voters belonging to all social strata. This applies in particular to the Emilia–Romagna region (capital city: Bologna), where it polled 48.5 percent of the vote in the 1976 elections, 1979: 47.3 percent). In Siena province (Tuscany) it got 57.5 percent (1979: 56.6 percent), and in seven other provinces (out of a total of ninety–four) its share exceeded 50 percent (1979: four out of ninety–four).

The degree of organizational penetration is also highest in Emilia–Romagna, where roughly 25 percent of the PCI's total membership is concentrated. Another 26.3 percent reside in Tuscany and in Lombardy (14.3 percent and 12 percent of total PCI strength, respectively), while membership consistency is much weaker in most of the other regions, particularly in the southern and northeastern parts of the country.[26]

In general, Italian public opinion does not associate the present PCI leadership with Stalinism or with the vicissitudes of the Comintern era, but tends to identify it mainly with the *Resistenza* fight against fascism in the 1922–45 period. It is common knowledge, moreover, that after 1943 the Communists were in fact the motor of the armed guerrilla struggle against Italian fascism and the German occupation forces. As a result they paid a much higher toll in human lives than any other *Resistenza* group. Although some non–Communist guerrilla brigades participated in these activities, the bulk of Italy's partisan troops was unquestionably supplied by the Communists, who (unlike their French comrades) clearly dominated the movement as organizers and fighters from the very beginning.

For this reason the PCI's *Resistenza* merits have become a constituent part of the Italian postwar republic's official legend of origination. Indeed, all political parties which support the Constitution concur in construing a direct causality between the defeat of fascism, attributed primarily to the *Resistenza* movement's heroism and sacrifices, and the foundation of the Republic, conceived as the end-product and culmination of the various *Resistenza* forces' joint efforts. The alternative possibility, to credit the victory over fascism and the foundation of the democratic republic to the military liberation of Italy and to subsequent political decisions reached by the Anglo-Saxon powers, has been practically discarded.

Never, therefore, was it seriously proposed to outlaw the Communists, because the Republic seemed so inextricably linked with the *Resistenza* struggle and was so deeply indebted to the movement's most zealous champions. Even after the PCI's undisguised relapse into abject subservience to the Communist Party of the Soviet Union (CPSU) during the years 1947–56, it did not fall into total political isolation on the domestic scene. By tireless repetition of the *Resistenza* myths and memories it has succeeded up to the present in keeping *Resistenza* solidarity permanently alive and influential across party divisions.

Resurrected as a mass party with a new patriotic image and national commitment sometime before the end of the war, the PCI reached its peak membership, 2.25 million, as early as 1947. Following Togliatti's directives, the party became present within every stratum or segment of the population. It was thought expedient, among other things, to keep the minimum ideological requirements relatively low, in order to realize this objective.[27] But also among the PCI's leadership group and among party officials of intermediate levels, attachment to the doctrines of Marxism-Leninism was generally much less dogmatic than it was among contemporary French or Spanish CP functionaries. All these factors aided the rapid expansion of the PCI after the war. As the process went on, the original "vanguard party of the working masses" transformed itself by stages into a broad popular party with a large following of faithful PCI voters.

Of great importance was the PCI's ability to find authoritative sources of revolutionary theory at home, provided by outstanding leaders of its own like Antonio Gramsci (1891-1937) and Palmiro Togliatti (1893-1964). It was much easier, consequently, for Italy's Communists than for their French or Spanish comrades to claim far-reaching political independence and to present their organization as a social-revolutionary party primarily guided by national requirements and realities. The assertion of ideological and organizational autonomy in relation to the CPSU, initiated by Togliatti, has been continued by his successors with remarkable persistence. Thoughts and statements borrowed from Gramsci were often refurbished and used as intellectual fortifications behind which subsequent advances toward political emancipation could be prepared.[28]

When Togliatti began to rebuild the PCI on the basis of his concept of the "new party" (*partito nuovo*), developed in 1944, as a nonsectarian mass party committed to a policy focused on national requirements, this concept was already closely linked to the notion of a specific Italian road to socialism.[29] After the end of the Cominform period (1947–56) Togliatti used an early opportunity in the fall of 1956 to define this particular "Italian way" of Socialist construction as a constitutional path, the gradual character of which he took pains to emphasize later (1962).[30] In his "Yalta Memorandum" (1964), he indicated that the PCI leadership intended to seize power in a step-by-step process without previous destruction of the "bourgeois" state.[31]

The conceptual model of the "dictatorship of the proletariat" was replaced by the alternative goal of the "hegemony of the working class" (or of the working people), the latter of course the specific concept of hegemony formulated by Gramsci with particular reference to the industrially advanced western societies. Similarly, the concept of the "historic compromise" was developed from Gramsci's theory on the necessity of forming "a new historic bloc" for specific revolutionary ends.[32] Permanently engaged in lively internal discussions on topical problems of political strategy and extremely keen to exert practical political influence on domestic affairs, the PCI leadership gradually developed a new attitude regarding constitutionalism, parliamentarism, and fundamental "liberal-bourgeois" rights and human liberties, which subsequently also found expression in party documents.[33]

As mentioned above, the Italian CP played a very active part in the drafting of the Constitution, which is still in force. In later years it never tired of professing its loyalty toward this fundamental law of the Republic, and since 1964 it has openly acknowledged the principle that by all means, no matter what kind of institutional or structural changes seem desirable, uninterrupted constitutional continuity must be ensured.[34] The PCI has therefore concentrated its revolutionary propaganda essentially on demands for radical changes in socioeconomic structures, without openly questioning the principles and institutions guaranteed by the Constitution. Its position that the fight for a radical transformation of socioeconomic structures is compatible with the Constitution itself is shared not only by many Socialists but also by prominent Christian Democrats, including Premier Giulio Andreotti.[35]

During the years when it was excluded from government participation at the "center" (that is, the national level) the PCI did not lack opportunities to demonstrate its capacity for responsible coalition partnership as well as its administrative competence at the municipal, provincial, and regional levels. Such occasions have always been regarded as very important tests, and most PCI representatives called upon to face the challenge did respectable jobs. Although the Communists soon began to establish extensive patronage and clientelistic networks of their own, Communist administrators and public offices controlled by them generally have a good reputation for only a minimum level of corruption and a particular concern for the citizens' worries. Not unjustly, the Italian CP recommends itself as the "party with the clean hands," and over the years this formula has proven to be the most successful of all Communist election slogans ever coined.

The PCI was able, indeed, to build up an impressive number of power bastions. At the beginning of 1978, three out of twenty regional governments (Emilia-Romagna, Umbria, Liguria) had Communist presidents. In three more regions (Piedmont, Tuscany, Latium) the PCI was the junior partner in a PSI-led regional government. Forty-nine out of ninety-four provinces were controlled by left-wing provincial administrations, in eighteen cases headed by a Communist president. Communist mayors governed not only Rome, Naples, Turin, Florence, and Bologna but also many other major cities. In twenty-one out of ninety-four regional and provincial capitals the mayor was a PCI nominee. In eighteen additional capital cities the Communists belonged to the majority coalition. Today more than fifty-three percent of Italy's total population lives in municipalities ruled by Communist mayors or by Communist-controlled administrative councils.

On the other hand, the PCI's electoral fortunes have always depended to a considerable degree on its nationwide appeal as the most radical and powerful opposition party in the country. After 1963, subsequent to the Socialists' entry into the "area of government" as the DC's preferred coalition partner, "leftist" votes of protest were all but monopolized by the PCI. Only from the 1976 general elections onward was some competition offered by the "petit-bourgeois" libertarian but anti-Socialist Radical party (PR—Partito Radicale: 1.07 percent) and by the ultraleftist Proletarian Democracy (DP—Democrazía Proletaria: 1.52 percent), which attracted minor parts of the "leftist" votes of protest. The PCI's comparative share amounted, however, to 34.44 percent (12,620,509 votes). In June 1979 the PR rose to 3.4 percent, and two ultraleftist tickets (PDUP, NSU) amounted to 2.3 percent, while the PCI's share dropped to 30.4 percent.

Many Italians found it easier to vote PCI after its attitude toward the CPSU became one of autonomy. This policy, initiated by Togliatti long before the CP leaderships of France or Spain ventured to follow suit, was not immediately recognized as a new or different factor by Italy's interested public. General awareness of these changes began to spread in 1968, however, following the outspoken protests addressed by the PCI leadership to the USSR and other Communist regimes in East Europe condemning the suppression of Czechoslovakia's Communist reform movement. The statements published in and after August 1968 by the Communist parties of France and Spain, which concurred with the PCI's critical reaction to the Soviet-led invasion of the ČSSR, were important elements in the development of what later became known as "Eurocommunism."

In objecting to the limitation or violation of human rights and civil liberties in the USSR and other East European countries, particularly in Czechoslovakia, the PCI leadership once more displayed a pioneering spirit and helped to induce some of its West European sister parties to make even more outspoken statements of their own. Italy's CP was the first one, moreover, to authorize the inclusion of writings by authors proscribed in the USSR (for example, Trotsky, Bukharin, Kautsky, Hajek, Šik, and so on) in party literature and to put out some of them in its own publishing house. All these initiatives contributed to strengthening the PCI's credibility as a democratic party in the eyes of many skeptics and helped to restore it as a potential coalition partner in the judgment of other parties, in particular of the Socialists.

Today the PCI is regarded by large segments of the Italian population as a radical–democratic, Marxist–inspired, but undogmatic reform party primarily interested in defending and amending the existing constitutional order.[37] This appraisal gained further ground when, in March 1972, Luigi Longo was replaced by Enrico Berlinguer as secretary–general of the party. According to data derived from opinion polls conducted in 1976, Berlinguer clearly held first place among Italy's most popular political leaders at that time.[38] And while earlier polls had shown that in 1970 roughly 45 percent of the respondents considered the PCI "a serious threat" to Italian freedom and believed that agreement with the Communists was "impossible," that figure dropped to 25 percent within four years, when the survey was repeated in 1974.[39]

Problems and Prospects of PCI Strategy

The foremost function of political leadership can be defined, in the context of normal party management, as the task of determining, on the basis of a binding general program or a set of specific political directives, a clear–cut and practicable order of priorities. Thereafter a number of operational choices have to be made in establishing the overall "strategy" to be followed. Any such general strategic blueprint must include, of course, a realistic strategy of alliances.

These rules apply with particular force to parties like the PCI, led through general–staff techniques by professional political leaders. If faced with a dilemma, such a party's general staff cannot forever avoid opting for one or several possible course of action. But every such choice will generate a multitude of secondary adjustments as soon as the inevitable revision of general policy concepts has been carried out.

Apparently such a basic choice was forced upon the PCI leadership by the Soviet invasion of Czechoslovakia in August 1968. For the PCI's top representatives, the military intervention was nothing but a great-power move launched by the Kremlin to replace the legitimate CP leadership of a fraternal Socialist country, which it happened to dislike. It was evident to the PCI leaders that in the case of a similar conflict of interests under analogous conditions, the Soviets could not be expected to treat the Italian CP's ranking functionaries with any more consideration than was granted to Dubček and other members of the Czechoslovak party's leadership.[40]

This experience could not but affect the PCI's attitude toward NATO, whose protective function became increasingly appreciated by its autonomy-conscious leaders. In his often-cited interview published immediately before the elections of June 1976, Berlinguer openly acknowledged what some of his colleagues had begun to admit much earlier in private, namely, that the PCI leadership had learned to recognize "also" NATO's useful function of serving as a "shield" for the construction of socialism in freedom.[41] In other words, after 1968 the party's general staff had come to define its specific mission (programmatic party objective) more precisely as the task of transforming Italy into a Socialist state under the conditions of NATO (and EC) membership in a medium or even long-range perspective.

Simultaneously, the PCI leadership is apparently trying to keep the option open for a possible EC defense union. For some time it has been advocating further efforts to develop the EC into a political union which should be "neither anti-Soviet nor anti-American," thus assuming a more or less neutralist attitude.[42] It seems, however, that the French CP's reactions to PCI probings on the EC defense union scheme have been discouraging. The PCF leadership obviously considers the incorporation of French nuclear forces into such a multilateral defense system to be a very thorny and in fact insoluble problem.

For the purpose of this analysis, attention will be focused, however, on the possible consequences for the PCI's strategy of alliances of its leadership's decision to accept Italy's NATO commitments as part of its binding programmatic party objectives. Several indications suggest a close connection between this crucial decision and the elaboration of the "historic compromise" strategy put forth by Berlinguer in fall 1973.

Berlinguer's proposals, dubbed by some participants of the fourteenth PCI Congress (March 1975) a "perspective" and by others an "offer" (addressed to the Democrazía Cristiana), signaled an inherent preference for a long-term cooperation pact with the Christian Democrats, though envisaging some kind of PSI partnership as well. By this preference Berlinguer clearly rejected the rival strategy of the "left-wing alternative," based on an alliance with the PSI against the DC. This conclusion is backed by much circumstantial evidence, by Terracini's immediate protest against the acceptance of the DC as the favorite ally,[43] and by the fact that the PCI never really tried to enlist PSI support for a joint effort resembling the *Pro-*

gramme commun elaborated by the French *Union de la gauche*. Apparently the PCI leaders did not even ask the PSI for consultations on this matter.

On the other hand, the PCI could not avoid tackling the problem of its own "democratic legitimation" vis-à-vis Italy's EC and NATO partners. Presumably this question was of primary importance in the deliberations which finally prompted Berlinguer to develop his new strategic conception. For if the PCI leadership really intended to make a serious bid for government participation, it had to expect that Italy's allies and EC associates would be alarmed by such a prospect. On balance, it could be assumed, however, that foreign objections to a cabinet formula including PCI ministers would be mildest if this cabinet were headed by a Christian Democrat premier, with the ministries of foreign affairs, of defense, and of the interior all led by DC appointees or, alternatively, by well-known PRI, PSDI, or PLI figures. Under such conditions, even the danger of a halt in foreign credits and investments or of a panicky flight of capital from Italy into other countries could be kept under control.

A government of the "left-wing alternative," in fact, would meet quite different reactions within Italy and abroad, if only because in it the PCI could not avoid assuming the role of senior partner, while the PSI's relative weakness would relegate it by necessity to junior partner status. The PCI leadership has no reason to want such a "solution" with its consequences: a period of uncertainty and suspense, capital flight, loan embargoes, investment boycotts, media polemics, instability, and so on. Neither is it interested, as is occasionally pointed out by PCI spokesmen in private, in taking over a completely rundown state machinery (comparable to the case of the Naples city government) or in administering the collapse of the country's economy, which the foreign response to the formation of a cabinet of a "left-wing alternative" might well bring to pass.

But obviously the Italian CP has been plunged into a deep crisis of identity by its opting for the "historic compromise," for "broad understandings" (meaning cooperation with the DC) also in the regions, for backing Premier Andreotti's conservative economic policies, and for advocating an austerity program requiring both PCI and trade-union support. This crisis was acknowledged by the party press[44] and was confirmed by the results of the administrative elections held in May 1978. Most section, provincial, and regional party secretaries appeared to be deeply worried by this state of affairs.[45]

They had to defend their party leadership against (ultraleftist) accusations of "parliamentary cretinism" and other forms of drifting toward "Social Democratism." In some cases PCI militants have joined the "Red Brigades." Many rank-and-file members sympathize with the terrorists and shield them against investigations conducted by party and trade-union functionaries at the party section, party cell, and workshop levels. The campaign of denunciation directed against the allegedly "revisionist" and "reformist" PCI leadership by ultraleftist papers like *Lotta continua, Quotidiano dei lavoratori,* or *Il manifesto* has considerable effect almost everywhere at the party base and in particular among the members of the PCI's youth league (FGCI—Federazione Giovanile Comunista Italiana).

At the party's "open left flank" a sizeable "ultraleftist area" has taken shape. It is kept under close surveillance by the PCI leadership, which has had to ward off repeated (although unsuccessful) attempts by groups in that political space to split the Communist organization.

One of the results of this ultraleftist challenge has been that the PCI's executive bodies have become increasingly anxious recently to keep relations with the CPSU as calm as possible. Presumably this concern is at least partly motivated by the belief that to be on good terms with the CPSU leadership provides the best kind of insurance against Soviet-sponsored efforts to split the PCI or to establish a new, less autonomous rival party on its side, in imitation of the Finnish, Swedish, or Spanish precedents. Moreover, the maintenance of regular party relations with the CPSU makes it much easier for the PCI to distinguish itself from organized "Social Democratism" represented in Italy by the PSI and the PSDI. On the other hand, the PCI leadership does not perceive any really compelling reason to abandon its present policy of active, critical presence within the international Communist movement. It would be, therefore, most unrealistic to expect the PCI to precipitate an open break with the Soviet leadership.

The New PSI: The Party of Democratic Socialism

Though there is a general proclivity among scholarly analysts to define postwar Italy's configuration of political parties as an "imperfect two-party system" (*bipartitismo imperfetto*)[46] or a "semipolarized two-party system" (*bipartitismo semi-polarizzato*),[47] political developments, whether in the country's parliamentary arena or outside of it, have always in reality been determined by three major parties. From the early postwar years to the present, DC and PCI could never afford to disregard the Socialist party's weight as an important third mass movement. Initially the Socialists (under the name of PSIUP) ranked second at the polls, for example, in the elections for the Constituent Assembly in June 1946, when they garnered 20.7 percent of the vote (PCI: 19 percent; DC: 35.2 percent). In organizational strength, the PSIUP also held second place that year, with more than 860,000 members (PCI: 2,068,300; DC: almost 700,000).[48]

The spectacular PSIUP schism in January 1947 gave the PCI the decisive boost and enable it to gain the dominating position on the left. For the left-wing Socialists (PSI), led by Pietro Nenni (the former PSIUP left wing), dropped into a subordinate role in relation to the Communists, a development due also to the fact that they conceived themselves as an autonomous party of revolutionary Marxists, if not Marxist–Leninists. Ever since 1934 the Italian Socialists had been closely tied to the Communists by a "pact for unity of action," concluded in Paris and renewed in October 1946. With Nenni, whom the Soviets honored in 1951 with a Stalin Peace Prize, many left-wing Socialists believed in those years that postwar developments would lead rather quickly to the full triumph of socialism under Soviet auspices everywhere in Western Europe.

Only after the twentieth CPSU Congress did the PSI begin to dissociate itself from the PCI. The unity of action pact was replaced by a less strong agreement on mutual consultation, although the principle of unity of action remained valid for the PCI–PSI partnership within their bipartisan labor federation CGIL (Confederazione Generale Italiana del Lavoro; membership figure for 1977: 4,316,177).[49] Contacts with the Social Democrats were reestablished at a meeting between Nenni and Giuseppe Saragat in the fall of 1956. In the general elections held in May 1958, the PSI made substantial gains, polling 14.26 percent (PCI: 22.72 percent; PSDI: 4.56 percent; DC: 42.35 percent) compared with 12.73 percent in 1953. But it took four more years before the PSI leadership accepted Italy's NATO membership in a Central Committee statement of January 1962.

In the meantime the reformist PSIUP wing had given birth to the Democratic Socialist party (PSDI—Partito Socialista Democratico Italiano), led by Giuseppe Saragat. This organization, immediately denounced by the Communists as a CIA puppet and still caricatured as such in the PCI's Almanac in 1972, joined the government in December 1947 and became a reliable pillar of the "democratic center" cabinets which administered the country until 1963, normally backed by a parliamentary majority based on a DC–PSDI–PRI–PLI coalition. Throughout, both the PSDI and the PSI remained member organizations of the Socialist International with equal status.

In the PSDI, a party advocating social reforms and progressive secularization, lawyers, teachers, university professors, administrators, and civil servants always played a dominant role. For many years it was characterized as much by its anticommunism as by its anticlericalism. For some time its labor wing held control, jointly with some PRI unionists, over the UIL (Unione Italiana del Lavoro; membership figure for 1977: 1,086,620),[50] a trade-union federation which came under preponderant PSI influence during the "hot autumn" campaigns of 1969–70. The PSDI's share of electoral votes was never very impressive (4.5 to 7.1 percent). In June 1976 it sagged to a scanty 3.4 percent (Senate: 3.1 percent), and obtained 3.8 percent (Senate: 4.2 percent) three years later.

When the left-wing Socialists entered the first Moro cabinet (vice-premier: Nenni) in December 1963, the PSI's reintegration into the "democratic camp" could be regarded as definitely accomplished. Simultaneously a period of "center-left" alliances began, destined to last for about thirteen years. It started with ambitious reform programs—plans and expectations which soon had to be drastically scaled down because of the rapidly deteriorating economic situation. In time, therefore, the crisis management functions of government became clearly predominant.

This was the setting in which the student and youth revolt started in 1967, followed by the "hot autumn" in 1969-70, along with outbreaks of neofascist violence and mysterious bomb explosions. Rumors and revelations concerning putschist activities and a suspected plot by reactionary forces within and outside the administration, allegedly working for the repression of social progress, gave rise to a psychosis which seized the entire left and crystallized into a specific theory of a conspiratorial "strategy of tension." Meanwhile, ultraleftist terrorists formed their first combat groups and common criminal violence began to reach alarming dimensions.

In spite of all this, the years of "center-left" rule were years of rapidly increasing mass consumption and of substantially rising standards of living for the working population. They were also years of general liberalization of social behavior and of considerable progress in the fields of secularization and emancipation. Beyond that, many significant reform projects were realized, including the codification of workers' and trade-union rights by the new "Labor Statute"; the legislation giving substance to the fifteen "regular" autonomous regions set up in 1970; the enactment of the divorce law; the introduction of the popular referendum; the creation of instruments for economic planning and price control by government agencies; the lowering of the minimum voting age to eighteen years; the legislation on public subsidization of political parties; and many other reform measures.

A certain initial stabilization of the general pattern resulted in December 1964 from the election of PSDI leader Giuseppe Saragat to the office of President of the Republic, for which the Communists' agreement had been previously secured. In October 1966 a new Unified Socialist party (PSU—Partito Socialista Unificato) was founded on the basis of a PSI-PSDI merger but proved to be shortlived. After the disappointing outcome of the elections of May 1968 (the combined 1963 PSI-PSDI percentage declined from 20 percent to 14.5 percent), both parties were separately reestablished in July 1969.

Owing to the unhappy merger experiment, the PSI suffered a series of severe setbacks. Although membership losses from left-wing defections were negligible, a considerable portion of the PSI electorate had lost confidence and turned to other banners. Many former PSI followers finally became PCI voters, often after supporting for a while the candidates of the left-wing PSIUP secession, founded in 1964 by Tullio Vecchietti and Dario Valori (both of whom jumped on the PCI bandwagon in 1972).

Within the PSI leadership unbridled factionalism led to the formation of five main subgroups. These engaged in strident controversies, competing for political predominance or profitable positions. But in spite of the Socialists' mishaps, it must be said that these were not chiefly the outgrowth of glaring political mistakes but rather by-products of their coresponsibility as a government party for the general development of the socioeconomic and political crisis.

It was only natural that some PSI leaders began to show signs of increasing nervousness in view of the growing danger of being pulverized between the grindstones of the PCI on the one hand and their DC coalition partners on the other side. They felt altogether betrayed when Moro, without previous warning, used a public speech on September 12, 1975, to address the Communists for the first time directly as possible interlocutors in future negotiations on programmatic agreements.[51] Soon thereafter the supporters of the ''left-wing alternative'' gained the upper hand within the PSI leadership. In the early days of 1976 this change of mood was followed by a PSI Executive Committee decision which blew up the parliamentary government coalition (including DC, PRI, PSI), toppled the ''two-colored'' Moro-Ugo La Malfa cabinet and thus caused the government crisis which led to general elections held on June 20-21, 1976.

The Socialists did not stick, however, to the call for a ''left-wing alternative'' as their key slogan for the election campaign. They launched a dual offensive instead, directed simultaneously against the DC and the PCI, but only to suffer another defeat. Although the PSI results (House: 9.67 percent; Senate: 10.23 percent) did not drop below the levels of 1972, losses in relation to the regional and provincial elections held in 1975 (12.1 percent) amounted to roughly 2.4 points. This failure triggered a young turks' revolt which compelled PSI National Secretary Francesco De Martino to resign in July 1976. His position was taken over by Bettino Craxi, a Nenni protégé aged forty-two, backed by a strong group of left-wingers under Claudio Signorile, aged thirty-nine. Existing factions (*correnti*) were dissolved by Central Committee edict and ''definitely'' abandoned two years later.[52]

It has always been difficult for the PSI to defend its identity against rival DC and PCI ambitions, rooted in the competing universalist pretensions of both these parties, and to hold its own ground as a mass party. For the DC and the PCI share a common tendency to monopolize power wherever possible on the basis of ideological premises. Both have been unflagging in their efforts to subordinate wider segments of society to their political and cultural hegemony. In the light of these experiences, the PSI's organizational and ideological renaissance, which began in early April 1978 with its forty-first party congress, must be reckoned among the most important developments on the Italian political scene in recent years.

Under the Craxi-Signorile leadership it did not take long for the Socialists to formulate a new program giving primary importance to a clear definition of the PSI's place in that scene, with particular reference to the principles of "democratic socialism." In this program[53] socioeconomic aims (progressive democratization of the existing socioeconomic order in conformity with a liberalistic type of socialism; reliable safeguards for individual rights and collective liberties) are closely connected with a firm commitment to ideological pluralism and a clear option for West European integration on the basis of a specific Social Democratic development model.

In confrontation with both the other major parties, the "new" PSI is obviously trying to establish itself as the mass party most sincerely pledged to social progress and to cultural and spiritual freedom. By advocating a policy of "national unity" to master the country's present crisis, the PSI has signaled a continuing preference for a broad emergency cabinet with Communist participation. Originally, the new PSI leadership had stressed that it would accept neither a revival of "center-left" coalitions based on preferential cooperation with the DC nor a government alliance headed by the PCI. After Craxi succeeded in early July 1978 in securing the election of a Socialist as President of the Republic, it was no surprise that the PSI's bargaining terms, in the opening phase of the 1979 negotiations over government participation, included the designation of a Socialist as premier. The former insistence on equal terms for PSI and PCI "responsibility sharing" (*corresponsabilizzazione*)[54] has been toned down very much since the Communists wrecked the five-party coalition in January 1979.

Essential to the definition of the "new" PSI's attitude toward the Communists are three areas where further changes are demanded as a prerequisite for an alliance of the "left-wing alternative" type.

1. The PCI is urged to revise its "special relationship" with the USSR and the other East European countries claiming to represent "real existing socialism," in favor of an unequivocal commitment to EC membership and cooperation within the community's West European and Atlantic environments.

2. The Communists are expected to participate in the realization of a West European economic union as envisaged by Socialist blueprints and to demonstrate "full solidarity" with those countries or "leftist" government parties (for example, West Germany's SPD and the British Labour party) pledged to such policy objectives.

3. The PSI holds that further PCI efforts to overcome Leninism are indispensable, given that the Communists appear to be still very much conditioned by ideological and political categories derived from Leninist tenets and principles.[55]

It is therefore most unlikely that a PSI-PCI alliance could be formed under the "left-wing alternative" banner within a short time frame. But the PSI continues to advocate the inclusion of the PCI in a broad coalition cabinet in order to give it a larger share in government responsibility during the present emergency. The main purpose of this plea is, presumably, to secure maximum Communist support for a medium-term national recovery program.

At present, in fact, the PSI occupies a genuinely key position on the domestic stage. A DC-PSI alliance would be strong enough to form a fully self-sufficient majority cabinet. Arithmetically, the seats held by the DC and the PSI groups in both houses of parliament would do for a solid government majority. The availability of additional coalition partners among the smaller parties of the "center" (PRI, PSDI) could be taken for granted.

Ever since mid-1976 the PSI has used its pivotal position quite effectively to accelerate the processes of adaptation which have begun to operate within both the DC and the PCI. Immediately after the elections held in June 1976 it was the pressure exerted by the PSI, in the main, which compelled the DC leadership to bring the ambiguous situation under control through the device of an ingenious no-nonconfidence (*nonsfiducia*) voting coalition including both the PSI and the PCI. This expedient allowed the third Andreotti cabinet (a *monocolore* DC minority cabinet) to obtain the necessary parliamentary support through prearranged abstentions when it was put to the vote, first in the Senate (on August 6) and thereafter in the Chamber of Deputies (on August 11, 1976).

Likewise, the PSI played an important part in drafting the program outline (*intesa programmatica*) agreed upon by the six member parties of the "no-nonconfidence" coalition, thereby giving substance to the PCI's participation in government responsibilities: with the approval of this program by the Chamber of Deputies in the early hours of July 16, 1977, the PCI's coresponsibility for the government's performance was raised to a much higher level.

Toward the end of 1977 the PSI and the PRI began to press strongly for the opening of the third phase of PCI reassociation, demanding the Communists' inclusion in a new parliamentary majority. Both parties helped to transform the program outline approved on July 16 into a coalition agreement to serve as general guidance for the fourth Andreotti cabinet (once more, a DC minority cabinet). This cabinet was inaugurated on March 16, 1978 (the day of the Moro abduction), on the basis of two votes of confidence supported by all the parties of the new coalition—DC, PCI, PSI, PSDI, PRI—in both houses with overwhelming majorities.

The powerful leverage commanded by the PSI was applied most convincingly on the occasion of the presidential election in June–July 1978: while blocking the entry of PRI leader Ugo La Malfa (a frequent critic of PSI policies) to the Quirinale Palace, Craxi brought both the DC and the PCI to agree on Sandro Pertini, a PSI candidate squarely opposed to the "historic compromise" design.

Looking Ahead: Forebodings of an Eternal Compromise?

As the Communists have been asserting ever since the early 1970s, it has become impossible to govern Italy without or against the PCI. Developments after the June 1976 elections fully confirmed the truth of this slogan, although the important part played by the PSI in strengthening the PCI's hand should not be ignored. But it is equally true that it would be even more impossible to govern the nation without or against the Democrazia Cristiana.

The DC has remained a large popular and mass party. In February and March 1978, party chairman Moro, backed in particular by Benigno Zaccagnini and other members of the National Secretariat, won a decisive victory, after long internal quarrels, over those groups within the DC leadership which had stubbornly opposed any cooperation with the Communists. Defeated at the same time were certain right-wing strategems whose promoters favored the transformation of the DC into a one-dimensional conservative party reduced in scope to the representation of middle-class, enterprise, and business interests together with those of Catholic fundamentalists and the clergy.

For the present, the Democrazía Cristiana continues to be also a party of Catholic wage-earners. In spring 1977 the CISL (Confederazione Italiana di Sindacati Lavoratori), a trade-union federation loosely associated with it, had 2,823,815 members.[56] Other DC working-class strongholds are the Catholic Workers Associations (Associazioni Cristiane Lavoratori Italiani). Although the ACLI were tormented by serious internal upheavals which in the crisis year 1969 threatened to wreck the entire movement, they finally were able to reconsolidate their ranks (present strength: roughly 500,000 members) and reestablished their former close ties with the DC.[57]

According to a survey conducted in early 1978, the DC's share of the factory workers' vote still seems to reach 26 percent (PCI, 53 percent; PSI, 11 percent; MSI, 4 percent; PSDI, 2 percent; PRI, 2 percent; DP and PR, 2 percent).[58] A breakdown of figures related to the regional and provincial elections held in 1975 indicates that 35.5 percent of the total voting strength of unskilled industrial and farm workers was attracted to the DC (PCI: 32.3 percent), which also obtained a 42.6 percent share of the total vote of skilled workers and farmers (PCI: 32.3 percent). On the whole, the social composition of the DC electorate is strikingly similar to that of the total national electorate.[59]

After the 1976 elections the leaders of the DC's "left-wing" elements (social reformers, "base" left-wingers, trade unionists, and so on) entered into an alliance with some of the most influential pragmatists (Piccoli, Andreotti) and "possibilists" (E. Colombo, D. Antoniozzi, V. Russo, and so on). National Secretary Zaccagnini proved to be a cleverer tactician and tougher fighter than originally expected. Although the "fundamental renewal" (*rifondazione*) of the party envisaged by him made little progress, the overall coherence of the leadership, at least, considerably improved. While up to 1975 the DC could be correctly described as a federation of ten or twelve strongly "personalized" sub-parties, there is not much left of the former clientelistic clans today.Most of them disintegrated and were absorbed by the two main groupings now identified most clearly with their to representatives: Zaccagnini-Andreotti-Galloni on the one hand and Fanfani-Forlani-Bartolomei on the other.

Within the DC leadership and its parliamentary groups (as well as on the regional and municipal levels) the process of rejuvenation has made remarkable headway. Roughly 25 percent of the DC deputies elected in 1976 were serving their first term in the central Parliament. A sizable group belonged to the militant Catholic movement Comunione e Liberazione (CL) which has found strong roots, particularly in some regions of northern Italy.[60] There is no doubt that the entire party has been roused by this league's activism and missionary spirit. But the DC leadership is also aware of the necessity to bridle CL zealotry whenever it might interfere with the party's political principles or strategy. Similar problems exist in relation to the DC's powerful free-enterprise and management wing, which repeatedly gave the impression of contemplating a party split in response to the gradual shifting of the DC towards positions of "leftist collaborationism."

In the wake of the DC's move toward "broad understandings" with the parties of the "classical left," the so-called buffer parties—Social Democrats (PSDI), Republicans (PRI), and Liberals (PLI)—have also effected similar shifts. As a result, practically all parties (excepting only the neofascist MSI, the National Democrats, and the Südtiroler Volkspartei) tend to behave, at present, as if they belonged to the "left."

The DC even reaped praise from the director of the PCI's official daily *l'Unità*, Executive Committee member Alfredo Reichlin. In a front-page editorial published on March 3, 1978, he saluted the victory achieved then by Moro and Zaccagnini over their own party's "anticollaborationist" wing as a significant step forward, adding that behind "the DC's seemingly motionless facade" a momentous "reshuffling of forces" had occurrred— the most important readjustment "since the times of De Gasperi's struggle with [his clerico-conservative antagonist] Gedda." He also paid tribute to Italy—meaning obviously the DC leadership—for having avoided, when challenged by crisis, choosing "the way hitherto always preferred in the capitalist world," namely the way of class repression and of tampering with the constitutional order, and of adopting instead a course "offering coresponsibility, granting democratic participation, and broadening the area of consent."

After this overture an understanding between DC and PCI became almost inevitable. But the prospect of a "marriage" of the two giants was particularly disturbing for the PSI. Its leadership's impetuous counter-moves were mainly motivated by its fear that close DC–PCI cooperation might lead first to the crushing of the PSI and finally to the elimination of all minor parties.

The "antirevisionist" groups on the extreme left felt equally menaced by what they consider the fatal consequences of such an alliance.[61] Spokesmen of the ultraleftists have denounced over and over again the alleged intention of the two major parties to establish in Italy a "protected democracy," allegedly on the West German pattern. Both parties are accused of seeking jointly the eradication of all political forces with truly revolutionary concepts and of working for the "Germanization" of Italy by a step-by-step operation.[62] Among these groups Moro not only passed for one of the intellectual authors of this strategy, but he was also believed to be particularly capable and determined to secure its speedy realization.

In December 1977 Senator Ugo Pecchioli, the PCI Executive Committee member responsible for internal security matters, commented on the presumed motives behind the offensive launched by "red terrorism" subsequent to the electoral triumph achieved by the PCI in June 1976. He attributed the spreading of political violence mainly to the impatience of youthful revolutionaries and in particular to their hotheaded incomprehension of the cautious circumspect attitude of the Communist party at a moment when the "working class" appears to have reached "the threshold of power" and time seems ripe for "a radical change" of "historical importance." Pecchioli made clear that the extremists' determination to exploit this situation for terrorist activities supposedly intended to spark off the "insurrection of the proletariat" was considered sheer "madness" by his own party. Pickets should be set up, he suggested, for the protection of factories against sabotage, and terrorists should be denounced to the authorities.[63]

According to Pecchioli's estimate the number of underground terrorists (*clandestini*) did not exceed 700 or 800 at the time, right-wing extremists included. They are supported by roughly 10,000 active auxiliaries from the ranks of Autonomia Operaia, a students' and punks' movement which only in some large cities (Rome, Turin, Milan, Genoa) has been able to gain a footing among industrial workers or within production plants. As Pecchioli further stressed, this group of militant helpers is surrounded by a much larger "zone of political solidarity" whose components include also most members of the ultraleftist organization Lotta Continua (set up in 1969) and similar associations.[64] Apparently the disbandment of the association Potere Operaio (founded in 1967), which disappeared in 1973, was "strategically" linked to the birth of the Autonomia Operaia movement in the same year.[65]

The "Moro strategy" of limited collaboration and burden-sharing with the PCI, applied by the DC leadership since mid-1976, should not be mistaken for a prelude to a surrender. For all the parties involved—DC, PSI, PRI, PSDI—this strategy is closely tied to the conviction that the PCI leadership must indeed be held coresponsible for many of the grievances of the Italian population, even more so because it has failed over a period of thirty years openly to account for its particular liabilities before the electorate. If the Communists were permitted permanently to monopolize the opposition role in times of crisis, it is argued, they would presumably continue to improve their position in each successive election and eventually overtake the DC as the "party of the relative majority" or even win the absolute majority of votes (and parliamentary seats). Therefore it would not be wise to muddle on as before without making an attempt to reduce the risks involved.

Once the PCI had become the "party of the relative majority" it would also be entitled, at least in principle, to ask for the premiership. In any case, its leaders would be in a much better bargaining position for negotiations with the other parties and potential coalition partners. Thus it would be considerably less risky and politically wiser, according to spokesmen of various parties, to admit the PCI to a regular government coalition as early as possible, before it might lost interest in a "historic compromise" arrangement and cease to content itself with junior partner status.[66]

Those DC, PRI, and PSI leaders who advocate the inclusion of the Communists in a government coalition, and eventually also into the cabinet,[67] see their admission mainly as a political deal obliging the PCI to shoulder full coresponsibility for unpopular government decisions: for the sacrifices a severe austerity program might impose on everybody; for curbing labor demands and other corporate interests; for the fight against unemployment; and for the struggle against the economic decay of Italy's southern regions. It is expected, moreover, that legislative and executive burden-sharing would accelerate the PCI's effective political integration.

Moro's "third phase" strategy was confirmed, although with some qualifications, in a programmatic DC document released by the Executive Committee on May 11, 1979. This "appeal to the voters," published three weeks before polling-day, reiterated the party leadership's commitment to a "policy of national solidarity" designed "to achieve, in view of the emergency, the broadest consent in support of the institutions and—facilitated by large parliamentary convergences—concordant exertions to reactivate development under conditions of democratic security." The declared goal of "democratic unity" should not be confused, however, with a desire to establish "unanimity-seeking government alliances," the document warned. Upholding the "realistic assessment" of the profound DC-PCI divergencies, which had "determined the well-known limits fixed by the DC, proposed and accepted when the agreements of March 1978 were reached," the Executive Committee emphasized its firm intention, sealed by a "solemn pledge" before the DC electorate, to refrain from "the formation of governments with PCI participation."[68]

Nevertheless, experienced observers outside the two mammoth parties are still afraid that both the DC and the PCI might get so accustomed to competitive cooperation that they would be tempted to establish a bipartisan "condominium" on that basis. They fear, to put it in a nutshell, that partnership agreements between DC and PCI could become a bad habit and degenerate into a kind of "eternal compromise" of power-sharing.

Notes

1. See tables "Redditi di lavoro 1970-1978, incrementi monetari e variazioni del potere d'acquisto," and "Retribuzioni nette e loro evoluzione in rapporto al salario dell'operaio specializzato dell'industria," *Corriere dell' Economia* (supplement to *Corriere della Sera*), May 24, 1979; Cesare Merzagora, "L'Italia è ricca...," *la Repubblica,* April 4, 1979.

2. Unemployment figures from Gilio Mazzocchi, "Crescono di 129 mila i disoccupati nel corso di un anno," *la Repubblica*, March 24, 1979: in January 1979 the total included more than 214,000 dismissed workmen or employees, almost 905,000 applicants for first employment, and 513,000 "other" applicants registered as housewives, students, or pensioners. See also Giovanni Russo, "Disperato Sud," *Corriere della Sera*, November 20, 1978, reporting a total figure of 1,381,000 unemployed, of whom 834,000 in the Mezzogiorno regions. See further the tabular survey for 1977-78 by provinces: "Disoccupazione: Giovani e adulti iscritti nelle liste di collocamento e disoccupati non disponibili," *Congiuntura Sociale*, CESPE Bulletin no. 2, February 1979, p. 12.

3. Target figures from "Bozza di programma triennale," presented by Minister of the Treasury Filippo M. Pandolfi to the Chamber of Deputies on Octber 11, 1978. A report on the economic situation, including a survey of performance in 1978, was given by ministers Pandolfi and Bruno Visentini on March 31, 1979 (*Il Popolo,* April 1, 3, 1979). See also Antonio Gambino, "Bilancio di un viaggio in URSS," *L'Espresso* 24: 7 (February 19, 1978); for the 1972-77 period Italy's real GNP increases averaged 3 percent annually (*la Repubblica*, October 5, 1978).

4. See "Reddito aumentato del 2, 6% nel 1978," *Corriere della Sera*, April 1, 1979. The rate of inflation computed for 1978 varies according to definition between 12.9 and 13.3 percent ("prezzi impliciti"); see *Il Popolo*, April 1, 1979.

5. See "Le cifre del sangue e del fuoco," *la Repubblica*, March 2, 1979, dossier no. 5 (La Violenza), based on figures released by the Ministry of the Interior.

6. See Stephen Hellman, "The Italian CP: Stumbling on the Threshold?" *Problems of Communism* 27: 6 (November-December 1978): 31-48, esp. pp. 36-38.

7. Draft version "Projetto di tesi per il 15° Congresso nazionale del PCI," *l'Unità*, December 10, 1978, supplement (ninety-one theses); final version: *La politica e l'organizzazione dei comunisti italiani. Le tesi e lo statuto approvati dal XV Congresso nazionale del PCI* (Rome: Editori Riuniti, April 1979).

8. Giorgio Galli, *Storia della Democrazia Cristiana* (Rome-Bari: Laterza, 1978), pp. 410-411, 476 (quoted from *Il Popolo*, July 21, 1975).

9. Pietro Scoppola, *La proposta politica di De Gasperi* (Bologna: Il Mulino, 1977), pp. 253-323.

10. Giorgio Galli, *Storia della Democrazia Cristiana*, pp. 61-64. Giorgio Bocca, *Palmiro Togliatti* (Rome-Bari: Laterza, 1973), p. 518, refers to consultations held in April 1947 between PCI Deputy Secretary-General Pietro Secchia and CPSU representative D. Shevlyagin on preparations for an armed insurrection, and later reported by Secchia himself.

11. Giorgio Campanini, *Fede e politica 1943-1951. La vicenda ideologica della sinistra d.c.* (Brescia: Morcelliana, 1976); Gianni Baget-Bozzo, *Il partito cristiano al potere. La DC di De Gasperi e di Dossetti 1945-1954* (Florence: Vallecchi, 1974); Paolo Possenti, *Storia della DC dalle origini al centro-sinistra* (Rome: Ciarrapico, 1978); Franco Rodano, "La questione democristiana," *Quaderni della Rivista Trimestrale* 13: 45 (Fall 1975): 3-74.

12. Giorgio Galli, *Storia della Democrazia Cristiana*, pp. 76, 143-147; Giuseppe Tamburrano, *L'iceberg democristiano* (Milan: SugarCo, 1975), pp. 58-63.

13. Giuseppe Di Palma, *Surviving without Governing: The Italian Parties in Parliament* (Berkeley-Los Angeles: University of California Press, 1977); Franco Cazzola, *L'opposizione di un partito di governo. Il PCI in Parlamento dal 1948 al 1972*, mimeographed conference paper, June 1973, 66 pp.; see also *Corriere della Sera*, November 21, 1973.

14. Enrico Berlinguer, *La "questione comunista" 1969-1975* (Rome: Editori Riuniti, 1975), vol. 2, pp. 609-639 (originally published in *Rinascita* 30: 38-40 September 28, October 5 and 12, 1975).

15. Antonio Tatò, ed., *Comunisti e mondo cattolico oggi* (Rome: Editori Riuniti, 1977), pp. 78-80 ("Per un patto di azione comune con la DC;" July 9, 1944, excerpt), pp. 94-98 ("Un accordo tra communisti e cattolici per un ampio movimento che salvi la civiltà umana dall'ecatombe atomica," April 12, 1954, excerpt), pp. 98-104 ("Il destino dell'uomo;" March 20, 1963, excerpt).

16. Enrico Berlinguer, *La "questione comunista,"* pp. 958-961 ("L'esercizio dell'egemonia politica proletaria," December 12, 1974,

excerpt); Luciano Gruppi, *Il concetto di egemonia in Gramsci* (Rome: Editori Riuniti, 1972).

17. Claudio Signorile, "Il Pci non è ancora un partito di governo," *la Repubblica*, July 28, 1978.

18. Eugenio Scalfari, "L'ultima intervista di Moro," October 14, 1978.

19. To the 15th PCI Congress Berlinguer reported that membership strength was 1,790,450 as of December 31, 1978; he openly acknowledged a decrease by 23,704 members since December 31, 1977; see *l'Unità*, March 31, 1979.

20. Giovanna Zincone, *I partiti tra due elezioni* (Turin: Guerrini, 1977), p. 137; DC membership figure for March 1976 (13th Congress): 1, 731, 241.

21. See *la Repubblica*, March 29, 1978 (41st Congress). A higher PSI membership total of 450,000 is given by *EUSO* 10 (December 1978): 13 (published monthly by the Confederation of the Socialist Parties of the European Community).

22. See *EUSO*; the much higher figure of 617,999 PSDI members recorded by Giovanna Zincone, *I partiti*, p. 115, for March 1976 (17th congress), although apparently taken from an "official" source, must be considered unreliable.

23. Giovanna Zincone, *I partiti*, p. 181; PLI membership figure for April 1976 (15th Congress): 138, 485.

24. See *Corriere della Sera*, June 14, 1978 (33rd Congress).

25. *Raccolta di dati sull' organizzazione* (Rome: Direzione PCI, November 1976), vol. 2, pp. 127, 147; *PCI '73. Almanacco del Partito comunista italiano* (Rome: Direzione PCI, 1973), p. 21: "51.5 percent of the section secretaries are workers."

26. *Raccolta di dati sull'organizzazione*, pp. 35-37 (figures for 1975).

27. Alessandro Natta, "La Resistenza e la formazione del 'partito nuovo,'" *Problemi di storia del Partito comunista italiano* (Rome: Editori Riuniti, 1971), pp. 57-83, esp. pp. 60-66.

28. This was most succinctly confirmed by PCI Central Committee member Lucio Lombardo Radice when he stated on behalf of his party's leadership: "We are all Marxists-Leninists-Gramsciists-Togliattiists—because they were all revisionists"; see G.R. Urban, ed., *Eurocommunism* (London: Maurice Temple Smith, 1978), p. 50.

29. Togliatti emphasized the PCI's task to find "our own way, the Italian way" to socialism for the first time explicitly in public at the party's organizational conference held in Florence in January 1947; see Palmiro Togliatti, *Il partito* (Rome: Editori Ruiniti, 1964), p. 116; Alessandro Natta, "La Resistenza," pp. 74-75.

30. See the text of the new PCI program adopted by the 8th Congress (December 1956) in *La dichiarazione programmatica e le Tesi dell'VIII Congresso del PCI* (Rome: Editori Riuniti, 1957). According to Paolo Bufalini's testimony (*l'Unità*, April 24, 1977) the draft version was written by Togliatti for immediate publication (October 14, 1956, supplement). For Togliatti's remarks on the PCI's "gradualism" see *X Congresso del partito comunista italiano. Atti e risoluzioni* (Rome: Editori Riuniti, 1963), p. 71 (address given on December 2, 1962).

31. Palmiro Togliatti, "Promemoria sulle questioni del movimento operaio internazionale e della sua unità," *Rinascita* 21: 35 (September 5, 1964): 1-4, esp. p. 4.

32. Luciano Gruppi, *Socialismo e democrazia* (Milan: Edizioni del Calendario, 1969), pp. 515-575, 655-702; and Luciano Gruppi, *Il concetto di egemonia in Gramsci*.

33. See especially the bilateral declarations published jointly by the PCI and the PCE in *l'Unità*, July 12, 1975, as well as by the PCI and the PCF in *l'Unità*, November 11, 1975.

34. Luciano Gruppi, "Le tesi di Lenin e di Engels sullo Stato," *Rinascita* 21: 30 (July 25, 1964): 27-28; "Problemi dell'unità del movimento operaio e socialista italiano" (Joint CC-CCC Declaration), *Rinascita* 22: 24 (June 12, 1965): 15-22; Antonio Tato, "I comunisti italiani e la Costituzione," *Almanacco PCI'76* (Rome: Direzione PCI, 1976), pp. 90-108.

35. Ruggero Orfei, *Andreotti* (Milan: Feltrinelli, 1975), pp. 164-165.

36. See "Partito comunista italiano '78," pp. 34, 37; "La 'mappa' del potere locale," *L'Unità*, October 28, 1978.

37. Wolfgang Berner, "The Image of the PCI as a Radical-Democratic Reformist Party," *Lo Spettatore Internazionale* 13: 3 (July-September 1978): 183-197; Robert D. Putnam, "The Italian Communist Politician," *Communism in Italy and France* (Princeton, N.J.: Princeton Univ. Press, 1975), pp. 173-217, esp. p. 214.

38. Vittorio Gorresio, *Berlinguer* (Milan: Feltrinelli, 1976), pp. 36-37.

39. Giacomo Sani, "The PCI on the Threshold," *Problems of Communism* 25: 6 (November-December 1976): 27-51, esp. p. 34.

40. Zdeněk Mlynař, *Nachtfrost* (Cologne-Frankfurt: Europaische Verlagsanstalt, 1978).

41. Interview by Giampaolo Pansa in *Corrierre della Sera*, June 15, 1976. Berlinguer repeated his statements on NATO in an interview given to Gianfranco Piazzesi (ibid., May 6, 1979) before the June 1979 elections.

42. Enrico Berlinguer, *La "questione comunista,"* pp. 872-882 ("Proposte e obiettivi di lotta per una nuova politica," Dec. 10, 1974, excerpts), esp. p. 878; see also Berlinguer's report in *XIV Congresso del Partito comunista italiano. Atti e risoluzioni* (Rome: Editori Riuniti, 1975), pp.

15–76 (March 18, 1975), esp. pp. 31–33 and his concluding address, pp. 617–637, esp. pp. 623–624.

43. Ibid., 396–400 (March 21, 1975).

44. "Il partito, oggi," *Rinascita* 35: 1 (January 6, 1978): 9–13; Gianni Cervetti, "La salute del partito," *Rinascita* 34 (September 1, 1978): 1–2.

45. See Giampaolo Pansa's interview with Bruno Ferrero, PCI regional secretary for Piedmont, "Perche noi del PCI stiamo perdendo l'appoggio della gente," *la Repubblica,* September 23, 1978; also Pansa's interview with Claudio Petruccioli, Deputy Director of *l'Unità*, ibid., September 27, 1978.

46. Giorgio Galli, *Il bipartitismo imperfetto. Comunisti e demo-cristiani in Italia* (Bologna: Il Mulino, 1966); and *Dal bipartitismo imperfetto alla possibile alternativa* (Bologna: Il Mulino, 1975).

47. Nicola Matteucci et al., "La situazione politica italiana e le sue prospettive," *Il Mulino* 27: 256 (March–April 1978): 177–252, esp. pp. 180–181.

48. Celso Ghini, *Il voto degli italiani 1946–1974* (Rome: Editori Riuniti, 1975), p.43; *Raccolta di dati sull'organizzazione*, p. 405.

49. Figure from *Rinascita* 34: 22 (June 3, 1977): 3.

50. Ibid.

51. Giorgio Galli, *Storia della Democrazia Cristiana*, pp. 411–412 (commenting on Moro's address, published in *Il Popolo,* July 21, 1975); see also Giovanna Zincone, *I partiti,* pp. 16–19.

52. Gianfranco Pasquino, "The Italian Socialist Party: An Irreversible Decline?" in Howard R. Penniman, ed., *Italy at the Polls: The Parliamentary Elections of 1976* (Washington, D.C.: American Enterprise Institute for Public Policy Research, 1977), pp. 183–227, esp. 221–222; see also Renzo Di Rienzo, "Psi/Si scioglie la corrente anti-Craxi," *L'Espresso* 24: 21 (May 28, 1978):11–12; Francesco De Vito, "Psi/Verso il congresso," *L'Espresso* 24: 12 (March 26, 1978): 24–28; "Il congresso del Psi," *L'Espresso* 24: 14 (April 9, 1978): 28–30; Salvatore Tropea and Fausto De Luca, "È nato il nuovo Psi," *la Repubblica,* April 4, 1978.

53. *L'alternativa dei socialisti. Il progetto di programma del PSI presentato da Bettino Craxi* (Rome: Edizioni Avanti!, 1978), p. 1.

54. The emergence of this PSI position is described in detail by Gianfranco Pasquino, "The Italian Socialist Party," pp. 202, 221–222.

55. Claudio Signorile, "PCI non è ancora un partito di governo," July 28, 1978, p. 3; see also the debate initiated in summer 1978 with Bettino Craxi's essay "Il Vangelo Socialista," *L'Espresso* 24: 34 (August 27, 1978): 24–29, 98.

56. Figure from *Rinascita* 34: 22 (June 3, 1977): 3.

57. Vittorio Monti, "Le ACLI verso un'alternativa diversa da quella socialista," *Corriere della Sera,* January 13, 1978.

58. See *L'Espresso* 24: 8:126.

59. Figures calculated on the basis of the 1975 election statistics and "party profiles" elaborated by Giacomo Sani, "The PCI. . .," p. 31.

60. See esp. Giancarlo Galli, *Il Piave democristiano. I protagonisti della DC che cambia* (Milan: Longanesi, 1978).

61. See Giorgio Bocca, *Il terrorismo italiano 1970–1978* (Milan: Rizzoli, 1978), esp. for the author's indictment against "*cattocomunismo*," pp. 7–22.

62. Mino Monicelli, *L'ultrasinistra in Italia 1968–1978* (Rome-Bari: Laterza, 1978), p. 131.

63. Arminio Savioli, "Una conversazione con il compagno Pecchioli," *L'Unità,* December 14, 1977.

64. Ibid.

65. Mino Monicelli, *L'ultrasinistra. . . ,* pp. 47–48, 116–117.

66. This line of reasoning was explained to the author by authoritative DC, PRI, and PSI representatives as early as January–February 1976.

67. As Premier Andreotti suggested in September 1978, the admission of PCI reprsentatives to the cabinet had to be delayed beyond "the conclusion of this experiment" (that is, the five-party "*intesaprogrammatica*") and "the end of the legislative period" (which meant mid-1981, at the time). At a later stage of the process, he added, with reference to the PCI, it might become even possible "to speak of alternation as the Socialists do" (see Beppe Lopez, "Che cosa ha detto Andreotti al 'Quotidiano dei lavoratori,'" *la Repubblica,* September 23, 1978.

68. *Il Popolo,* May 12, 1979. Earlier, the DC National Council (composed of more than 180 members) had endorsed a more rigid version of the "Appeal," on April 21. It contained a pledge "never" to enter a government coalition (that is, cabinet) including the PCI or to accept other forms of DC-PCI partnership equivalent to "joint management of power" (see *Corriere della Sera,* April 22, 1979). Although publication of the "Appeal" was scheduled for April 25 (see *Il Popolo,* April 22, 1979), its original version apparently was held back for revision by the DC executive committee (forty-three members).

3

Ambivalence Yet Again Unresolved: The French Left, 1972-1978

Ronald Tiersky

Introduction

For six years after the Socialist party (PS) and Communist party (PCF) signed a joint governmental program in 1972, French politics was dominated by the possibility that the united left might win a national election and alter basic government policy and even the very structure of the French economy and society.

Facing the potentially historic elections of March 1978, however, the French "Union of the left" coalition of Socialists, Communists, and left radicals divided radically against itself. Because of this, although other factors had some influence as well, the left lost an election it had been earlier heavily favored to win. In losing the election the left also lost its chance to reorder French society. Owing to the quite extraordinary nature of the alliance, the internal tensions resulting from its defeat have been also extraordinary. Today, despite protestations of "left-wing unity" which leaders are politically obliged to sound, the "left" in France is moribund. Its future is, more than ever, a mass of contradictions and paradoxes. In a sense, survival itself is at issue.

Heading toward the 1978 elections, the alliance of French left parties failed to resolve, either for public opinion or more importantly for itself, its dominant problem—an ambivalence about going into government and about the uses to which government power should and could be put. Furthermore, ambivalence about governing divided not only the left as a whole against itself (that is, Socialist and Communist disagreements); it also divided each party within itself. To a surprising extent, even the mass organizations which had supported ardently the goal of a left-wing government—in particular the two socialist labor unions (CFDT and CGT)—ended up similarly struck by this seemingly unconquerable schizophrenia regarding not only how the left should govern, but whether it should govern at all.

The French Left Yesterday and Today

The "left" in France is a mythic beast. Since the Great Revolution of 1789, it has reemerged regularly out of what right-wing writers have sometimes termed *le pays réel,* a virtuous civil society opposed to *le pays légal* of corrupt governments and regimes. The left's purpose has been to promise, or to threaten, French society with greater social justice and a radical redistribution of wealth. As in other European countries, whereas French center and right-wing doctrines generally have called for greater liberty, the ideologies of the left have demanded first of all equality (as the means to social justice) and fraternity (in the form of working-class solidarity become the bond of general social cohesion). At the same time, in France as elsewhere, there have been not only moderate but also authoritarian extremes of both right- and left-wing doctrines, based on theories of irreconcilable social conflict which obliged the conclusion that the good society could be achieved only through repression of the "other" France.

Ever since French radicalism, the dominant middle and late nineteenth century left-wing doctrine, began to prevail decisively in its struggle for political and social secularization (permanent establishment of the Republic, permanent republican and democratic primary school system, the Dreyfus affair, formal separation of Church and State in 1905), socialism in one form or another has taken over as the predominant left-wing world-view. For a moment at the *fin de siècle*, it seemed that syndicalism would be the most powerful expression of this dream of egalitarian justice and community. But the anarcho-syndicalism of the pre-World War I *Confédération générale du travail* (CGT) could not in the nature of real politics have prevailed. "Party socialism" in the form of the *Section française de l'internationale ouvrière* (SFIO), which in 1905 unified the Guesdist, Jaurèsian, and other socialist currents into a single party, thereafter focused left-wing politics at the national level. The SFIO's quick ascendancy over syndicalism was obviously prepared by the early weakness of French labor unions (weak both in the sense of anarcho-syndicalism's political naivete and the relatively low level of unionization and representativeness of French unions generally).

The SFIO, along with nearly all other European socialist movements in the Second International, entered a profound crisis at the time of World War I at once over the issues of whether or not to "participate in a bourgeois government" (a false problem far from irrelevant even today) and, more importantly at the time, whether socialists should accept the war: that is, whether "working-class internationalism" should prevail over "bourgeois nationalism"; whether French workers, to use again the imagery of the time, should kill German workers for *la patrie*, or should instead unite with the European working class to effect the international proletarian revolution predicted by Marx and his successors for half a century.

As a result of the entangled disappointments of the Great War and the less-than-great peace, the Bolsheviks, victorious in Russia, found certain elements of Western European socialism in each country eager to join the

Communist International which they founded in 1919. In France, where anticolonialism and to some extent pacifism were already strongly associated with anticapitalism and antiimperialism, the French Communist party at its foundation in December 1920 immediately posed a formidable challenge to the dominant Socialist party, the now "revisionist" SFIO which had supported the war in a government of "national union."

I and other writers have analyzed elsewhere the history of Socialist-Communist rivalry on the French left since 1920, separating out the conjunctural ambivalence and ambiguities, and stressing the fundamental enduring differences.[1] Here, one need only say that the periods of left-wing alliance (Popular Front, 1934-38; "tripartism" with the Christian Democratic MRP, 1944-47; the "Union of the Left" since 1972, with the small Movement of Left-wing Radicals [MRG]), as well as the periods of hostility (the 1920s; during the Hitler-Stalin pact, 1939-41; during the cold war; off and on during the "Union of the Left"), have been conditioned more by the basic characteristics of each party than by circumstances. In a word, one understands more about French left-wing politics if one begins with the basic differences between Western European socialism and communism than if one masters the *histoire événementielle* of their various moments of conflict and cooperation. This fact implies a second: that the central issues dividing French socialism against itself in 1977-78, aside from matters of detail, are still the same disagreements which arose from the SFIO's choices in World War I and from the PCF's "bolshevization" in the 1920s and the crystallization of Stalinism in the 1930s.

However, this is not to say that both the PS and PCF in 1978 won victories of a sort by remaining true to themselves. On the contrary, the fact that the French left's central divisions have seemed indestructible seems to me, in a way analyzed in detail below, a considerable success for the Communists and failure of the Socialists.[2] The Communist party, largely through that persistence which is one of its admirable qualities, has obliged the French left-wing "audience" (and thus the Socialist party as an "actor") to speak a vocabulary and accept a symbolism derived at once from nineteenth-century political mythology and from international Communist experience, an anachronistic political discourse which serves the PCF well in its struggle against overwhelming odds, and which prevents the Socialist party from "being itself" or rather "becoming itself" politically. The Communist party, as I will argue below, is in a paradoxical sense France's classic "industrial party," a class-based anticapitalist party. The French Socialist party refounded in 1971 has seemed on the verge of becoming a "new" type of party, in some way uniquely a product of advanced capitalist political economy and postindustrial social structure.[3]

In another way, however, the PCF's success in 1977-78 in reimposing the traditional terms of left-right politics in France signifies its own greater failure. The Communist party, to the extent it remains within its old appeals and old limitations, is fated to wither as its historic social bases are transformed by macrosocial and economic processes. The Socialist party, to the extent it destroys the Communist quasi-monopoly of determining political discourse on the Left, can "become itself," that is, it can become the dominant party on the left, able to rally its social bases and pursue the policies to which it aspires by occupying a large and at present only partially exploited terrain which opinion polls consistently detect in contemporary French political consciousness.

The French left has been, indeed, to use a notorious Communist slogan, a political space where "unity is struggle." In this battle with the Socialists for dominance, and ultimately for survival, one is inclined to believe that unless the PCF makes a decisive adaptation to French and West European society—a "Eurocommunization" of the PCF which has been heretofore ambivalent and without deep enough roots—the Communist party in the long run can only lose. The Socialist party, on the other hand, can win, particularly if it is able to change more to its own favor the terms in which the struggle is fought.

One basic PS characteristic in the 1970s has been political ambiguity, or, some would say, duplicity—the necessity of speaking a Communist-derived language from one side of its mouth (that is, to challenge the PCF as the dominant socialist industrial party) and a new socialist language (*autogestionnaire*, decentralist, ecologist, and so on) from the other. Given the unusual dilemma of despising one's allies more than one's opponents, the PS, it may be said, did not surprise so much by its failure in the 1970s as by its near-success. This would be somewhat misleading, however. That so many Frenchmen remained loyal to the "Union of the Left," or rather that so few defected following the vicious internecine struggle launched by the Communist party in summer 1977, indicates that the desire for a left-wing government, or more precisely a vaguer desire for some alternative in governmental majority and policy, was widespread and rooted deep in French opinion after two decades of Gaullist-Centrist monopoly. Moreover, the policy it desired was indicated at least in the negative by the fact that the left-wing electoral gains in 1972–77 (over 10 percent) were made almost exclusively by the new Socialist party (along with minor gains by ecologists and the far left). At the same time, the Communist party and the small third partner in the "Common Program," the MRG, stagnated and center and right parties declined outright. A further indication was found in the fact that the last-minute voter shift away from the "Union of the Left" preceding the March 1978 elections came almost entirely at the expense of the Socialist party.

In other words, by 1978, after six years of left-wing alliance, no sector of French opinion had rallied to the PCF, indicating that even if the

Communists were perceived as somewhat less dangerous to public liberty than before, few voters had changed their minds about Communist policies or about the nature of the Communist party as such. On the contrary, a significant number of voters moved to the Socialists and were even willing to trust them, under certain conditions which were ultimately not fulfilled, to control the PCF in a coalition which would govern the country and implement policies of radical reform.

Our task in the rest of this chapter will be double: first, to sketch more in detail the basic Socialist-Communist differences, the tendencies within each party, as well as in the smaller political parties or groups in the outer corona of the left. Second, to evaluate the post–March 1978 situation according to the historic question posed above: does the "French left" still exist?

French Socialism and the New PS

François Mitterrand remarked in summer 1977 that the Socialist party's singular problem at that point was that "it is obliged to do everything at once." More precisely, the PS's problem was the necessity of *attempting* to do everything at once.

What goals did the Socialist party leaders have to reconcile? Essentially there were four: (1) the problem of consolidating the new PS, which in itself meant a three-fold task of resolving deep internal disagreements over policy, finding a leadership capable of winning national elections, and building strong party organization; (2) controlling the Communist party's influence on alliance policy and on coalition strategy and tactics; (3) maintaining the Common Program's list of radical reforms while winning the sympathy, or at least the neutrality, of the rest of France as well as of France's western allies, both "social democratic" (especially the SPD and Labour governments) and "capitalist" (the United States); (4) conceiving a cabinet including Communist participation and capable of governing the country successfully in case of victory—a task which concerned Mitterrand alone, for he alone had the decisive voice in this.

The problem of government personnel was a particularly portentous dilemma. For one thing, extraordinary leadership would be required to face a postvictory situation that seemed certain to present itself as a crisis. In addition, few of the PS leaders had had high-level governmental experience (and this two decades ago under the Fourth Republic), while the present Communist leaders had basically none at all at the national level, the PCF's last experience in government having ended three decades ago, in 1947.

Further analysis of this extraordinary situation can be left for later. Let us say only the following by way of introduction: the Socialist party setback in 1977–78 in a sense consisted precisely in its inability to achieve everything at once. Our analytical task, then, is to dissect the bundle of partial successes and failures, to sift out key elements in order to see how, altogether, they added up to defeat.

The Socialist party in France, as noted above, was known until 1969 as the SFIO. Under its two longtime leaders Léon Blum (1919–1940) and Guy Mollet (1946–69) the SFIO conceivably could have become a permanently dominant party as did the Labour party or the SPD. Between the Word Wars, however, it governed only once, bedeviled considerably by the *fin de siècle* left-wing taboo against cabinet participation, whose persistence allowed the Communist party a preventive accusation of "class collaboration" whenever SFIO leaders seemed interested in going into government with "bourgeois" parties. The Popular Front was basically an SFIO-led antifascist left-wing coalition, in which the two other main partners were the newly strengthened PCF and the Radical party. The latter party was a remnant of the nineteenth-century battle for laicism, and its quintessentially "stalemate society" leaders played a role in Third Republic coalitions far beyond what was merited by their electorate or organization. Its legacy provided the splinter "Movement of Left-wing Radicals" for the "Union of the Left" in 1972.

Léon Blum's Popular Front government, despite several major social reforms, failed in its central task of halting the movement toward a Franco-German war.[4] This failure is not attributable to any single event or element, and one should mention several reasons here, not only because of their importance in the Popular Front's travail but, more importantly, because they are an example of the way in which certain fundamental Socialist-Communist characteristics have guaranteed persistently the French left's impotence to go beyond joint policies at any given moment. For one thing the Socialist leadership under Léon Blum was, as usual, deeply split within itself. And what in routine times can be a fruitful pluralism became in a time of crisis a paralyzing inability to agree, hence to act. Divided over how far and how rapidly to extend domestic economic reform and, more imperatively, over how to react to the related problems of German militarism and the Spanish Civil War, the SFIO leaders failed to act together, let alone to control the divisions within the larger Popular Front coalition or in the French situation as a whole. The dominant French social classes and their political representatives were of course dead set against, and at a certain level even scandalized by, this first "socialist" French government. It is hardly necessary to add that other western governments were not enthusiastic, either. Finally, the Communists, who could have done at least something to give the Popular Front a better chance, were obliged, in the nature of their fundamental policies, to weaken the Popular Front from the inside: first of all to promote the double-game of Soviet foreign policy (toward the Third Reich, the Spanish Civil War, and Western Europe in general) and, second, to preserve the PCF's credibility as a radical "vanguard" organization vis-à-vis the SFIO, by agitating for more extreme domestic reforms from a government it claimed to support, though not to the point of threatening the more important interests of the international Communist movement.

In the tripartite period at the end of World War II the same essential Socialist and Communist tendencies produced essentially the same results. The political landscape, to be sure, had been radically altered by the war and the victorious Resistance. In particular, the addition of General de Gaulle and the newly emerged West European Christian Democracy (in France the MRP) to the SFIO-PCF *retrouvailles* for a time promised a basic change in the structure of French and European political life. But in France, as throughout Europe, the competition of several mutually exclusive political grand designs (Gaullism; Christian Democracy; the idea of a French Labour party without the Communists designed expressly to marginalize them; the contrary idea, for a reunified Socialist-Communist party) worked to destroy them all. Soon General de Gaulle resigned and retired to Colombey-les-deux-Eglises. French Christian Democracy (the MRP) rather quickly lost popular support, suffering a rapid decline in the Fourth Republic and total obscurity in the Fifth. The Socialists and Communists in 1945-46 renewed their historic disagreements over differing socialist visions and, hence, international alignments. By 1947 the left-wing split had become once again radical.

The political system of the Fourth Republic, in short, quickly came to operate much like the Third Republic's, even if some of the central actors were new or had new profiles. Yet the Fourth Republic, as many historians have written, might well have endured were it not for the successive crises of decolonization out of which came General de Gaulle's establishment of the Fifth Republic in 1958.[5] Furthermore, during the Fourth Republic's renewal of "musical chairs" government at the top, French social structure and the French economy had begun—despite, and in part also facilitated by this—deep changes and modernizations outside the narrow spotlight of politics-as-usual.

Whatever the case may be, the political costs of decolonization weakened the Socialist party more than the other parties dominant in the Fourth Republic political game. The Communists in particular were rather successful in perpetuating the myth of their pure anticolonialism,[6] a bit of subterfuge hidden further by the SFIO's agonized public fall from its own anticolonialist tradition, one which seemed to echo the SFIO's abandonment, in 1914, of its anti-militarism and its working-class internationalism.[7] The new Socialist leader, Guy Mollet, had assumed party leadership from Léon Blum in 1945-46 on the basis of shortlived Guesdist-type radical policy commitments. By the final years of the Fourth Republic, the former secondary-school English teacher from the Pas-de-Calais had added a turnaround on the key issue of Algerian policy to his generally lukewarm reformism in the postwar decade: During the "Republican Front" government which he led in 1956–57 (a center-left coalition which, as was inevitable during the cold war, excluded the Communist party), Mollet even achieved a reputation as a staunch *Algérie Française* advocate.[8]

The SFIO was thus largely a spent force by the time the Fifth Republic was established out of the crisis of military colonial revolt in Algiers. The Socialists, haunted by an authentic desire for socialism and in turn terrified by the suspicion that Bolshevism was the only possible revolution, had persistently failed to overcome their historic ambivalence about government and its purposes. They were ambivalent also about international politics, where both the goal of socialism and the SFIO's authentic pacifist and anti-colonialist traditions prevented any but an ambiguous accommodation with the West against the Soviet East, when finally, in 1947, a choice was imposed on a party otherwise much better suited to indecision. Furthermore, the SFIO's strong secularism (Mollet's first career as a teacher was symbolic: not for nothing was the SFIO reputed to be a "party of *instituteurs*") rebuffed the Christian progressive public set adrift by the MRP's failure. This was potential support which at least might have slowed the SFIO's decline in the 1960s or given it greater currency with which to bargain with other political parties during its replay of de Gaulle's *traversée du désert*.

A complex sequence of events made these same Christian progressives, by the middle 1970s, a significant element in the success of the reborn Socialist party. This rally of certain *militants chrétiens* was derived to a considerable extent from the labor movement, [9] and in particular from the *Confédération francaise democratique du travail* (CFDT) which in 1964 split as a majority faction from the parent *Confédération francaise des travailleurs chrétiens* (CFTC), adding in 1970 a Marxist-sounding program to its traditional Christian social reformism. This radicalization of the CFDT, it can be added, was but one delayed effect, and perhaps not the least important in the long run, of the "events of May" 1968.

The mixing of strong secular and religious traditions in the new PS was by its very nature incomplete and a further source of internal tension. Nonetheless, the CFDT-PS connection has given the Socialist party in recent years a potentially large measure of influence in the organized working class, an essential leverage if the PS is to challenge successfully Communist ideological and organizational hegemony on the left. The CFDT turn to class-struggle doctrine thus both helped and hindered the PS. On the one hand, it authenticated the Socialists' radical credentials and provided a burgeoning militant industrial base, while on the other hand it prevented the PS from developing politically as freely as it might otherwise have done. In particular it encouraged the PS leadership to adopt a socialist rhetoric closer to that of the Communists, reinforcing a preexisting tendency to summary anticapitalism and implying that social progress could come only in the form of a "rupture" with the established order.

It may be argued that the epoch-making event of twentieth-century left-wing politics in France was the Communist seizure of the major labor union, the *Confédération générale du travail* (CGT), in 1945–46.[10] It is probably also true that the basic ingredient of Communist persistence in France since 1947 has been not so much the party itself as the union. The CGT, because it is an efficient professional organization which gets results that working people can measure, indirectly produces excellent Communist party militants, spreads Communist party doctrines, and maintains a broad Communist party influence in the major productive and social mobilizing sectors of the society. Given the large public sector of the economy, whose employees are organized mainly by this union, the CGT is a force which has obliged Gaullist and Giscardist governments to accord the Communist point of view a continuous day-to-day importance much beyond that of any other opposition organization. Thus the recent Socialist party penetration (whatever its insufficiencies and inconveniences) of the labor movement through the CFDT gives the non-Communist left a long-term chance to counter the core of Communist strength at the base level. Because of its *own* internal incoherencies, however, the CFDT accepts its Socialist party relationship only with great ambivalence. Torn by dogmatic Christian social, Marxist radical, and even residual anarcho-syndicalist tendencies, the CFDT commitment to the Socialist party has been weakened yet further by its doctrine of union independence from party politics. However laudable, this CFDT position is an advantage to the PCF-CGT tandem in the Socialist-Communist organizational struggle for dominance on the left.

Whatever support this recent labor movement influence may eventually provide, the Socialist party which was recreated in 1969–71 from the SFIO was first constructed upon other pillars.

The first, an "antipillar," was the fact of a political space left vacant, an opportunity. Gaullism, even during the reign of the General himself, had changed from a very broad and interclass—in short, sociopolitically amorphous—movement of national union to save the Republic and French destiny into a much more narrowly based socioeconomic conservatism and strident political nationalism. Whatever de Gaulle's intentions of fostering a society founded on participation and *concertation*—a "third way" neither capitalist nor socialist—he never used influence or applied force sufficient to render his initiatives more than interesting doctrine. One can object, of course, that compelling national and international interests (rapidly ending the hopeless Algerian war and creating the "right" kind of European community) obliged a regrettable choice in priorities. Nonetheless, the narrow Gaullist-led victory in the 1967 elections and the social explosion in spring 1968 were evidence that a massive current in French opinion wanted "change," whatever that might mean in terms of actual policies.

Despite their unprecedented scope, the "events of May" ended finally as a demand for reform rather than revolution. Although the revolutionary Marxist far left enjoyed a spectacular and shortlived popularity at this time, and although as a consequence of May 1968 a certain number of young activists joined the Communists because they seemed the only "serious" radical force, the otherwise perplexing dramatic demobilization after such a departure indicates that it was more a traditional *jacquerie* by French society against the state than a class war episode, although elements of both are clear.

The new Socialist party emerged ambiguously at its 1971 Epinay Congress, with a radical doctrine, inspired at once by the traditional and the innovative aspects of May 1968, and a leader, François Mitterand, whose past doctrine had been many things but certainly not that. The party's swift political ascent—from 10–15 percent of the electorate in 1969 to 25–30 percent in the opinion polls in 1977 and 23 percent of the actual 1978 vote—was due in considerable measure to this very imprecision of image and intent, which allowed potential supporters to comprehend the PS as they wished.

Leaving aside even the moderate Christian reformist element which rallied the PS in 1974, not all of the remaining Socialist *electoral* renaissance derived necessarily from the Communists or the far left. On the contrary, many of the new PS voters in the 1970s came from a variety of constituencies seeking a progressive, modernizing left–wing party. In the French context, this meant a party that would (1) create some plausible alternative to the tired Gaullist majorities, and (2) produce reforms based on new or emerging clienteles and problems.[11] At the same time, the fact that the reestablished Socialist party was built upon the old SFIO permitted it to retain two other moderate clienteles which the Mollétiste leadership had not yet frittered away: one was the historic anti–Communist Socialists, whose tradition was born in the split at Tours and who resonated still with the radical phrase-mongering which marked each SFIO congress until the end; and the other more important source of strength for the new organization, the traditional SFIO local government power–holders, a clientele (particularly strong in the *Nord* and *Pas-de-Calais*) built up over a half-century and impregnable even to Communist militancy.

These were the new PS's reformist, or at least moderate, constituencies. On the party's left wing the renaissance came from a young, hard–core socialist base which had earlier been either Communist or far left (Trotskyist or Maoist) and which had drifted toward the Socialist party renewal because both the PCF and the extremist *groupuscules* seemed to have demonstrated their limitations in May 1968. The most important elements organized into the Center for Socialist Study and Research (CERES), some of whose leaders paradoxically had originated politically in extreme right-wing chauvinist and colonialist groups.

The CERES leaders quickly exerted a crucial radicalizing policy influence, just as the PS leadership fixed its program in 1971–72 and signed the "Common Program" with the Communists in June 1972. Thereafter, it became a separate organization within the party, provoking serious conflicts with the Mitterrand group. The key CERES capacities, as far as Mitterrand was concerned, were two: an organizational militancy which the new party needed badly, and an ideological fluency which the party leadership (wisely or not) accepted, giving the PS a shortcut appeal to the post-1968 young generations. The CERES organizational and ideological predilections gained a reputation as "proto–Communist." It is true that the CERES had promoted several Communist-style conceptions. Besides certain organizational characteristics relevant mainly to internal CERES affairs, the PS commitment to a "rupture with capitalism" has owed much to CERES aggressiveness. Yet the CERES, which has controlled one-fifth to one-fourth of the party organization, is much less important electorally and has had much more influence *within* the party than on public opinion. Its skills and its very presence have served quite clear political interests, including a certain negation of Communist intimidation of great value to the older SFIO leaders.

The CERES describes itself as the "hinge" which can join together "social democracy" (the PS tradition) and "Stalinism" (the PCF tradition). This updated vanguardist notion has been developed into a strategy for radicalizing the PS economic program and demanding de-Stalinization of Communist politics. Thus for the CERES *both* the PS and the PCF are vital to its own "new" strategy for socialism; and, as Jacques Julliard has put it, the CERES has believed more in the "Union of the Left" than in the PS itself. (Moreover, it is not surprising that the Leninist-influenced CERES people despise "social democracy" above all else.)

The failure of the left in 1978 and the breakdown of the PS–PCF alliance make it difficult to predict future CERES policy and influence. The CERES-Mitterrand coalition against Michel Rocard and Pierre Mauroy at the April 1979 PS congress is hardly a long-term solution for party leadership. But in retrospect one is astonished at how much effect, above all ideologically, it had during the 1972–77 "Union of the Left." For one thing, the CERES served for five years, with whatever reluctance, as a cover for François Mitterrand's left flank. Small as it has been, the CERES caused serious problems for the Communists by its own rather successful radical rhetoric. With its passion for vanguard politics, the CERES contributed to the Socialist doctrine which successfully pressured the Communists into debating vanguardist pretensions in the public arena. Could the PS also be a vanguard party? Had it even replaced the PCF? For half a century the Communists had been more or less able to ignore blithely challenges to its claim to be the only authentic revolutionary socialist party in France.[12]

Finally, and most centrally, the Socialists found a leader of truly national stature, the necessary catalyst in joining together all these disparate elements in the new PS. François Mitterrand, who had been politically compromised more than once in his various manifestations as a Fourth Republic *ministrable*, emerged from the 1971 Epinay Congress and the following three years of consolidation as the "Great Federator" of the party.[13] To be sure, the "Union of the Left" (basically any alliance putting together the Socialist and Communist parties) was a project not unique with Mitterrand.[14] But clearly no other leader possessed the "personal equation," to use de Gaulle's language, necessary to bring off such a complex, ambiguous, and audacious undertaking.

In the 1965 presidential elections François Mitterrand, an all-party left-wing candidate assisted by the presence of several Center and other candidates, unexpectedly forced General de Gaulle into a run-off ballot. Mitterrand was at that point neither a member of the SFIO nor had he yet embraced socialist doctrine. In 1974, now both a socialist (though not a Marxist) and leader of the PS, he was again the joint left-wing candidate. He lost the presidency by less than 1 percent; Valéry Giscard d'Estaing won it with the avowed intention of shifting the governing majority's base and of bringing the Socialists into the government sooner or later. Then, in 1976–77 local elections, the PS under Mitterrand's leadership surpassed the Communist party electorate for the first time since the 1930s, by about 26 percent to 21 percent.

In 1977–78, however, both the Socialist party surge and François Mitterrand's long-term plans were deflated, sapped by a bitter struggle with the Communist party within the alliance and by a crucial if minor defection in popular support from without. Some of the last-minute PS vote loss was no doubt the traditional last-minute electoral desertion of the left, but some was caused by what the Socialist-Communist struggle revealed about the nature of the alliance and its member parties. In the logic of circumstances as they seemed in early 1977 (left-wing dynamism, Western economic problems and their consequences in France—heavy unemployment, inflation and stagnation of production and private investment), the "Union of the Left" seemed hardly capable of losing the 1978 elections. The key element in producing this difficultly achieved result was precisely that over which Mitterrand (whose personal authority in elaborating and executing PS strategy between 1971–1977 was overwhelming) had the least control and foresight: the Communist leadership's capacity to make a radical choice against the Socialists, and hence against a left-wing victory.

Many observers agree (although owing to the still remarkable Communist secrecy we cannot be certain) that while the PCF leaders could not entirely have excluded, even right up to the first ballot, the possibility of victory in March 1978, sometime in the previous half year they chose to try to prevent it. Because such behavior violates so radically our practical sense of what a political party is about—above all else the pursuit of power—the issue is extremely controversial and its significance is essential: in what ways, and to what degree, do the French Communist leaders want a "party not like the others"? It would perhaps be accurate to say that up to a point sometime in 1977 the PCF leaders still wanted to win, but only on their own terms. After that point, it is probably more accurate to say that, despite their contrary rhetoric, the Communist leaders acted to *prevent* a victory which they felt might ultimately be an historic defeat for the Communist party. The key move was to sabotage the alliance with the Socialists. An explanation for such a radical choice will lead us eventually back to a restatement of the essential characteristic of French communism historically, and of the PCF's failure to push sufficiently quickly or profoundly its evolution from this past before it was faced with a moment of truth.

Like the Socialist party, the French Communist party for the past decade has acted out a fundamental ambivalence about government, with conflicting conceptions of what the party should be, what the party should seek to accomplish, and how the two can be related. Using ideological shorthand, one can say that the PCF in the 1970s oscillated between its traditional Leninism–Stalinism and its recent tendencies toward Eurocommunism.

The dominant mode of PCF psychology and action traditionally has been what I call Leninism–Stalinism. The PCF was "bolshevized" in the 1920s and adopted a Leninist conception and organization of the Communist party as the "vanguard of the working class." The PCF was "Stalinized," in the decade after bolshevization began in 1924, along with Soviet politics itself, even as it was being Leninized. The thoroughness of the PCF's Stalinization set it off from other European Communist parties, for example the postwar Italian Communist party, which accepted Leninism–Stalinism in theory but for various reasons worked out organizational patterns in practice much more adapted to the liberal character of Western European societies. Even after it grew from a small party of a few tens of thousands in the 1920s to a party of 200,000 to 300,000 in the 1930s, the PCF maintained two key elements of the Leninist doctrine which many other western Communist parties chose to avoid or ignore.

The first was a dogmatic proletarianism, or *ouvrièrisme*. This doctrine of hero-worship of the working class (or at least of its idealized image) produced results for the newly arrived Communist party in France because socialist and anarchist *ouvrièrisme* was by the 1920s already a French left-wing tradition of more or less half a century. *Ouvrièrisme* inside the PCF was a kind of terrorism about members' social origins, among other things giving privileges to real or pretended workers once they got into the struggle for advancement in the leadership or in the party bureaucracy. A natural *ouvrièriste* corollary was intimidation of the poor bourgeois (usually a teacher or an intellectual) who joined the party out of an honest desire to "betray" his class. The second Leninist doctrine which also saturated French Communist psychology was the preference for a small, closed, and highly disciplined party as opposed to a larger, less selective, and less tightly directed organization. This policy of extremely close supervision, a rigid *encadrement,* or encapsulation of the party apparatus, was meant, at least at first, to produce the Leninist ideal of a party "organizational weapon," a strike force which could be quickly mobilized, hitting at a specified target and with a specific political intent. However, in practice this choice worked out to be not a strategy for action but rather an iron corset whose essential purpose was to maintain the boundaries of a subculture.

In addition to the *ouvrièriste* and subculture mentalities which dominated French Communism historically, a third element in the PCF tradition was not so much Leninist as Stalinist: "unconditional loyalty" to the Soviet Union. This meant in practice that the PCF acted mainly as an arm of Soviet foreign policy rather than seeking to establish and to attain its own goals.

This "tripartite" PCF tradition was consolidated at the end of World War II as the Western–Soviet antifascist alliance disintegrated and Europe was divided at the Iron Curtain, suffering the perhaps necessary consequences of U.S.–Soviet, liberal–Communist great power confrontation. At this moment the French Communist movement withdrew into a political ghetto for fifteen years, "drawing up the wagons in a circle," so to speak. The French Communists established a largely impermeable "counter-society" whose chief purpose was to propagandize Soviet foreign policy (for example, the "Peace Movement," the "Stockholm petition"), nourishing itself politically on its own passion while waiting for the Soviet system, as Khrushchev told them with perhaps not entire hypocrisy, to "prove its superiority to capitalism."[15]

During the fifteen years following Stalin's death in 1953, the French Communist party nevertheless began to produce—however sporadically and however more slowly than other West European Communist parties, especially the Italian CP—internal pressures toward erosion of its by now much discredited tradition. Resulting both from the de–Stalinization controversy throughout the international Communist movement and from domestic political considerations, the French Communists began to preach a less dogmatic socialist doctrine, based on a gradually enlarged legitimation of social diversity (that is, a weakening of *ouvrièrisme*) and less political determination. (Not only did the USSR fail to overtake American productivity but it began to be permitted to doubt whether, again as Krushchev had boasted, "the grandchildren of the Kennedy generation would indeed play under a red flag"). Following the Soviet-led invasion of Czechoslovakia in 1968, which profoundly shocked all the nonruling CPs including the PCF, the French Communist leaders moved more quickly to innovate. This meant first of all the assertion of decision-making autonomy from Soviet control, the PCF's major step toward "Eurocommunism." In late 1975 the PCF publicly switched sides against the Soviets in preparatory meetings for the 1976 international Communist conference at East Berlin. The point of no return on the question of party autonomy was crossed apparently in this episode.[16]

With unsettling rapidity thereafter, the PCF's self-criticism of certain traditional doctrines and policies became more than simply negative. Growing criticism of Soviet defects was augmented with apparently conciliatory policy changes on French national defense and the European Community. The PCF's "new policy" included neither violent revolution nor, as the Twenty-second PCF Congress announced in early 1976, a post-revolutionary "dictatorship of the proletariat."

In short, the break with its solid Stalinist tradition required the French Communist leaders to develop a coherent political strategy and conception of the PCF as a *party of government*, that is, a party which might reasonably expect to win power electorally and therewith to face the problems of a "transition to socialism." Herein lies the explanation for the PCF's obstinate, and finally successful, attempts from the early 1960s to draw the Socialists into a governmental program alliance—despite the possibility of thereby creating a potential rival. In order to have some coherent vision of power, the Communists accepted the necessity of compromise electoral and program alliances in which they were not likely, at first, anyway, to be the preponderant force. The PCF then had to win gradual political supremacy and, ultimately, to realize its grand vision of a new society. Thus in the "peaceful transition to socialism" doctrine the Leninist idea of the vanguard party was merged with the problem of becoming a serious government party aspirant in the Republic.

Curiously, it now became apparent how contradictory in certain ways were Leninism and Stalinism in their consequences for nonruling Communist parties. Whereas Leninism was a mode of thought more or less entirely centered on the problem of winning power (making the revolution, moving from opposition to government), Stalinism, with its primacy of foreign CP loyalty to Soviet goals which might or might not fit their own, turned out to be monumental conservatism for nonruling Communists. Remaining loyal to Stalin and the USSR implied a party of permanent opposition; really to seek power for themselves would involve breaking loose from Soviet-style "proletarian internationalism." In this sense, the

PCF's determination in the 1960s and 1970s to enter the government was *itself* one aspect of de-Stalinization. This and related changes in the *ouvrièriste* and *encadrement* traditions (enlarging the party, loosening the requirements for members, asserting that socialism "in French colors" need not imply the disappearance of non-socialist elements of society) were, furthermore, in harmony with developments in several Western European (and the Japanese and Australian) Communist parties which in the middle 1970s began to be called "Eurocommunism." Were the "ideal-type" Eurocommunism to be realized, it would in practice be autonomous of Soviet control, nonviolent and reformist in method if still radical in intent, and perhaps even politically liberal inside the party, although the latter seems to be the most difficult characteristic for any would-be Eurocommunist party to produce.[17]

When the Communist leaders signed the "Common Program" in 1972 with the PS and the Left-wing Radicals (MRG), the PCF was by far the strongest party—not only organizationally, as one had come to accept as natural, but also electorally. Had the new Socialist party not been temporarily so weak, its leaders very possibly would have avoided signing such a program which, just as the Communists had intended, acted to limit the party's choices and movement significantly in the following years. In any case, between 1972–76 the Communist electoral superiority was erased. The Socialist party, building on the various elements discussed above, became not only the dominant *leftist* party electorally but also, according to the results of local elections in 1976 and 1977, the largest electoral party in France. Moreover, it was the only party in ascendancy in the country (the Gaullist decline was particularly impressive), and the only party whose political logic aimed at breaking through the 30 percent barrier, that is, becoming a dominant government party.

This was the disconcerting new relation of forces perceived by the Communists in 1977, and they did not accept the new Socialist superiority, even though in 1972 they must have recognized two probabilities in the "Union of the Left" strategy: that left-wing gains for obvious reasons would go mainly to the Socialists, and that the PCF would enter a government, if at all, as a junior partner of the PS, electorally and in terms of parliamentary seats. What the PCF leaders finally could not tolerate, however, was the fact that their party made virtually *no electoral gains at all* in 1972–77, notwithstanding the above-cited successful massive enlargement of the party, while the PS moved ahead remarkably. This political reversal on the left was all the more dangerous because the Communist "vanguard party" identity or pretense itself was at stake, and therefore the credibility of the PCF's entire "peaceful transition to socialism" strategy, the basis of its vision of power for the long term. This, after all, was the first time in French Communist history that its leaders claimed that transition to socialism was the immediate practical task. The price of possible success, however, being possible failure, the paradoxical attraction of permanent opposition for a vanguardist party is evident.

In 1974, following Mitterrand's near victory for the left (especially for the Socialists) and several unexpected Communist failures in by-elections in the fall, the PCF leadership had launched a vicious old-style Communist attack on the Socialist party. Two years later it cranked up the Leninist-Stalinist attack machine again, following new Socialist gains (and despite even the first significant PCF gain, in local government control, as a result of the 1977 municipal elections) and Mitterrand's refusal to agree quickly to initial Communist proposals for updating the 1972 joint program for the 1978 elections. By summer 1977 the five-year PS success and the relative PCF stagnation had placed the Communist leaders in a dilemma which went far beyond immediate problems. In choosing their tactical and strategic attitude toward the Socialist party at this point, the Communists, in the nature of the situation, were also choosing between their still powerful tradition—the dogmatically working-class, organizationally elitist, and psychologically Stalinist "vanguard party"— and their tentative new Eurocommunist tendencies which, at least in the Italian and Spanish Communist versions, seemed to imply a strikingly less monopolist pretense of vanguardism as well as permanent social and political pluralism.[18]

In a phrase, the political risk to the party in choosing the new over the old, the immanent PCF over the ancient, was too great for the leadership to take, at least at this point in the party's strategy and internal struggles—or at least this appeared to be how the leadership itself conceived the alternative. However, one could argue that, by any realistic political calculus, the PCF was throwing away a chance which might never come again. If so, the Communist leaders had gotten cold feet, psychologically unprepared to follow through on their own strategy, a plan for innovation, power, and structured reform policies which meant, symbolically, a definitive choice of Eurocommunism over Leninism-Stalinism.[19]

During the past few years, many observers have suggested the hypothesis that the PCF must change its appeals or face an inevitable "historic decline," because its traditional social bases are in some places withering away. The PCF has in the past combined a strong "modernist" working-class base with a "traditionalist" disprivileged clientele to maintain over a fifth of the total electorate. However, in France today the industrial working class is declining as a relative percentage of the labor force, as in other "postindustrial" societies, and the less modernized sectors of society are declining numerically as a whole. While the PCF surely can continue to count on most of its industrial working-class and functionary sector, it must replace its losses and even expand elsewhere. The Communists must change appeals (that is, ultimately themselves) in order successfully to compete for new political clienteles, which in any case will not be the traditional industrial working–class proletariat at the center of Marx's calculation of the likelihood of socialism. In 1977–78, however, the PCF leadership chose to conserve the party's established position rather than trying to better it—the latter possible only by going to government. This was done by constantly upping the stakes to "maximalist" positions in renegotiating the Common Program, by attacking the PS's credibility as a genuine socialist party in cases of disagreement, and consequently by sabotaging both the program and left–wing alliance as a whole. All the while the Communists insisted, of course, that they were loyal to the goal of left–wing unity.

This extraordinary Communist behavior served also to limit Socialist party gains, by scaring off *moderate* Socialist voters (who counted on a strong PS to control the PCF) and *radical* Socialist voters (who saw alliance with the Communist party as a guarantee of the PS's radical intentions and who therefore accepted the Communist accusation that the Socialists, "as before," had "turned to the right" at the crucial moment).

The primary Communist motivation seems to have been a conclusion that political gains from a left–wing government tenure would go mainly to the Socialists, while the Communists would gain substantially less, stagnate, or even decline—in short that the 1972–77 pattern would persist. The Common Program, furthermore, had been written in 1972, and its growth-based, "productivist," that is, substantially Communist economic logic, would have been impossible to carry out in present circumstances. Thus it would either have been abandoned hastily or repudiated from the beginning by a Socialist leadership in a position of force. Here again the Communists stood to lose more than the Socialists, inasmuch as it was the PCF's traditionalist ideology of the "transition to socialism" which now seemed irrelevant in the face of long–term growth, energy, and inflation/unemployment dilemmas in the West. How could one have peaceful, democratic nationalizations on a massive scale, how could one raise rapidly and drastically the minimum wage and other economic and social guarantees, if the French economy clearly could not finance State activity suddenly on such a scale? In addition, to avoid office—and the drama of renunciation or disaster— would allow the Communists to continue to claim the West's economic difficulties are simply a function of capitalist economic tendencies, and therefore to reject all discussion of generalized austerity policies (contrary to the Italian Communist attitude, it is significant to note). The Socialists, whose commitment to the program strategy had been questioned continuously by the Communists themselves, had a much smaller political stake in the credibility of its "transition to socialism" ideology. The Socialist position of strength and initiative in a left–wing government, furthermore, would have rendered an ideological revision once in office a decline in Communist "vanguardist" prestige: The Communist leadership would appear incapable of controlling the Socialists, a fact perhaps reassuring to the rest of French society but devastating to the all-important relationship between the PCF leaders and their base. Altogether, an electoral victory of the left in 1978 paradoxically could have been an historic Communist defeat in the contest with the Socialists for left-wing dominance, with all the historic "socialist" and "vanguardist" prizes included. The PCF could well have found itself in a permanent minority position on the left, from which its "historic decline" would have seemed a logical consequence.

Ultimately, however, even the Communist success in holding down PS gains in 1978—and thus preserving a certain equilibrium (22.5 percent PS to 20.3 percent PCF) on the left—may only have delayed rather than avoided the PCF's relative weakening. The permanence of Socialist electoral superiority seems somewhat less likely one year after the 1978 elections (the June 1979 European Parliament elections showed even a slight reduction in the gap), but the Communist failure to make electoral gains for almost two decades says something fundamental about the PCF's long-term prospects. In any case it seems clear that the PCF's choice in 1977–78 has destroyed for at least several years any possibility of government participation—and perhaps then only if its leadership has changed. On the one hand the present PCF leadership, after all it has done in the past fifteen years, could hardly accept one or a few portfolios in a government which it did not control. On the other hand it is even more unlikely that any governing coalition, with or without the Socialists, could now have the minimum confidence in Communist loyalty necessary to govern with this group of PCF leaders as a more or less full partner.

What is basic here, in conclusion, is to reemphasize that in choosing defeat and a renewal of traditional attack politics vis-à-vis the Socialists, the PCF—*precisely by throwing into question its pretension to be a serious and legitimate government party aspirant*—has damaged seriously its vanguardist pretense. This damage, and its ramifications, are likely to have certain lasting debilitating effects on the rank and file. During the 1978 "Union of the Left" electoral campaign, and even more so since, the Communists have behaved not as a potential government party but rather once again as a party of permanent opposition—the PCF version of which has been traditionally Stalinist to its marrow.

What of the rest of the French political spectrum, as it fits with the analysis just made? One is tempted to begin: *Le centre est mort*; *vive le centre*! *Ça change, mais ce n'est peut-être plus la même chose.*

The traditional centrists in French politics—the Radical party, Christian progressives, and motley of liberals, republican "peasants," and "democrats for progress"—have been unable in the past decade to escape the logic of electoral bipolarization. The Movement of Left-wing Radicals, which signed on *contre nature* with the PS and PCF in the 1972 "Common

Program" and in the "Union of the Left," waited all of about one hour after the polls closed the evening of the second ballot in 1978 before diving into what American journalistic jargon of the 1960s unfailingly called an "agonizing reappraisal." For all intents and purposes the MRG failed utterly to make a go of its 1972 decision to join the socialist left, and whether it now remains in the left, joins the PS outright, splits, or rejoins its parent Radical party in President Giscard d'Estaing's new "Union for French Democracy" (UDF) is not of necessary consequence politically, although, as in the "Union of the Left," its small electoral weight (3 percent) could give it crucial leverage in certain circumstances.[20]

The major question on the other hand is whether President Giscard d'Estaing will be able to "govern France in the center," as he has put it. Politically, this would mean three things: that Giscard move successfully away from the Gaullists (RPR) to some extent, escaping the tactical *emprise* of former Prime Minister Jacques Chirac; that Giscard strike a bargain with the old center remnants still outside the UDF; and, most importantly, that he make some connection with the Socialist party, or perhaps some parts of it, should the PS not hold together. This prospect of course remains hypothetical at this point. No one pretends to know what form a Giscard-Gaullist split might take, let alone a "new center" with the Socialists, who will maintain a "Union of the Left" discourse until the 1981 presidential elections now that François Mitterrand has beaten back challenges to his leadership. Giscard seems to be correct, judging by various opinion polls, that the French people would now support a moderate change-oriented new center or center-left political orientation, and that the current political bipolarization—at least in its extremism—ill reflects French society. Yet it will not be a simple matter to achieve a government "in the image of the nation." Too much anticapitalist and antiwestern politics have had their effect as a result of the 1972–78 Common Program alliance. And the bipolarization, in its early stages as much the result of institutions (for example, the electoral laws) as of ideologies, was exacerbated thereafter as much by the governing majority's short-sightedness and cupidity as by either a left-wing "totalitarian temptation" or some illusory socialist fraternity.

Conclusion: The Eternal Return or a New Beginning?

Historians decades hence may find it surprising both politically and culturally that in the middle 1970s the conditions had developed in "bourgeois" France for an attempted "peaceful transition to socialism" based on the nationalization of industry and credit. Four key elements had, in particular, been put in place: a potentially majority electoral alliance of Communists, Socialists, and smaller groups; a program agreement to launch massive changes in economy and society; a French public opinion prepared either to support or to endure the experience; and tacit acceptance of the "experiment" by other western governments. The protagonist "Union of the Left"—shot through with internal incoherence, based on unstable public support, and faced with a single, tragic precedent, the Allende Government in Chile—raised the possibility of an historic moment in French history. It would not necessarily have led to "socialism." It would in any case have been a leap into the radically unpredictable—highly promising in the eyes of some observers but without doubt also highly dangerous.

The French left, however, failed to create history. It neither won the March 1978 elections nor, therefore, began whatever it might have begun as a government coalition. Moreover, the cause of the left's defeat, finally, was more its own actions than any unforeseen resilience of the incumbent governing majority or the hazards of social and financial-economic conditions. To put it bluntly, the French left, just when it might have won the chance to test in practice its old socialist dream, subverted itself. But the left, one must add, has subverted itself in France repeatedly for over half a century. Was 1978 then a semblance of "eternal return," a new instance of the popular "iron law" of French politics: *plus ça change, plus c'est la même chose*? Less metaphysically, we can put the question this way: do the old mentalities still prevail today, despite the new defeat? Is the French left still, after what was perhaps only an *accident de parcours*, made up of the "old" parties conducting the "old" struggles?

It is reasonable to suggest that the very idea of the "left" in France was substantially discredited in 1977-78. For one thing, at least a generation of left-wing leaders and militants has been deeply marked by the self-produced failure to test out the "rupture with capitalism" logic when it seemed finally possible to do so. For another, the "Union of the Left," the idea of a Communist-Socialist alliance for a "transition to socialism," may never again be so convincing as it was in the middle 1970s—either for party leaders or the long-suffering and eternally disappointed anticapitalist rank and file. In the short term, the "Union of the Left" is moribund. For the longer term, credibility of the "peaceful transition to socialism" mystique may be decisively attacked.

The new defeat of traditional industrial working-class political culture in France may have broader ramifications as well. Merging with recent renewed left-wing criticism of Stalinism, of Leninism, and even in some cases of the Marxist base itself, the failure to take advantage of favorable conditions (obviously no one could have expected an "easy" time for the Left) is likely to weaken the cult of the working class and of its supposed destiny to take power in society to create a new and just order called "socialism." In short, the 1978 failure conceivably is a harbinger of an

eventual supersession of traditional French left-wing industrial politics—
class struggle and anticapitalist—as a whole. "Socialism" in France clearly
must either succeed or die at some point in time (contrary to Marx's theory,
these are not inevitably the same). The 1978 disillusionment seems to me an
omen.

However, because the left's promises remain untested by experience,
and because the Socialist and Communist parties remain with roughly equal
electorates, it is far from clear that traditional French leftism will not
survive for some considerable time. The extrapolation of present tendencies, confused as they are, leads only to the conclusion of "ambivalence yet
again unresolved." Yet it is interesting to analyze certain alternatives for the
left, though again it will be impossible to judge with any rigor their probabilities of realization.

First, the "Union of the Left," despite everything pointed to above,
may be resurrected. This would no doubt require new leaders in one or both
parties, however, and even then the possible circumstances are difficult to
envisage. The 1981 presidential elections, for which the Socialists and
Communists have already promised separate candidates at the first ballot,
may not—despite its majority logic—produce a new "Union of the Left"
for the second ballot and a commitment to govern together. In any case, a
new Socialist–Communist alliance would be unlikely to produce the kind of
detailed program, radical or not, which the Communists continue to proclaim a sine qua non of left-wing credibility, but which the Socialist perceive increasingly as a recipe for disaster by contract. It is only a seeming
paradox to say that this kind of "Union of the Left"—the old formula of a
popular front alliance based on a Cartesian Jacobin program—is precisely
the matrix of Communist recidivism in 1977–78: that is, the PCF may
choose not to go to government *even with* such an alliance and such a
program. But certainly, as long as the Communists remain locked into their
traditional politics, they have no justification for going into government in
a credible way except a clearly radical left-wing coalition.

The traditional Leninist-Stalinist logic may thus be said to have served
the PCF again in the recent past, but in the process to have mortgaged its
future. The Socialist party, to the contrary, has been and remains *handi-
capped* by the old, Communist-dominated logic of French left-wing
politics. The "transition to socialism" mystique has been an iron corset
which is increasingly less tolerable to the PS to the extent that it today is
once again electorally equal to or stronger than the PCF. The "old" PCF is
a motor which can be geared up only to the "old" left-wing industrial politics drive-shaft: the Communist vanguard role doctrine, the myth of unique
working-class destiny, and their combination in the seductive imagery of
the "left" and its "struggle for socialism." Indeed, to the extent one can
say that class conflict and the arguments about "capitalism" and "social-

ism" have been the characteristic politics of continental Western European industrialism in the century of industrial growth and of the *Communist Manifesto*, it becomes clear in what sense the Communist party has been in France the industrial party par excellence, or rather the party of industrial politics. For one thing, the PCF's major social base—salaried workers, whether industrial or bureaucratic, private sector or public sector—was the "new class" produced by early and maturing capitalist industrialism. Furthermore, no other French party has embraced industrialism ("productivism," to use an anti-Communist epithet) as has the PCF, not surprising in a capitalist society traditionally so ambivalent about industrialism as the French. And given the historic French ambivalence about the desirability of capitalist industrial society as a whole, it is not a paradox that the major protagonist of industrial-derived politics should be antisystem. Finally, the PCF's major issue or political *problématique* has been precisely the double perspective of salaried workers in industrial society: on the one hand the defense of acquired interests difficultly achieved, and on the other hand the laudable and enticing vision of a society in which the basic social tendencies of European industrialism as a whole—class conflict, centralized power, and certain unforeseen dissatisfactions with economic and social democratization—no longer establish the matrix of political conflict.

In short, the PCF choice in 1977–78 was, literally, recidivist.[21] Fear of risking a painfully acquired and maintained capital of popular support and bureaucratic security incited the inner party leadership to choose again the PCF's traditional identity as the archtypical, if not necessarily the most morally or socially praiseworthy, industrial class party in France. To be sure, many Communist leaders realized in the 1960s and 1970s that they had to adapt the party to contemporary social and political developments if in the long term the PCF were to prosper or even perhaps simply to evade an historic decline.[22] But, for reasons I have sketched above and analyzed elsewhere in detail, they did not go fast enough or far enough to "Eurocommunize" French communism, arriving at the major PS–PCF confrontation of 1973–76 insufficiently committed to their own strategy and apparently ignorant of many of its implications.[23] The "Union of the Left" alliance, the keystone of French Communist strategy for the 1970s, progressed in these years only because the Socialist party progressed. The Communist strategy was working, but for the Socialists. In 1977–78 the PCF leaders were faced suddenly, and for them unexpectedly, with the choice of continuing their "new industrial party" or "Eurocommunist" identity—though under conditions less favorable than anticipated, but still acceptable in a purely rational political calculation—or of going back to the "old" Communist industrial party logic of permanent Stalinist anticapitalist opposition. Rather than calculating with power realism alone—that is, mortgaging the long term in favor of the short—one suspects that something more was involved: an incapacity to face the risk of innovation under less than ideal circumstances.[24] However, the traditional PCF—a defensively oriented, pro-Soviet party of permanent opposition which lived on immobilism in French politics and society, rationalized by vanguard party rhetoric—no longer suffices unto itself. To the extent the Communist leaders prefer a policy of rigid conservation of the party's traditional identity and, hence, social bases over goals of legitimation and power, the PCF will remain both in permanent opposition and in danger of seeing its Fifth Republic electoral stagnation become a slow but nonetheless certain decline.

There is of course a possibility that the French Communist party may suddenly produce an authentic and totally committed "Eurocommunist" leadership. But it is unlikely to do so, for two reasons: for one thing, the new popular support it might expect to win seems attracted more to the Socialist party; thus a new PS decline seems necessary to a radical innovation in French Communist leadership. More important, however, is the fact that the traditional machinery in the party still works admirably for the traditional purpose, namely, to prevent innovation. This was imposed on skeptics beyond any shadow of a doubt by the relative ease with which the supposed great crisis in the part after the 1978 defeat was squashed, a trend further confirmed by its Twenty-third Congress in May 1979.

The Communist party, therefore, seems for the next several years to have only the choice between one strategy for power (a radical left-wing alliance) and one strategy for permanent opposition. Of course this is not necessarily to say—as the precedent of 1977-78 shows—that the PCF will be more loyal to the "Union of the Left" idea in the future than the Socialist party. Yet the new PS has other possibilities as well.

Ever since the taboo against cabinet participation was violated by the SFIO in the Popular Front, the Socialist party has been basically a party of government. It remains so today. But despite the fact that the Mitterrand leadership has legitimized itself more in terms of winning power than of some precise radical vision of a new order in society, the PS since its founding Epinay Congress has nonetheless, like the PCF, acted out a deep ambivalence about government power and its uses. However, whereas the Communist ambivalence has been a matter of seeking power or avoiding it, the Socialist ambivalence has been a matter of two logics, both of which led to government.

On the one hand the new PS *had* to be built as a vehicle to realize the traditional prophecy of French industrial leftism: that is, a party whose purpose was to lead the working class to socialism. France being what it is, in other words, the new PS was obliged to base its strategy one-half on a challenge to the PCF's role as the dominant protagonist of anticapitalist industrial politics. However, there were two dangers in emphasizing too strongly this particular "face" of the new PS: first, the Communist party could hardly be battled successfully solely on its own terrain; second, a quick failure to weaken the PCF on its own turf would have created conditions in which the new PS might swiftly have gone the way of the SFIO, that is, become an unsuccessful social democracy. Therefore, the Socialist party also had to grow on social bases other than those in which Communist allegiance was hegemonic if it seriously intended to become the dominant party which Francois Mitterrand's strategy and goals implied. A coherent strategy for reestablishing the government party goal of French socialism (this, after all, was Mitterrand's essential contribution to the PS renewal) thus required that the new PS take the struggle with the Communists also onto a new *champ de bataille*, which we may call here the terrain of advanced capitalist and postindustrial politics.[25]

The PCF, because of its still fundamentally unswerving commitment to the Marxist working-class myth and to a Soviet-derived conception of socialist political economy (even, heretofore, in the PCF's most Eurocommunist moments), can essentially be only a traditional anticapitalist working class industrial party, a Leninist or *ouvrièriste* Jacobinism. The Communist ambivalence about government—the "old" and the "new" logics, Stalinism and Eurocommunism, refusing power and seeking power—can be basically characterized as two partially overlapping conceptions of classic French leftism. The Socialist party ambivalence, on the other hand, is the attempt (and, first of all, the political necessity) to be *simultaneously* a traditional anticapitalist industrial party and an innovative antistatist or postindustrial party.

Let us define the innovative aspects of the PS by two rudimentary criteria. First, it has constructed an ideology that addresses new problems, or at least new forms of old problems. Its "self-management" socialist doctrine—*autogestion*—concentrates on the decentralization of state authority and on self-management of socialized enterprise. Second, the PS's political logic leads away from traditional class politics and parties, or at least class parties of the type associated with the period of capitalist industrialization and centralization (based rather clearly on a single class— the working class—or on a heterogeneous group of class and strata relationships which form, at least in the eye of popular opinion, a single class—the bourgeoisie). The temptation is immediate, given this second criterion, to consider the PS in the 1970s as no more than a special type of "interclass," "catch-all," or "popular" party. Yet it has been neither—or rather not only—a cross-class aggregator of sundry interests and opinions, nor a broad-based though nonetheless basically lower-class "popular" party. This new political logic and agenda have particular appeal to what many have labeled, not entirely unsuccessfully, "new class" or "postindustrial" social categories. Here we need simply list the key groups cited in such analyses: highly skilled "new working class" and "new middle class" salaried personnel in technology–intensive industries; the new scientific, technical, and intellectual strata in the tertiary sector; the growing stratum of salaried middle and upper management personnel; politicized ethnic, race, and other "single–issue" groups (also, women organizing corporatively to gain specific women's rights in divorce, child–bearing, job remuneration, and so on); and finally, but, in view of their numbers at any given time not least, new young voters and especially university students.

The Socialist party electorate in 1978 seemed a "catch–all" electorate. It was the only one among French parties to reflect closely the socioprofessional distribution of the population:[26]

	French Voters	PS Voters
Agriculture	9%	8%
Small business and artisans	7%	5%
Upper management and professions	9%	8%
Middle management and salaried employees	20%	25%
Workers	28%	31%
Retired or inactive	27%	23%
Total	100%	100%

Since the Fifth Republic's inception, only the Gaullist party between 1958 and 1962 was representative of the population sociologically to this degree. Gaullism's "catch–all" tendency at this point in its history is indisputable.

Yet it would be hasty to conclude that the PS electorate was or is now simply a sum of the lowest common denominators in the political sociology of French society. On the contrary, the PS was rebuilt in the 1970s on the basis of radical rhetoric, and, more essentially, on an alliance with the Communist party. This is hardly the program and the strategy of a catch–all party. Superimposed on the variety of Socialist voters today is a duality noted by the analysts of the above–cited survey: "To those who vote Socialist because of ideological conviction and who believe in the leadership's discourse and in the action of party militants, has been added. . .a large mass of 'uncommitted' voters; the latter are not predisposed to a Socialist vote but have done so as a rejection of the other parties, or by lassitude."[27] To be sure, the "new party" hypothesis about the PS is not limited to saying it is exclusively an immanent expression of a new political agenda. On the contrary, the argument is complex, derived in part from evidence that its electorate is not basically "catch–all," but rather demonstrates the dual character—traditional and advanced capitalist, industrial and postindustrial, old and new left—of the Socialist renewal as a whole.

In addition to the duality of the PS electorate, the ambivalence in question is found also in Socialist party doctrine, a combination of Jacobin anticapitalism and "new left" antistatism. On the one hand the PS has used a traditional anticapitalist industrial politics imagery of "class front" alliance (not very convincing because of the Socialist ambivalence on this very point), combined with a new *autogestion* or "self-management" version of socialism, which never quite evades giving the impression that the main obstacle to self-management is not corporate power or the bourgeoisie but centralized state power. The contradictory character of Socialist party doctrine has been located indirectly in another way by Jacques Julliard. Because of the popular success of the *socialisme autogestionnaire* idea, says Julliard, there are now *deux discours de la classe ouvrière* in France, two languages and imageries of working-class politics.[28] He might have added that one of these languages—that of classic anticapitalist "productivism"— is *common* to the Socialists and the Communists and is the political orismology of their struggle for similar or overlapping social support, the historic territory of the French left.[29] The other language, however, is at this point still proper to the Socialist party. It is far from clear whether the Socialists will be successful in imposing their version of the "new" politics on a left-wing public so long in the thrall of the PCF's version of socialism—that is, the final working-class struggle and victory in capitalism.[30] For the moment one can say that the idea of a *socialisme autogestionnaire* has had such a wide appeal in France (even among certain professionally advantaged categories that did not vote PS) because, as we now see, it is a symbolic bridge of "old" and "new" antisystem politics—at once anticapitalist and anti-statist, productivist and antibureaucratic, for economic planning yet also for decentralization. Moreover, if there is a *socialisme autogestionnaire* there is also, at least in theory, an *autogestion* without socialism, the latter meaning here collectivization of the means of production and distribution. Thus those Frenchmen who aspire to an end to the devastating silent civil war in France are attracted by the hope that the ground is being prepared for some future agreement on at least the proper questions in French political life, if not necessarily the workable answers.

Even if the French Socialist party fails ultimately to emerge as a dominant party in French politics by fully "becoming itself," the observer of political life in advanced industrial societies has been necessarily keenly aware of its development in the 1970s. For half a decade the PS embodied, among many other things, a new political agenda. Its present difficulty, its unwillingness or rather its seeming incapacity to exploit certain evident advantages over a recidivist Communist party, demonstrates two points. The first is a characteristic of modern democratic parties as a whole—the tension between program and government, between ideology and effectiveness. The Communists justify their internal regime of "democratic central-ism" with this contradiction, arguing that social democratic parties will inevitably be unable to resist cooptation or political castration by the system. The latter is an equivocal argument at best, and an adequate analysis of the problem of "democratic centralism" would require a separate essay or book. However this may be, the brutal and debilitating leadership struggle currently under way in the Socialist party is at once a sign of its liberal character and a political windfall to the Communist leadership, which is able to point up the weaknesses of political liberalism to its rank and file without being responsible for a fair presentation of the alternatives.

The second point is a characteristic of French politics proper: the resilience, against tremendous social and political pressures, of a Communist movement which has been able for too long to command the destiny of the French left, and therein the destiny of French politics, through its traditional and characteristic modus operandi, the power of veto.

Notes

1. On the pre-1972 period see Tiersky, *French Communism, 1920–1972* (New York: Columbia Univ. Press, 1974) and the annotated bibliography therein, especially the studies by Annie Kriegel. It is too early yet for a comprehensive history of the "Union of the Left" period 1972–78 to be possible. See below for several noteworthy studies with limited purposes.

2. The old Socialist party—the SFIO—changed its name to *Parti socialiste*—the PS—as part of its refounding in 1969. Alain Savary was a transition leader during 1969–71. At the 1971 Epinay party congress Francois Mitterrand became the leader.

3. See note 25 for a discussion of this terminology.

4. It has been characteristic of French political life for almost two centuries that in crisis situations of a certain dimension the typically stalemated (and threatened) established powers call on a political savior, an "heroic leader" or *homme de recours,* endowing him with emergency powers to deal with the immediate disaster created by routine stalemate politics. The price, never fully or permanently paid, is in each case the possibility of a new general policy or even a new regime (as in 1958). The Popular Front, even though the result of elections, had nonetheless certain characteristics of a *coalition de recours,* emergency leadership of a traditional French type. Less controversial historical examples are Napoleon, Clemenceau, Pétain, and General de Gaulle. (On this theme of "heroic leadership" in French political history generally, see Stanley Hoffmann, *Decline or Renewal? French Politics Since the 1930s* [New York: Viking Press, 1974].) Significantly, despite a severe economic recession, the "Union of the Left" in the middle 1970s was never perceived as a recourse in crisis. The Communists tried dearly, and failed, to play on this chord, another aspect of their traditionalism.

5. See, for example, Bernard Brown, "The French Experience of Modernization," *World Politics* 21 (April 1969): 366-391; Raymond Aron, *France: Steadfast and Changing* (Cambridge: Harvard Univ. Press, 1960); Jacques Fauvet, *La IVe république* (Paris: Fayard, 1959); and Jacques Julliard, *Naissance et mort de la IVe république* (Paris: Calmann-Levy, 1968).

6. See Jacob Moneta (pseudonym), *Le PCF et la question coloniale, 1920-1965* (Paris: Maspero, 1971); Jacques Doyon, *Les soldats blancs de Ho Chi Minh* (Paris: Fayard, 1973); and Emanuel Sivan, "Leftist Outcasts in a Colonial Situation: Algerian Communism, 1927-35" *Asian and African Studies* 10:3 (1975).

7. Here, as elsewhere, we lack an integrative historical study of the Socialist party. A useful book on this period of SFIO foreign policy is Harvey Simmons, *French Socialists in Search of a Role, 1967-67* (Ithaca: Cornell Univ. Press, 1970). A very detailed study of prewar SFIO foreign policy is Richard Gombin, *Les socialistes et la guerre, 1919-1939* (Paris: Editions Mouton, 1976). The Christian Democratic MRP was less damaged by the colonial issue than by its own internal incoherence, and by competition from Gaullists (during their period of radical opposition, 1947-53), and later by the Poujadist populist movement.

8. François Mitterrand, at this time a non-Socialist *ministrable* who at one point was Minister of the Interior, also became stigmatized as a supporter of the attempt to retain French colonies. Memories of the colonial issue die hard in French political culture, and Mitterrand's position at this time has been one significant limit on his popularity within the left since the presidential election of 1965, notwithstanding his skillful incarnation of the aspiration to left-wing "unity."

9. In particular after the *"Assises du socialisme"* convention (October 1974), which brought not only trade union support but also the key leaders of the small but dynamic Unified Socialist party (PSU), including Michel Rocard, to the PS. See the proceedings of the *"Assises,"* in *Pour le socialisme* (Paris: Stock, 1974). A group of important "Christian" intellectuals, often writing in the journals *Esprit* and *Faire*, also moved toward the PS. Besides articles therein, see Robert Chapuis, *Les chrétiens et le socialisme* (Paris: Calmann-Levy, 1976), for a representative viewpoint.

10. The Communists first moved to take over the CGT during the Popular Front. As a result of the second and successful attempt, in 1945-46, the independent but socialist-leaning *CGT-Force ouvrière* (known since as "FO") was formed by the minority in 1947. For the past decade, however, the laicized and radicalized Christian labor union, the CFDT, has been the more directly identified with Socialist party leanings.

11. In short this meant a party that could occupy the empty political space left both by the shrinking Gaullist appeal and by the PCF's immo-

bilism, that is, its failure to win back the traditionalist–nationalist voters it lost to Gaullism in 1958 or to solicit successfully the "modernist" vote (as the Italian Communists had begin to do by the early 1970s).

12. Another beneficiary of the weakening of Communist credibility was the far left, which appears to have achieved a stable electorate which the PCF no longer controls or has great hopes of coopting (about 3 percent in 1973 and again in 1978).

13. Mitterrand played a crucial personal role with talent and subtlety, but one must add that the underlying basis of federation—holding together the PS factions against each other and also often against Mitterrand's sometimes overweening authority—was the institution of a directly elected, politically powerful President of the Republic and the logic of majority-oriented bipolarization it set in place in the regime as a whole.

14. Here I am talking of non–Communist leftists. The PCF had been after a "joint program" with the Socialists since the early 1960s. Achieving it, given the fundamental anticommunism of the elctorate and of the Socialists as well, was a considerable PCF success.

15. On the PCF tradition of Soviet loyalism, *ouvrièrisme*, and strict democratic centralism see my chapter in Rudolf L. Tökés, ed., *Eurocommunism and Détente* (New York: New York Univ. Press, 1978). On the "countersociety" see Annie Kriegel, *Les communistes français* (Paris: Seuil, 1970, 2nd ed). On the Peace Movement and the PCF as an arm of Soviet foreign policy during this period, see Marshall Shulman, *Stalin's Foreign Policy Reappraised* (New York: Atheneum, 1969). For more general views of French Communist foreign policy, see Donald L.M. Blackmer and Annie Kriegel, *The International Role of the Communist Parties of Italy and France* (Cambridge: Center for International Affairs, 1975).

16. See Tökés, ed., *Eurocommunism. . .*;Lilly Marcou and Marc Riglet, "Du passé font-ils table rase? La conference de Berlin, juin 1976," *Revue française de sciences politique* 26: 6 (December 1976); and Kevin Devlin, "The Challenge of Euro-Communism," *Problems of Communism,* January–February 1977, pp. 1–20.

17. On the problem of internal party liberalization and democratization, see Neil McInnes, *The Communist Parties of Western Europe* (New York: Oxford Univ. Press, 1975), chapter 3; and Ronald Tiersky, "The Problem of Democratic Centralism," in Heinz Timmermann, ed., *The Communist Parties of Southern Europe* (forthcoming, 1979, in German and Italian editions).

18. This is not the place to discuss the democratic content of the Italian and Spanish Communist conceptions of working-class "hegemony."

19. In the chapter in Tökés cited above, I termed the newly autonomous PCF—national-chauvinist in certain matters and Stalinist in others—

a "Gaullocommunism." The point is that party autonomy does not result necessarily in identical "Eurocommunist" policies. The term "Gaullo-communism" symbolizes, among other things, the PCF's continued anti-European Community and anti-NATO biases, very different from the more forthcoming positions of the Italian and Spanish Communist parties toward the EC and existing Western defense arrangements.

20. Since the left-wing alliance had only a narrow majority in the 1977–78 opinion polls, the MRG's 3 percent seemed to matter a great deal. It was the MRG leader Robert Fabre who provoked the final public break-down of the "Common Program" negotiations by walking out September 14, 1977, taking Socialist and Communist leaders alike by surprise.

21. It would be wrong, however, to say the PCF here simply repeated a supposed refusal of power during the "events of May" 1968. The 1968 rejection of an insurrectionary move was justified by the "objective relation of forces" (including NATO), if nothing else. In 1978, on the other hand, a strategy of going to govenment was implied precisely by the antiinsurrection choice of a decade earlier.

22. As the Italian Communist leaders recognized even earlier. The French Communist adaptations came too late and too unconvincingly to produce even modest immediate electoral gains. Paradoxically, the Socialist party would have been better served perhaps if the PCF had also progressed somewhat during 1973–76.

23. For detailed analysis of this period of complex development and uncertainties, see my "French Communism in 1976," *Problems of Communism,* January–February 1976, and chapters in the *Yearbook on International Communist Affairs* for 1976 and 1977.

24. Neil McInnes has remarked that one of the characteristics of Western European Communist leaders traditionally has been the tendency, derived perhaps from simplistic ideas about historical determinism, to underestimate the opposition they faced in the long run. Another possibility is that this interpretation is too generous, that many Communist leaders never really believed they would come to power, or gave up this belief early on—which would go some way to explain the strength of Stalinism in relation to Leninism in a given party.

25. In this brief chapter I will not analyze the concepts of "advanced capitalism" and "postindustrialism." My aim is merely to be suggestive, to use the hypothesis of an immanent "new politics" to substantiate the discussion of pressures for "new" parties, and, by implication, a fundamental realignment in the party system as a whole. The fact of *refounding* the Socialist party in France—a true refounding rather than a quick change of label, as has gone on incessantly in the French Center and Right parties—seems to me at once symbol and substance. The literature of various conceptions on the "new politics" is too vast even to summarize here. A few

recent studies of developments in European left-wing parties which I have
found particularly helpful are Leo Panitch, *Social Democracy and Industrial Militancy: The Labour Party, The Trade Unions and Incomes Policy
1945–1974* (Cambridge, England: Cambridge Univ. Press, 1976); Peter
Lange, "The PCI and Possible Outcomes of Italy's Crisis," in Luigi
Graziano and Sidney Tarrow, eds., forthcoming; and the overview analyses
in Philippe Schmitter, ed., "Corporatism and Policy-Making in Contemporary Western Europe," special issue of *Comparative Political Studies* 10:
1 (April 1977); and Alan Wolfe, "Has Social Democracy a Future?"
Comparative Politics 11: 1 (October 1978): 100–125.

26. See the survey research cited in *L'Express,* April 14, 1979, pp. 75–78.

27. Ibid., p. 78.

28. See his rich polemical essay, *Contre la politique professionnelle*
(Paris: Seuil, 1977).

29. Soon after signing the "Common Program" in 1972 François
Mitterrand announced at a meeting of the Socialist International that the
new PS could hope to attract as many as 3 million voters from the Communist party (the PCF had about 5 million altogether).

30. The French version of the "Internationale" does indeed begin:
"C'est la lutte finale. . ."!

4

The Spanish Left: Present Realities and Future Prospects

Eusebio M. Mujal-León

The parliamentary elections held in June 1977 marked the beginning of what promises to be a long and difficult struggle to build a stable democracy in Spain. Once before, in the third decade of this century, that challenge and opportunity were present: for a variety of reasons, not the least of which was the fact that representatives and supporters of the right and left saw each other as evil incarnate, the experiment did not work. The Civil War captured the tragic inability of the two Spains to coexist, much less work together. In the nearly forty years of autocratic rule under Francisco Franco that followed, things changed significantly. No one can overlook the impact profound social and economic changes have had on Spanish society in that time, but it has been the maturity and the degree of statesmanship exhibited by the *clase política*—encompassing both the Establishment and the Opposition—which have been of decisive importance in the almost historically unique peaceful transformation from dictatorship to democracy. A final verdict as to the success of efforts to consolidate democracy is hardly possible today, but it is fair to say that a key element in that enterprise will be the degree to which the working class and those political parties which have made the clearest claim to represent it are incorporated into the emerging political system.

This chapter will explore the prospects for the consolidation of democracy in Spain from the perspective of the left and particularly of those two parties—the *Partido Socialista Obrero Español* (*PSOE*) and the *Partido Comunista de España* (*PCE*)—whose preeminence on the left has been amply demonstrated in the two national and one municipal election celebrated so far in the post-Franco era. Adolfo Suárez and his centrist coalition (now party), the *Unión de Centro Democrático* (*UCD*), won the parliamentary elections in June 1977 and again in March 1979, but did not do so well in the municipal races a month later. There, the left in its national and regional manifestations made a good showing and in the aftermath of those elections nearly 70 percent of the Spanish population lives in *municipios* with mayors elected by the left. No one should underestimate either the tenaciousness with which the UCD and Suarez will hold on to power or the difficulties the PSOE and PCE will face in consolidating their positions, but it is evident that the importance of the left in Spanish politics will only increase as time passes.

This chapter will consist of three parts: the first focusing on the reasons

I should like to thank the Social Science Research Council for support during 1977 and part of 1978. Thanks are also due Ray Caldwell, Enrique Guerrero, and José María Maravall for their comments and suggestions on an earlier draft of this chapter. Responsibility for the views presented here is mine, of course.

for the emergence of the PSOE and PCE as the most important parties on the left in June 1977; the second, on the Socialist-Communist struggle for hegemony on the left in the months after those elections; and the third, on the possible evolution of the situation there and in the country more generally in the wake of the parliamentary and municipal elections in the spring of 1979.

The Emergence of the PSOE and the PCE in post-Franco Spain

The first free election of the post-Franco era was unkind to most of the groups striving for political space on the left. The only real winner in the contest was the PSOE, with its candidates receiving over 5.2 million votes and capturing 118 seats in the newly elected *Cortes*. The Communist party, the only other party not to be swamped by the reinvigorated Socialists, nevertheless trailed the PSOE badly, winning about 1.7 million votes and twenty deputy seats. Between them, the PSOE and PCE captured nearly 88 percent of the Lower House seats the left won in 1977. For everyone else— except the center-left *Pacte Democratic*, led by Jordi Pujol in Cataluña, which received 17.2 percent of the vote in that region, and the autonomist, extreme left coalition known as *Euskadiko Eskerra* with 9.4 percent of the vote in the province of Guipúzcoa and 5 percent in the Basque provinces more generally—the results were dismal. *The Partido Socialista Popular/ Unidad Socialista* (PSP/US) coalition led by Enrique Tierno Galván nationally and various Socialist leaders in their respective regions captured less than 5 percent of the national vote and elected only six deputies, three of whom were from Madrid. Various Social-Democratic groups, some running separately and others in coalition, received less than 200,000 votes, or just slightly over 1 percent of the total. The extreme left did only slightly better: the four coalitions these groups put forward attained 1.5 percent of the vote.[1]

Some observers may have been surprised with the performance of the PSOE (nationally, of course, it was the *Unión de Centro Democrático* coalition led by the incumbent premier Adolfo Suárez which came in first, with 34.7 percent of the vote and 165 deputies) but the results were generally within the range suggested by various polls released in the last month or two preceding the election. Of course, some in the extreme left groups believed to the bitter end that their voters simply did not want to reveal their intentions before the balloting; the Social Democrats could not imagine how the moderate Spanish voter, whom one survey had indicated was only slightly less conservative than his West German counterpart, could vote for a party like the PSOE, which claimed to be Marxist; and the Communists could only with great difficulty accept the notion that the PSOE was in a position to deprive them of the fruits of their long and patient efforts during the years of clandestinity.

Several factors help to explain the remarkable performance of the PSOE and the failure of the Communist party to translate into electoral terms the influence it had exerted during the 1960s as the best organized opposition force in the country.

For one thing, the Socialists were for the most part successful in presenting themselves to their rank and file as revolutionary Marxists while putting themselves across to a more moderate electorate as a party with a genuine and deep commitment to traditional western, democratic values. They received support not only from those who did not believe in the moderate and democratic intentions of the Communists and from assorted leftist elements who found the moderation of the PCE distasteful and the radical rhetoric of the PSOE more to their liking, but from an electorate that by and large considered the PSOE credibly reformist. The PSOE was a party with a historic past but with a youthful leadership. That combination of *memoria histórica* and dynamic leaders (none of whom was into middle age) came together in June 1977. Unlike the Communist party, the Socialists also had no previous, embarrassing ties to Moscow which they had to explain away. Their leaders had not been, like Dolores Ibárruri and Santiago Carrillo, active during the Civil War and this was certainly an advantage in a situation where nearly everyone who fought them had something to hide now.

And yet, the reason for the failure of Eurocommunism Spanish–style to catch on with the electorate did not lie simply in the ability of the Socialists to preempt what would have been its political space. Also relevant was the fact that although the PCE had undergone a dramatic transformation in the years after 1956—becoming in the present decade the point party of what has come to be called the Eurocommunist movement—this transformation had not been entirely unambiguous.[2] The PCE simply could not convince large sectors of the electorate that its Eurocommunist outlook was more than a simple and expedient tactical shift. Indeed, one survey published in early 1978 by the newsmagazine *Cambio 16* indicated that 26 percent of those who voted Communist in the election did not believe something called Eurocommunism existed and another 31 percent expressed ignorance as to the meaning of the term.[3]

The results of the June 1977 election also reflected the inability of the Communists to resolve the contradictions between their claim to be a revolutionary force committed to the radical transformation of the regime and the reformist practice which had characterized their policies over the course of two decades. Under the leadership of Secretary General Santiago Carrillo, the PCE had expanded the broad front orientation it had developed during the Civil War, issuing a call for national reconciliation and urging both sides to put the divisiveness of that conflict behind. The strategy was certainly successful in the sense that it softened the image the party had among the new generations which had not experienced the Civil War, but the analysis which lay behind this strategy also helped in some ways to undercut the long–term effectiveness of the initiative. Here we allude to the claims PCE leaders made in the late 1950s and early 1960s about the nature of change in Spanish society. Predicting the imminence of the overthrow of the regime, the Communists argued that profound social and economic change which would put Spain on the road to socialism would necessarily accompany that transformation. Any effort to reform the authoritarian political structures from within, they went on, was destined to fail. When predictions about the substance and form of change did not materialize, party leaders hardly shifted gears. They quietly dropped the idea about changes in the social and economic structure being inevitable in the short run, but continued to say that the end of the regime was still near, would come in relatively peaceful fashion, and could not be frustrated by a reformist faction within the regime.[4] Clearly the PCE was trying to please everyone and maintain the *élan* of militants working under difficult conditions within Spain as well. Unfortunately, it displeased a good number of people. Critics on the left objected to the politics of national reconciliation, seeing in its emphasis on peaceful change a capitulation to the bourgeoisie. More moderate elements did not altogether trust the Communists and never quite understood how the party could couple its insistence on moderation with the demand that the structures created by Franco be torn down and replaced. It was not until the end of 1976, much too late to do anything about the rise of the PSOE and their own isolation, that party leaders admitted the success of Adolfo Suárez. Even then, the admission was grudging and, in one speech in March 1978, Carrillo would brush aside criticism of his and his party's performance by saying that the Communist analysis had not yet been demonstrated to be incorrect.[5]

Despite our emphasis on the Communist failure to recognize the capacity for maneuver open to some elements within or close to the regime, we should not overlook either the important role the PCE played in the opposition to Franco or the significant strides the party made in the years after 1939 to break out of the ghetto into which it had been cast after the Civil War.

Employing a strategy premised on the utilization of all legal possibilities and the penetration of those organizations with a mass clientele, the Spanish Communists built up an impressive underground structure. Their strategy was particularly effective in the labor movement, and Communist activists, acting in generally uncoordinated fashion at first, sought to infiltrate the *Organización Sindical,* the fascist–style substitute for a free trade union movement. The first returns on this strategy came in 1951 on the occasion of a public transport boycott in Barcelona: the movement spread with surprising speed to Madrid and the Basque country and only came to an end when the government and employers ceded to many worker demands. The Communists were quick to seize credit for the movement, although, in fact, it was spontaneous and no organization was in control, with workers of all persuasions participating. The 1951 strike was significant because it marked the first time since the end of the Civil War (the general strike which paralyzed the Basque country in 1947 was really the last gasp of the Civil War) that workers had been bold enough to strike.[6] In many ways, it signaled the birth of the new Spanish working class—a product of the industrialization and development Spain embarked upon in the 1950s and 1960s.

Labor had been monopolized in the pre-Civil War period by the Anarchists and the Socialists. Both of these movements, organized into the *Confederación Nacional del Trabajo* (CNT) and the *Unión General de Trabajadores* (UGT), suffered a harsh repression in the first fifteen years after the Civil War. Decimated by the regime and unwilling as a matter of principle to participate in the vertical *Organización Sindical*—the UGT argued those who participated would only be coopted and thus ultimately help legitimize the regime—both organizations (in large measure) lost touch with the new working class emerging in the country and were unable to develop new cadres. The impact this had on the labor movement was most clear in Cataluña, virtually a fiefdom of the anarcho-syndicalist movement in the pre-Civil War period and an area where the CNT had an important influence into the early 1950s. Two decades later, only a shell of that organization remained and it was the Communist-controlled *Comisiones Obreras* (CC.OO.) who were hegemonic in the region.

The organizational vacuum which had developed in the labor movement had been filled from early on by Church-affiliated Catholic Action groups and by the Communists. Both of them played a role in most of the strikes which shook Spain in the years 1958–63. One aspect of the growth of working class dissent was the emergence of the phenomenon known as the *Comisiones Obreras*. This movement originated and expanded in the context of the changes in the collective bargaining law in 1958: under provisions enacted that year, negotiations for contracts no longer had to be carried on under direct government intervention but could be engaged in at the individual factory level. One index of the impact of this change—which revolutionized the system of industrial relations in Spain and energized the role of the *jurados de empresa* and the *enlaces sindicales,* whose election was in the hands of the factory workers—may be given by statistics showing that whereas in 1958 contracts negotiated under the new system affected less than 20,000 workers, by 1962 that number had risen to 2.3 million.[7]

The Communist party did not control the *comisiones* at the outset. Indeed, that movement was originally a rather spontaneous development where Catholics, Socialists, Anarchists, Communists, and even Falangists participated. Over time, however, the Communists distinguished themselves by giving the nascent organization the provincial, regional, and national infrastructure it needed, developing many new cadres in the process.

Participation in the *Comisiones Obreras* was also advantageous to the Communists because it encouraged contact with Catholic labor activists. This was important from the PCE's point of view because it would help break down the Catholic Church's support for the Franco regime and also perhaps prevent the emergence of a strong Christian Democratic party in the post–Franco era. Such a turn of events might even lead to the creation of a Catholic left party which would incline toward alliance with the Communists and Socialists and put Spain in a post–*compromesso storico* phase. In all of this, it should be noted, the PCE was quicker than the PSOE in shedding the anticlericalism which had always been so much a part of the Spanish left.[8]

With respect to Catholicism as with respect to the labor movement, the Communist leadership misjudged the efficacy of their party's efforts. Certainly, *comisiones* activists could penetrate the vertical syndical structure set up by Franco but it was not that easy to take over the structure, particularly given the repression and other obstacles placed in the way by the regime. Similar things could be said of the Catholic Church. Undoubtedly, there was a great deal of dissent and resentment toward the regime expressed in the lower levels of the clergy (especially those living in working–class neighborhoods and regions where nationalist sentiments ran high) but it was unlikely that this ferment could dramatically shift the balance of forces in the episcopal councils. With the appointment of Cardinal Tarancón as primate of Spain in 1969 and particularly after his confirmation as archbishop of Madrid in 1971 and subsequent election as president of the episcopal conference, the tide had certainly turned against the most inveterate supporters of the regime within the hierarchy. A break with Franco was never in the cards, however, except on the one or two occasions when the government was clearly too bold in its violation of the rights accorded the Church by the August 1953 concordat with the Vatican. Catholic leaders wanted more independence from the regime in the troubled waning years of the Franco era, but the hierarachy saw little benefit to be gained from too active an opposition to the regime. Church interests, the government subsidy to the clergy, and the virtual monopoly it held on elementary and secondary education had to be protected as well.

The Socialists had had less success in adapting to clandestinity than the Communists. Twenty years after the end of the Civil War, the PSOE was still an important component of the anti–Franco opposition, but repression had heavily damaged the party and by the late 1960s its organization had atrophied considerably and nuclei of Socialists remained active only in Asturias and the Basque country.[9] Repression was only partly responsible for the withering away of the PSOE in Spain. Another factor which helps explain this development was the obsessive belief the PSOE leadership in exile developed that some sort of foreign intervention would be decisive in defeating Franco. Such trust had been understandable in the immediate post-World War II years (although misplaced even then) but the Socialist leaders held on to this notion twenty years after the end of the Civil War. As late as 1956, PSOE Secretary General Rodolfo Llopis predicted the imminent overthrow of the Franco regime because, as he explained, the axis of the Atlantic Alliance had shifted from the Republican government in the United States to the Labour government in Great Britain. Also working against the revitalization of the PSOE organization was the almost obsessive anticommunism which became the hallmark of the exile leadership. It should be understood that Socialist leaders who had lived through the Civil War and had experienced firsthand the virtual destruction of their party because one part of the PSOE (and its youth wing) passed into the Communist party may well have had cause for prudence in their relations with the Spanish Communists. But the Llopis leadership used the past as a bludgeon with which to attack not only the PCE but those Socialists within Spain who advocated including the Communists in discussions leading to the creation of any anti-Franco front. Every Socialist congress since 1944 adopted a resolution ruling out any sort of alliance with the Communists or other totalitarian forces. It was not that Socialists living in the country were ready to leap into the arms of the Communist party—there was a good deal of distrust and resentment of the perceived Communist tendency to claim credit for initiatives undertaken by all the opposition and also for the effort the PCE made in the late 1950s to infiltrate the *Agrupación Socialista Universitaria*[10]—but simply that the Communists were one of the most resolute opponents of the regime and this could hardly be ignored. The new generations of workers and students reaching political maturity in the Franco era could not understand anticommunism as visceral and unflinching as that which the exiled PSOE leaders preached, particularly when it so resembled what the regime said and was used as a tool to keep power within the organization in the hands of the exiles.

One manifestation of the loss of influence suffered by the PSOE during this time was the emergence of a variety of national and regional groups within Spain, each seeking to lay claim to the political space of democratic socialism. A few words about the most important of these groups are in order.

The *Frente de Liberación Popular* (FLP) was one of the first to challenge the PSOE. Much impressed by the example of the Algerian FLN and the Twenty-sixth of July Movement in Cuba, the FLP presented itself as a radical alternative to both the Communists and the Socialists. The first of many movements whose membership consisted of many radicalized Catholics, the FLP (known as ESBA in the Basque country and the FOC in

Cataluña) participated actively in the various strike movements of the late 1950s and early 1960s and joined with the PCE in the convocation of a *journada de reconciliación nacional* in May 1958. The group had a very ambivalent attitude toward the Communists. On the one hand, it criticized the PCE for not being revolutionary enough, proclaiming it would show the Communists how to make the revolution; on the other hand, many of its members could never quite overcome a marked inferiority complex with respect to the Communists and constantly looked over their shoulders at what the PCE was up to. The FLP suffered various splits and reincarnations before disappearing in the late 1960s, after which its former members could be found in any number of parties. Some, like Nicolás Sartorius and Alfonso Carlos Comin, ended up in the PCE, others went into the PSOE, and still others, like José Pérez Llorca (who headed the UCD parliamentary group), were to enter the government party.

Another group, this one with loose ties to the PSOE but not trusted by the exile leadership because it appeared to have a certain proclivity for joint actions with the PCE, was the aforementioned *Agrupación Socialista Universitaria*. Founded in 1957, the ASU attained a certain audience within the Spanish university and became the spawning ground for several men who after Llopis's ouster in 1972 would become important figures in the PSOE.

A third group consisting primarily of intellectuals, university professors, and professionals coalesced around the figure of a prestigious *catedrático*, Enrique Tierno Galván, who in 1965 had been deprived of his chair at the University of Salamanca. He and his supporters (organized in what was called the *Frente Socialista Unido Español* in 1964, the *Partido Socialista del Interior* a few years later, and, finally, in 1974, the *Partido Socialista Popular*) had on-again, off-again relations with the PSOE in exile. Looking to replace Llopis and his organization within the country, the PSI nevertheless appeared to side with the exiled leader in 1972 when dissidents took over the leadership of the PSOE. Subsequent recognition by the Socialist International of the dissident group (since an October 1974 congress in Suresnes led by the Seville lawyer Felipe González) left the PSP in something of an embarrassing position and, in an effort to gain some leverage with respect to the PSOE, the Tierno group joined the Communist-inspired opposition coalition known as the *Junta Democrática*.

We should also note in this context the presence of various groups associated with Dionisio Ridruejo until his death in June 1975. A former Falangist, Ridruejo was in many ways the Spanish Djilas and his intellectual evolution from fascism to liberalism and then to democratic socialism earned him the respect of many oppositionists and the enmity of many former comrades. Determined to shift the axis of Spanish socialism away from its Jacobin tradition and toward social democracy, Ridruejo created the *Unión Social Democrática Española* with Antonio García López in

1974. It was the moral authority of Ridruejo which held the group together; after his death it split into numerous parts, losing whatever possibility it might have had for influence on the left.

Regional socialist groups also proliferated on the political scene during this period. Many of them had an ephemeral existence and consisted of little more than a name and a group of friends. Nevertheless, some of these groups found a fertile soil in the lack of responsiveness by the exiled leadership to rising demands among political activists in various regions of Spain for self-determination and autonomy. Historically, the PSOE had never been known for its sympathies in this regard: Catalan nationalists, for example, never forgave the Socialists for voting against a statute of autonomy for their region in 1932. Some efforts were made by these groups to set up a national coordination, but only in June 1976 did many of them come together in the *Federación de Partidos Socialistas.* The latter never became a party but remained a loosely structured federation of groups whose claim to political relevance would be shown to be rather tenuous: after June 1977, the PSOE absorbed all but one of its important components.

Disenchantment with the Toulouse-based Llopis leadership grew deeper in the course of the 1960s as it became apparent that the PSOE was losing what remained of its influence in the opposition. A concerted challenge to Llopis by discontented PSOE members residing in Spain and some exiles occurred at the Eleventh UGT Congress in August 1971 at which time, and over the objections of Llopis, the delegates—reacting in part to the challenge laid down to the opposition by Franco when he decreed martial law at the time of the trial of Basque separatists in late 1970—voiced support for the creation of a united opposition front which would include the Communists. At previous congresses, Llopis had been forced to acquiesce in raising the number of seats militants in Spain could have on the Executive Committee. Finally in 1972, dissidents within the country—men like Pablo Castellano, Enrique Mugica, and Felipe González—were ready to join others in exile for an all-out push against his leadership. Overcoming various procedural obstacles set in the way by Llopis (he and his four supporters in the Executive Committee first demanded the convocation of an extraordinary Congress and then opposed the celebration of the scheduled one in August 1972), the majority of the executive convoked a congress which Llopis did not attend. The delegates replaced Llopis as head of the party and adopted several decisions. The most important of these were the abolition of the secretary-generalship, the establishment of a collegial directorate to run PSOE affairs, the withdrawal of the automatic veto the PSOE had put to collaboration with the Communists, and the transfer of control of funds to the interior. Llopis denounced the congress, celebrating his own version, the Twelfth Congress, in December of that year. The Socialist International responded by suspending the participation of its

Spanish affiliate until the legitimacy of either group had been established. A commission appointed in early 1974 chose by a nearly unanimous vote (only the Social Democratic party of Italy abstained) to grant official recognition to the group which had seized control from Llopis. That decision flowed from the realization that Llopis was opposed by the great majority of Socialists residing in Spain and a large proportion of the members in exile, but it also reflected the judgment of the International that it was in Spain and not in exile that the fate of Spanish socialism would be decided. For this struggle, the younger, more dynamic elements which made up the opposition to Llopis were much better placed.

The decision by the Socialist International to grant the PSOE recognition had important consequences. It insured West German and Swedish organizational, financial, and moral support (the latter should not be underestimated: the West German embassy in Madrid intervened forcefully on behalf of the PSOE when Felipe González's passport had been withdrawn prior to his attendance at the SPD Congress in Mannheim in 1975, and the next year, when the Spanish government did not want to give permission for the celebration of a PSOE Congress in Madrid, similar pressures were successfully brought to bear on Suárez and King Juan Carlos) for the PSOE and guaranteed that, all other things being equal, the party would stand heads above the other groups calling themselves Socialist. Put on guard by developments in neighboring Portugal, the West Germans in particular used the *Friedrich Ebert Stiftung* to provide training programs for PSOE cadres and labor activists.

Many rival Socialist groups subsequently attacked the PSOE for its "social-democratic" orientation and subservience to Bonn. Whatever judgment one cares to make about these criticisms depends in large measure on one's ideological and political persuasions. What can hardly be overlooked here, however, is that a good bit of pique and resentment over the international connection of the PSOE was involved. Some of the groups which criticized the PSOE most vociferously had been trying for years to enter the International and, had they succeeded in doing so, would gladly have accepted whatever financial and organizational assistance the Social Democratic parties in Western Europe would have offered. Moreover, a party like the PSP, one of the most ardent proponents of a "Mediterranean" socialism, could hardly cast stones. On the one hand, the party was willing to consider the Ba'th party in Iraq and Mu'ammar al-Qadhdhafi in Libya to be members of the Socialist fraternity; on the other, the PSP appeared (and the June 1977 election confirmed this) to derive most of its support from sectors of the population impressed by the very moderate figure and style of its president, Enrique Tierno Galván.

The PSOE was most vulnerable to criticism with respect to the regional question. Although personal antipathy played a role in the decision of someone like Alejandro Rojas Marcos in Andalucía to challenge the national party, the fact is the PSOE, as has been mentioned earlier, had traditionally been inattentive and, in some cases, outright unsympathetic to regional demands. A discussion of the reasons for this is certainly beyond the scope of this paper. Suffice it to point to the strength of the anarcho-syndicalist movement in pre–Civil War Cataluña as one factor which may have inhibited Socialist adoption and defense of the cause of federalism.

Conversations between the PSOE and various other groups aiming at the unification of the Socialist movement began in 1974 soon after the International granted exclusive recognition to the PSOE. The parties held talks for nearly a year, with little progress made on substantive issues. Many of the other groups charged the PSOE with negotiating in bad faith, arguing that it saw in the conversations and in participation in the so–called *Conferencia Socialista Ibérica* primarily a way of defusing an uncomfortable problem. The others in the CSI demanded that the PSOE renounce its claim to exclusive participation in the Socialist International, dissolve its federations in the various regions where CSI members were active, and turn over responsibility for the collection and distribution of funds to a collegial organ set up by the CSI. Unwilling to comply with these conditions, the PSOE withdrew from the organization in April 1975. It subsequently entered into negotiations with the PSOE faction headed by Llopis known as the *históricos*. Conversations went on into the summer of 1976 but eventually broke down when the Llopis groups refused to attend a reunification congress for which delegates would have been chosen on the basis of membership. A final flurry of negotiations with an eye to unity occurred in early 1977 with the PSP and groups in the FPS. PSP leaders proposed to the PSOE that the two parties agree on a proposal for joint electoral lists and that unity should be discussed after the election. Emboldened by the success of its congress in December, to which most of the ranking figures of International Socialism came, the PSOE refused and insisted on having a framework for organic unity set up prior to the election. The party had more success in its negotiations with two groups within the FPS. With the *Convergencia Socialista de Madrid,* it agreed to fusion after waiving (something it had always refused to do before) the requirement that all PSOE members join the UGT. The PSOE formed an electoral coalition with the Joan Raventós–led *Partit Socialista de Catalunya.* This last alliance broke the shaky unity of the FPS and insured that the PSOE would do well in the important Catalan provinces.

The shift in the leadership of the PSOE from exile to the forces in the interior and the recognition accorded that party by the International were important factors in bringing about the rebirth of the PSOE and of a unified Socialist movement in Spain. Also of critical importance were the nature and length of the transition to the post–Franco era. Unlike in Portugal, there was no dramatic change in government and the success of the *reform política* pursued by Adolfo Suárez also permitted the more moderate groups in the opposition like the PSOE to develop their infrastructures and to gain public recognition before a first electoral test. There was more than a grain of truth in the complaint voiced by many Communist leaders in 1975 and 1976 that the regime showed the PSOE a certain toleration. Whether this was because the government preferred the PSOE or because (as is more likely) it was in some way pressured by the PSOE's powerful international friends to take it easy on the Socialists is not altogether clear. On the one hand, many in the government did want the presence of a relatively strong Socialist party, one which would marginalize the Communists; on the other, a good number of them were also convinced that the PSOE with its radical rhetoric and Jacobin tradition would never fit the bill. This ambivalence led to government negotiations with regional Socialist groups, with the *históricos,* with the PSP, and with various Social Democratic groups, but the government was always careful not to burn all its bridges to the PSOE. The Suárez government came closest to challenging the PSOE outright in January–February 1977 when, apparently breaking a tacit agreement with Felipe González and his party, it legalized the *históricos.* The maneuver appeared to have been part of a plan by Interior Minister Rodolfo Martín Villa and other officials to spark a coalition between ex–Falangists converted to certain socialistic ideas and the most moderate Social Democrats. Some feel that there was no plan at all in this direction and that the move was really a way of pressuring the PSOE to opt for participation in the upcoming election. The reaction of the PSOE, in any case, was so virulent that, if the plan existed, it was abandoned.

By late 1976 and early 1977, the PSOE had moved once again to claim the mantle of leadership on the Spanish left. The party had been successful in wresting the political initiative in the opposition from the Communists and, if the latter had viewed the decomposition of the PSOE under Llopis with a certain self–satisfaction,[11] they now could feel the shoe on the other foot. Communist leaders now had to live down predictions made several years earlier to the effect that the PCE would exert a hegemonic influence on the left in the post–Franco era.[12]

The Struggle for Hegemony on the Left
after the 1977 Elections

In the aftermath of the June 1977 election, the Spanish political panorama had been clarified significantly. What started out as a *sopa de letras* with some 200 parties had been narrowed down to two large and two small national parties and another two or three regional ones of some importance.

It did not take long for the sparring between the large and the small party on the left, the PSOE and PCE, to begin. The Communists made their point of view clear in the analyses they published. Throwing down the guantlet to the PSOE in almost insulting fashion, PCE leaders described the Socialist vote as "disposable," "transitory," and "not militant" and made clear their intention to battle the PSOE for the same political space on the left. At a Central Committee session in late June, the party defined its objectives: consolidate the nascent democratic institutions *and* stop the PSOE from consolidating its position as the left alternative to the Suárez government.

In pursuit of those objectives, PCE leaders proposed the creation a *gobierno de concentración nacional* with the participation of the UCD, PSOE, Catalan and Basque minority groups, and the Communists. All would come to terms on a *pacto constitucional* and an economic recuperation program to last four or five years. The Communists insisted again and again during the summer and fall of 1977 that only such a government could rally the popular support necessary to stymie those interested in destabilizing Spanish democracy, but behind their warning about the dangers of polarization lay the PCE's rationale for collaboration with the UCD against the PSOE.

Both the UCD and PCE shared a common interest in impeding a possible accession to power by the PSOE. Suárez, of course, wanted essentially to remain in power, but the Communists—who did not mind this for the present—also wanted to prevent the UCD and PSOE from consolidating their electoral postiions and cementing a bipolar political system in Spain. The PCE had to be careful in how it went about achieving these objectives however. It did not wish to pursue a strategy whose consequence would be the weakening of the UCD, as this would probably result at once in a strengthening of the PSOE and of the more conservative forces in the UCD and on the right more generally. The alternative, then, was to insist on a policy of consensus. The adoption of such a policy had the advantage of helping to consolidate democracy in the country and of encouraging the PSOE to come to terms with the UCD. In exchange for Communist efforts in this regard, Suárez and his party would insist that in any negotiations the Communists would participate as equals. The *Pacto de la Moncloa*—an economic austerity package and political agreement signed in October 1977 and whose name derives from the residence of the premier where the negotiations took place—was the most explicit manifestation of this confluence of interests between the UCD and PCE. The Socialists gave their consent to the *pacto* only reluctantly and refused to agree to a Communist proposal that a commission representing the parties oversee implementation of the accords. The PSOE wanted the government to bear full responsibility for implementing the agreements and did not want the focus of political struggle in Spain to shift from the Parliament (where they were all represented) to supraparliamentary commissions, where they would have the same weight as the Communists.

Outmaneuvered by the center and the PCE, the PSOE responded to these developments by vigorously attacking the government, demanding that municipal and general elections be quickly convoked, and working to unify the various Socialist groups under the PSOE banner. That strategy was successful in many parts of the country—groups from Cataluña, Aragón, Valencia, and to some degree Andalucía fused with the national party—culminating in May 1978 with the entry into the PSOE of the PSP and the elevation of Tierno Galván to the post of honorary president. In the labor sphere, a similar effort was evident with the integration of an important part of the third-largest union in the country, the *Unión Sindical Obrera,* into the UGT in late 1977.

Indeed, labor was and continues to be the main battleground for the PSOE and PCE. The Communists, as we have noted earlier in this chapter, had developed an important presence in Spanish labor movement in the 1960s and 1970s through the influence they exerted in the *Comisiones Obreras.* PCE leaders had confidently expected their party would turn its longstanding efforts at penetration of the official *Organización Sindical* to profit and would one day simply assume control of the national labor structure. The success of the Suárez *reform política* foiled those plans. In the months after Franco's death, the *Comisiones Obreras* was shown to be an organization which despite its claim to independence and autonomy was firmly under the influence of the Communist party (in mid-summer 1976 it came out that twenty-one out of twenty-seven individuals on the CC.OO. National Secretariat were members of the PCE) and the Socialist-led UGT had the opportunity to build a much-needed infrastructure.

The rather impressive PSOE performance in June 1977 (remember the Socialists received triple the number of Communist votes) provided a shot in the arm to the UGT. Many Socialist labor activists, anxious to give their party an advantage in dealing with the Communists which no other Latin European Socialist party had had since the end of World War II, looked for the UGT to develop a hegemony in the labor movement analogous to the one the PSOE had begun to build in the political sphere. The Communists, for their part, were keenly aware of the need to hold the line in the working class: a UGT triumph in the upcoming syndical elections would be a serious blow to any hopes the PCE had of reversing the "correlation of forces" on the left.

The animosity between Communists and Socialists that had already become evident in the Cortes and had been exacerbated by the Moncloa agreement grew even more acute as a result of competition in connection with the syndical elections. Many issues separated the two unions. On the issue of the *pacto*, for example, there was sharp division, with the UGT criticizing the agreements (more than the PSOE, in fact) and the CC.OO. expressing its wholehearted approval of it from early on. Other issues on which they were at odds related to the claims the UGT made about the *patrimonio sindical* confiscated by the Franco regime in 1939 and to the question of whether the delegate lists for the syndical elections should be closed or open.

The UGT favored closed lists and argued that such a procedure, by encouraging the identification of the worker with a union instead of an individual, would not only render an accurate reading as to the implantation of individual unions but would also encourage the creation of a stable industrial relations system in the country. Behind this argument, of course, lay the conviction that trade unions were the best instrument for the defense of the rights of the working class. Closed lists would also make it easier for the UGT to attract that workers' vote which had gone to the PSOE in June 1977. *Comisiones* and Communist labor activists had a different point of view on this issue. Drawing on a lengthy tradition of work-place *asambleas* and a disdain (tempered over time, however, by the necessity to consolidate control of the union) for trade-union structures, the CC.OO. called instead for a system of open lists.

The dispute over which system should be introduced intensified as the UGT accused the government of favoring *Comisiones* by seeking to adopt the system that organization desired. That the government did not want a UGT victory in the syndical elections is quite clear. That it wanted the CC.OO. necessarily to win, much less. Some individuals in the government (primarily Minister of Labor Jiménez de Parga, whose brother worked for the *Comisiones* and was vice-president of the Soviet-Hispanic Friendship Association) may have preferred such an outcome, but those close to Suárez and with real influence in the government were less interested in promoting the Communist-led union than in keeping the UGT down and in confusing the labor situation to the point where the UCD could promote either its own trade-union alternative or a third force independent of both the Communists and Socialists. That confusion was the underlying objective of government labor policy became readily apparent when the Suárez government issued its decree regulating the syndical elections. The law set up a system of closed lists in enterprises with more than 250 workers (approximately 30 percent of the syndical electorate) and open ones in factories with fewer than that number. In the latter, moreover, there was no requirement that the prospective delegate's syndical affiliation appear on the ballot, and this permitted the government subsequently to claim that many of the delegates in those factories were independents.

After several months of delay, negotiation, and procedural squabbling, the syndical elections began in early 1978. The voting lasted well over three months and final results were never fully disclosed. Available results, however, indicate that *Comisiones* came in first nationally, with between 38 and 44 percent of the delegates elected compared to between 27 and 31 percent for the UGT. *Comisiones* won most clearly in the regions of Cataluña (particularly in Barcelona), Asturias, Madrid, and in parts of Andalucía. CC.OO. did best in factories with less than fifty workers and its margin with respect to the UGT was least in those with more than 250.[13] Compared to *Comisiones*, UGT just did not have enough cadres: its policy of non-participation in syndical elections under Franco hurt the union and the harm was only partially overcome by the training program it ran with some of its Western European counterparts. Although the UGT did not do badly, particularly if we keep in mind it had members active primarily in Asturias and the Basque country in the early part of this decade, on balance CC.OO. has to be considered the victor. The Socialists had hoped—it is unclear whether they really believed it was possible—to duplicate their June 1977 showing, and for the Communists to more than hold their own dealt a serious blow to PSOE expectations.

Our consideration of the politics of the left in the post–June 1977 period would not be complete without an analysis of what for want of a better word we might call the ideological/propagandistic offensive which the PCE undertook in order to improve its popular standing. Because of space restrictions, we shall limit our consideration of this, focusing first on the polemics with the Soviet Union sparked by publication of the book *"Eurocommunism" and the State*, written by Santiago Carrillo, and his visits to the USSR and the United States in the fall of 1977; and, then, turning to a discussion of the Ninth Congress of the PCE in April 1978 and the decision adopted there to abandon the term Leninism. Although all these initiatives had a serious and substantive side, we should not overlook the fact they were also public–relations gambits undertaken by Carrillo and others in the PCE in an effort to make up the ground the Communists had lost to the PSOE in June 1977.

"Eurocommunism" and the State, published shortly after the tripartite summit of Spanish, French, and Italian Communist leaders in Madrid in March 1977, will not be remembered for the originality or depth of its analysis. The political importance of the document derives from the fact that for the first time a secretary–general of a Western European Communist party put his name to a book which so bluntly assailed the Soviet Union, coming very close to denying the socialist nature of the USSR and declaring that profound structural transformations were necessary there before the Soviet state could be considered a "democratic workers' state."[14] The Russian reaction to this polemical blast did not come right away. For whatever reasons, only in late June and after the Spanish elections, did the Soviet journal *New Times* publish a vitriolic personal attack on Carrillo

(had it come before, he only half–jokingly suggested, the PCE might have done better in the elections), accusing him of propounding ideas which "accord[ed] solely with the interests of imperialism, the forces of aggression and reaction."[15] Some saw in the attack an effort by the Soviets to force Carrillo's ouster, but what is more probable is that the CPSU was more interested in trying to isolate Carrillo and his party from their Western European counterparts.

In the summer of 1977, relations between the PCE and CPSU stood at an all–time low, worse even than when the Soviets had encouraged Enrique García and Enrique Lister to split from the Spanish party in the aftermath of the Czech invasion in 1968. With many observers wondering what the next step in the conflict might be, the Spanish Communists announced in the fall that a PCE delegation would attend the sixtieth anniversary celebrations of the October Revolution in Moscow. Both sides appeared to have an interest in tempering the dispute. For the Soviets, having as heterodox a party as the PCE come to Moscow would help reinforce the by now much-worn idea that the Soviet capital was still the mecca of the international Communist movement. The Spanish also had an interest in attending: Carrillo planned to visit the United States in late November, and a trip to Moscow would give his foreign initiaitves a sense of balance and, perhaps, help undercut criticism within the PCE and among some Western European Communist parties that he liked to grandstand and was too extreme in his criticism of the CPSU.

Carrillo and the Spanish delegation arrived in Moscow a few weeks later, and then, in a move which made the PCE leader an international cause célèbre, the Soviets did not permit him to speak. Press accounts of the incident generally placed responsibility on the CPSU or on some faction in its leadership, but there is evidence which suggests that Carrillo was not quite an innocent victim and that the affair was really more a public–relations effort worked out in anticipation of the Carrillo visit to the United States and designed to reinforce the impression, domestically and internationally, that the Spanish leader was the most anti–Soviet and thus the most Eurocommunist personality in Western Europe. Indeed, what better way to start a trip to the United States than to have been rejected so publicly by the Russians? This aspect of the incident becomes particularly relevant if we remember that Carrillo and others in the PCE expected, incorrectly, as it turned out, to have direct contacts with the Carter administration once he arrived in the United States.

It was during his trip to this country (he spoke at several major universities and at the Council on Foreign Relations in New York) that Carrillo first mentioned the possibility that during its Ninth Congress, scheduled for early 1978, the PCE would drop the appellation Leninist and define itself simply as a "Marxist, democratic and revolutionary" organization. The proposal, like the foreign policy initiatives undertaken by the PCE with the publication of *"Eurocomunismo" y Estado* and the visits to the Soviet Union and the United States by Carrillo, had as its principal objective a quest for votes and democratic credibility.

In the weeks and months preceding the congress, the first legal one held since 1932, when the PCE had only some 5,000 members, party leaders sought to make sure the debate on dropping Leninism did not get out of hand and, particularly, that it did not catalyze too great a debate on the content of Communist policies since 1956, when Carrillo had assumed a dominant position within the party. Carrillo and others in the leadership of the PCE in some ways underestimated the emotive power of the Leninism issue within the PCE. It was one thing to abandon aspects of Leninism in practice, as the party had increasingly done in the years after 1956, and quite another to formally recognize that rejection and to develop a substitute doctrine. Some of those who opposed Thesis 15 (the proposal to drop Leninism) wanted the PCE to uphold as still valid such fundamental Leninist notions as the armed seizure of power and the dictatorship of the proletariat. Others who were less nostalgic and recognized how much the world had changed since 1917 saw no necessary contradiction between Eurocommunism and Leninism, properly understood. However, they wanted the party to be clear about its objective of eventual working–class hegemony and desired a full–fledged debate on Leninism and its implications to promote the development of a coherent "Eurocommunist" alternative. Those who thought in this fashion were to be found primarily in Asturias, Andalucía, Cataluña, and Madrid. They feared that electoral avarice would lead the party quietly to drop some fundamental principles. Still others in the party, a distinct minority, however, would have liked to abandon Leninism entirely, but voted with those who opposed both Thesis 15 and Carrillo because they felt only a thorough airing of this issue would permit the PCE to rid itself of the residue of forty years of Stalinism.

In the end, the tradition of democratic centralism carried the day and only in some of the provincial conferences—those in Madrid, Asturias, and Cataluña—did Carrillo and his supporters face anything resembling a real challenge. The congress, it should be stressed, was much less controversial than many observers imagined it would be. Despite its predictability and the inordinate amount of attention paid to the Leninism issue, however, the Ninth PCE Congress was an important event because it signaled the beginning of a renovation in the Spanish party. Of the 160 members of the Central Committee elected there, fifty–six are new to that body, as are fourteen of the forty–six in the Executive Committee. One development, whose implications are not yet clear, was the rise in the influence of those in the PCE active in labor affairs. Over a quarter of the new Central Committee is composed of people with *Comisiones* backgrounds (the percentage of those with working-class origins in the CC is over fifty), and seven CC.OO. Leaders now sit on the Executive Committee. This influx of labor activists into the highest ranks of the PCE is in no small measure due to the fact that in most parts of the country—Cataluña was an exception—those active in the labor movement distinguished themselves as the most dependable supporters Carrillo had outside the apparat. Many of them, we can be sure, were less than enthusiastic about some "Eurocommunist" tenets, but they sided with Carrillo primarily because they felt that was the best way to control the debate within the party.

The Elections of 1977 and Beyond

The Communists had been able in the months after June 1977 to work out a mutually satisfactory arrangement with the UCD to block the PSOE. The arrangement worked for nearly a year and a half and lasted during the negotiations for the new constitution.[16] As a result, such traditionally thorny issues as Church–State relations, the monarchy, education, and the devolution of power to the regions were for the most part satisfactorily resolved or papered over to be dealt with at a later time. But, while consensus politics had some very obvious advantages, its limits were also apparent. A recrudescence of terrorist activity, a growth of discontent within the military, and citizen boredom with what appeared to be endless parliamentary debates tarnished the image of nearly all the parties by late 1978. The disenchantment peaked with the constitutional referendum in December. Although those voting overwhelmingly approved the charter, abstention was high, averaging 30 percent nationally and attaining dramatic proportions in the Basque country.

The Socialists, ever more convinced that Suárez was becoming weaker and susceptible to being ousted from power and the UCD split, stepped up their drive for new elections. In what came as a surprise to some observers of the Spanish political scene, Suárez picked up the gauntlet, dissolving the *Cortes* and calling for parliamentary elections for early March 1979, to be followed by municipal ones a month later. He chose that sequence so as to prevent the left from capitalizing on what everyone anticipated would be a good showing in the major Spanish cities in local elections: this had happened once before in April 1931 and the result had been the abdication of Alfonso XIII and the onset of the Second Republic. Under the terms of the new constitution, Suarez did not have to call elections. Although the UCD did not have a majority of votes in the *Cortes*, he could have opted for investiture. The constitution provided for two rounds in any such vote. To win the first, a premier–designate had to gain an absolute majority of the votes cast, but on the second round a plurality of votes would suffice. Given the improbability of agreement among the other parties and the likelihood of Communist abstention, Suárez had little to fear on this score.

The decision to call new elections, therefore, represented quite a gamble on the part of Suárez. True, only he had access to the polls performed by the *Centro de Investigaciones Sociológicas*—a polling organization attached to the office of the premier—and these probably confirmed his suspicion that most of the undecided voters, some 40 percent of those queried by pollsters, would in the end opt for his party, particularly given the growing national concern over terrorism. The realization that without elections any minority government would have had to face up to constant Socialist demands for a return to the polls and that in this atmosphere making headway against mounting social and economic problems would be virtually impossible probably also helped make up his mind. So did the desire to rule without having to rely on agreement with other forces, particularly the Communists.

Although most polls in early 1979 showed the PSOE to be ahead among those Spaniards who had already made up their minds about whom to support, the Socialist party was not as well-oiled a machine as people supposed or party leaders let on. For one thing, although the Socialist-backed UGT had come in second to the Communist *Comisiones Obreras* in the trade-union elections celebrated in early 1978, the union had not done anywhere near as well as Socialist leaders had originally predicted and had even slipped since that time. The party, perhaps overly confident of victory over Suárez, had also fallen behind in its organizational reinforcement and consolidation. Many in the PSOE did not take this problem seriously even after senatorial by-elections in Asturias and Alicante in May 1978 showed the Socialist vote hurt by abstentions. Moreover, the unification of the various Socialist currents under the PSOE banner had not come off as smoothly as hoped and a part of the regional Socialist electorate resented the unification. There had also been a good bit of grumbling in the ranks about a González remark to the effect that at its forthcoming Twenty-eighth Congress the party would drop the reference to Marxism from its program. A more profound political miscalculation probably had to do with the Socialist decision to attack Suárez as a slightly disguised continuation of Franco. Suárez, it could hardly be denied, had made his career under the *ancien régime*, but only the most shortsighted could deny the decisive role he had played (along with King Juan Carlos) in bringing democracy to the country. The Socialists, in effect, also overestimated their ability to overcome in two years the effects of four decades' hostile anti-left propaganda. In this respect, a story appearing in *Cambio 16* is eloquent: campaigning in a town twenty-five miles from Madrid, a UCD candidate put a pin with her party emblem on the coat of a prospective voter; before she consented, the voter asked if one could be put in jail for wearing it.[17]

There was a good deal of talk in Spain prior to March 1 about possible coalition governments with most of the speculation focusing on the so-called "grand coalition" between the UCD and PSOE. Suárez, of course, did not call the elections to share power and sources close to the UCD insisted during the campaign that, were their party to win 160 seats in the new *Cortes*, it would form a minority government. A coalition government, it should be stressed, would have benefited neither Socialist/UCD partisan interests nor those of democracy in Spain. It would only have muddied the political waters at a time when clear-cut alternatives, put aside in part because of the exigencies of the transition from Francoism, needed to be emphasized once more. The Communists, it goes almost without saying, would have welcomed the opportunity to claim the mantle of opposition to a UCD-PSOE government.

The election results, it turned out, vindicated Suárez's political judgment. His party received slightly fewer votes than in 1977 and captured only 168 seats (less than an absolute majority), but he beat the Socialists decisively. With many of the deputies elected on the right wing *Coalición Democrática* ticket and even some Catalan nationalists ready to support him—provided, of course, certain conditions with respect to autonomy for that region are met—Suárez should be able to govern effectively for the full four-year parliamentary term. For the Socialists, on the other hand, the election results represented a significant setback. Their leaders had been confidently insisting that the PSOE was a viable *alternativa de poder* and would in the end capture more votes, if not seats in the *Cortes*, than the UCD. The PSOE elected 119 deputies and won approximately 5.3 million votes, an increase of 100,000 relative to 1977, but the figure is misleading. The combined PSOE/PSP vote in June 1977 had been over 6 million and Socialist leaders had thought that the unification of the two parties would have a "multiplier" effect and bring even more votes to the Socialist banner. They miscalculated. Indeed, PSOE losses were especially pronounced in Andalucía—where the *Partido Socialista de Andalucía* and its leader, Rojas Marcos, took advantage of the perhaps too evident PSOE disdain for regional sentiment in the area and came back strongly from a weak performance two years earlier—and in the Basque country. In the latter region, the Socialists were hit hard by abstentions in working-class districts and lost ground to nationalist groups. The more moderate *Partido Nacionalista Vasco* won seven of the twenty-six deputies the region sends to the Congress, and two more radical groups with ties to ETA—*Euzkadiko Ezkerra* and *Herri Batasuna*—won four.

The Communists did somewhat better this time around, increasing their share of the vote slightly, from 9 to 10 percent, and its total by nearly 200,000 votes. Nevertheless, the party could not have been overly cheered by that performance. Communist leaders had expected their party to really "take off" this time around. Instead, and despite the vicissitudes noted above, the PSOE generally held on to its voters and the Communists, although placing over 10,000 *Comisiones Obreras* activists on their parliamentary (and later, the municipal) lists, were still unable to translate their syndical influence into votes. At the same time, the Communists could and did take great comfort from the fact that the Socialists failed in their effort to consolidate their hegemony on the left. In this respect, the elections were an important step forward in the breaking of the bipolar dialectic which had emerged after June 1977.

Suárez and the UCD won the March 1979 parliamentary elections in rather convincing fashion, but the left bounced back from that defeat to emerge victorious from the municipal contests celebrated a month later. Following the pattern established in most Western European countries, Spaniards tended to shift their support in local elections to parties of the left. The UCD came in first in twenty-six out of fifty-three provincial capitals and did well in small and medium-sized towns and cities. The parties of the left, on the other hand, and as was to be expected, turned in their best performances in the most populous cities. After agreement between the Socialists and Communists nationally and between those two parties and the PSA in Andalucía generally to support the party with the most votes in a given city, they now control more than 1,500 *ayuntamientos* or city halls, where, as we indicated at the beginning of this chapter, over 70 percent of the population resides. Socialist mayors govern in Madrid and Barcelona, thanks to Communist support, while a Communist does so in Cordoba and the PSA in the symbolic capital of Andalucía, Seville.

The rather impressive performance given by the left in the municipal elections did much to take away the sting from the defeat in the national parliamentary contest. Although Suárez and his administrations are not without significant leverage in the *municipios*—the UCD finds itself for the most part frozen out of government at that level—the party and Suárez still have influence through the *gobernadores civiles*, who are named by Madrid, and the UCD has taken over many *diputaciones provinciales*, whose members are elected by the municipal councilors in a given province and where the councilor from a small town has the same electoral weight as one from a large city. The parties of the left will now have the opportunity not only to demonstrate their competence in administration but also to use their control of the municipal arena to build still fledgling organizational structures.

The entry of the left into many city halls was the result of a post-electoral agreement between Socialists and Communists, an agreement which PSOE leaders might not have felt compelled to make had they not misjudged their chances against Suárez so badly. The announcement spawned fears among observers of the Spanish political scene not only that a new Popular Front which would polarize the country was in the offing but that it would be only a matter of time before the Communists would completely outmaneuver the PSOE and become the dominant force on the left. Let us explore those possibilities more closely.

It would be foolhardy to deny that the conditions for a Popular Front (or whatever name an alliance of the left would take) exist in Spain. For one thing, the Socialist and Communist electorates overlap to a significant degree, and this reality of electoral geography encourages understandings such as the one only recently seen. For another, important ideological differences which have always separated the two parties have narrowed and there is little in Socialist doctrine as it has been articulated by the PSOE up to this point (particularly if we take as a reference point the program approved at the Twenty-seventh Congress celebrated in Madrid in December 1976) which is dramatically at odds with the Eurocommunist tenets defended publicly by the PCE. A further evolution on the part of the PSOE toward "Social-Democratic" positions is, of course, not out of the question, but as the debate over Marxism at the Twenty-eighth Congress in May 1979 demonstrated, those who wish to move in that direction will not have an easy time of it. For its part, the PCE already crossed its Rubicon (or at least gained much public-relations mileage from saying it had) in April 1978 when delegates to its Ninth Congress dropped Leninism from the party program. Although Eurocommunism has certainly not caught fire in Spain, the image of moderation projected by the PCE and its leaders makes it difficult for the PSOE not to collaborate with the Communists. Although important areas of competition (particularly in the municipal arena and in the labor movement) will exist between the two parties, many signs point to growing ties and unity of action between PSOE and PCE.

And yet we should not be too quick in supposing either that this outcome is inevitable or that the pattern will follow the experience of the 1930s with little or no variation. Clearly, a good number of Socialist leaders and voters do not want the *entente* to prosper much beyond what exists today, and that electorate could react negatively to further consolidation of the alliance. It is not all that clear, however, that the Communists (that is, the dominant faction associated with Santiago Carrillo) simply want a new edition of the Popular Front. Collaboration between the PCE and UCD against the PSOE in the months after June 1977 was in many ways a marriage of convenience, but for Carrillo and his associates alliance with Suárez and the UCD was part of a more long-term strategy designed to force the Socialists and the UCD into a government of national salvation or cooperation, into a Spanish version of the *compromesso storico*. They have not abandoned that objective. Indeed, although the Communists have been rather cautious in their discussions of medium-term strategy, it would appear that the constitution of such a government remains their primary

objective. Carrillo still looks for Spanish politics to follow much more the
Italian rather than the French example and probably believes that with a bit
of luck the PCE might find itself in a situation by the mid-1980s comparable more or less with that of the PCI. The keys to the situation would be an
increase in the Communist vote and a weakening of the UCD and PSOE.

Obviously there is no guarantee that any of these conditions will be
met, but it may be worthwhile to consider how the Communists perceived
their future possibilities. The PCE views the UCD as the Christian Democratic analogue in Spain, but considers that party to be in some important
ways more vulnerable than the Italian DC. The DC and UCD are, in the
Communist analysis, typical but very effective multi-class parties which
have straddled the political and social center, thereby frustrating the designs
of the Communists and the left more generally. Christian Democracy relied
on the Catholic Church and its parallel institutions for an infrastructural
support base in the years after World War II. Because it retains that dimension even today, the DC is a very difficult opponent for the PCI. In Spain,
however, the task may be easier, the Spanish Communists believe. The
power base and the source of infrastructural support for the UCD come
from participation in and control of the government. Because the UCD
does not have the religious component, however, this makes the UCD less
resilient and more vulnerable in Communist eyes. PCE and PSOE entry
into the government would allow the left to begin the job of breaking and
weakening the hegemony of the UCD within and over the state apparatus.
Along with this, obviously, would come the weakening of the UCD as a
party and the isolation of its most conservative sectors.

For the scenario to be realized, not only must the UCD be weakened
over the next four or five years but the Communists must also reduce the
margin separating them from the PSOE. The Communist party has not
been particularly successful in having its brand of Eurocommunism
accepted by the Spanish voter, however, and to a large extent whether or
not the PCE advances electorally in the future will depend largely on Socialist mistakes. As we noted earlier, some observers of the Spanish political
scene view the recently concluded municipal agreement between Socialists
and Communists and the crisis precipitated by the resignation of Felipe
González at the Twenty-eighth PSOE Congress over the question of
whether or not to include a reference to Marxism in the party program
(González did not want to do so) as the first steps on the road to the emas-
culation of the Socialist movement in Spain. Today we can hardly predict
whether the PSOE will be able to withstand the Communist challenge in
Spain or whether it will be able to avoid the fate of the Italian Socialist
party, but it may be useful to discuss some of the problems the PSOE has as
its moves to consolidate an incipient (but weakened) hegemonic position on
the left.

One of these has to do with the style of politics PSOE leaders have
favored up to this point. Many people outside and in the Socialist party had

been surprised in June 1977 by the performance of the PSOE and, perhaps because the party garnered so many votes with so little apparent effort. Socialist leaders were confirmed in their view of politics as a game of parliamentary seats and little else. Certainly, many PSOE leaders paid lip service to the importance of strengthening their syndical presence and of developing an influence at the municipal level, but in retrospect it is evident that the party did not do enough about these issues in the months after June 1977. This was an unpardonable omission for an organization which claimed for itself the role not only of *alternativa de gobierno* but of *alternativa de poder*. The parliamentary arena was but one area where political influence could be manifested, and it is clear that PSOE leaders not only claimed but expected too much would flow from 29 percent of the vote and 118 deputies. In this, they left themselves at a distinct disadvantage with respect to the Communists, who parlayed a much smaller vote into a proportionately greater influence. The Socialists have not yet really penetrated into the Spanish social fabric and it is for this reason that the struggle for hegemony on the left will focus on the municipal arena. The PSOE has mayors in over 1,000 cities but little so far in the way of organizational structures (within and outside the party) to compete with the neighborhood and housewife associations which the Communists in large measure control. If the Socialists lose this battle and that for syndical influence as well, it will only be a matter of time before the margin separating them from the Communists shrinks dramatically.

Another problem area confronting the Socialists has to do with the ideological clarity and organizational cohesion of the party. This problem was highlighted at the Twenty-eighth PSOE Congress in May 1979 when delegates overruled leadership efforts to give the party a more moderate accent and instead approved a motion to include Marxism in the party program.[18] Defeated by a two-to-one margin on the question, First Secretary Felipe González surprised the delegates by refusing on the following day to run for reelection. That decision, coming after three days of exhaustive debates, threw the party into turmoil and led to the appointment of a five-person steering committee to handle party affairs until an extraordinary congress met in late September 1979 to decide the Marxism issue. There González carried the day, only slightly the worse for wear, agreeing to some suitable compromise language and to greater diversity within the executive committee. In the intramural battle which preceded the congress, González had an important advantage over the more radical PSOE faction. None of its leaders (and the list must include longtime Socialists like Francisco Bustelo and Pablo Castellano as well as those who came in from the PSP, like Tierno Galván) matches González in personal popularity among PSOE rank and file.

Moderate voters might now be more reassured as to the intentions of the PSOE, but the party could also experience the splintering and factionalism which has bedeviled and so weakened the Italian Socialist party.

Watering down the Socialist commitment to basic Marxism could be a Pyrrhic victory if the party does not work harder at establishing its social presence and articulating an alternative which is quite distinct from that of the government party.

Spanish socialism has always had a Jacobin wing, but this problem has been exacerbated in the last two and a half years by the tremendous growth the party has experienced. It has gone in that span of time from a membership of 8,000 to one of more than 200,000 and this has caused problems both organizationally and politically. Despite this growth, however, the PSOE is still woefully short of cadres. This shortcoming must be remedied if the party is to meet the Communist challenge. Earlier, we alluded to the difficulties the PSOE faces in the municipal sphere. Here let us insist that similar problems exist in the trade-union movement. The Socialist-led UGT has not developed as rapidly as many had expected and the absence of cadres is evident there as well. It has had severe organizational problems in Aragón, Galicia, Santander, and the Basque country (to name only the most prominent places), with a good deal of resentment clouding its relationship with the National party. Suárez has not made it easy for the UGT to consolidate its structures.

As a result of the defeat suffered in March 1979 and the crisis which erupted at the Twenty-eighth PSOE Congress two months later over the Marxism issue, Spanish socialism has entered a period of introspection and doubt. The picture we have sketched of the party suggests it will have a difficult time consolidating a hegemony on the left. It is nevertheless important to emphasize that the PSOE is today in much better shape than many observers of the Spanish political scene would have been willing to wager in the twilight of the Franco era and that many of the difficulties it faces now are the result of its very emergence as the second most important force in the country.

The Communists view the PSOE with a mixture of condescension and envy, confident still that they are the only truly "serious" force on the left. Unfortunately, from their point of view, whatever mistakes and failings the Socialists have made, these have not led to a corresponding electoral growth on the part of the PCE. In an area like Andalucía, for example, the PCE can be cheered that the PSOE lost so many votes to the PSA. But are those votes only marking time before journeying on to the Communist banner? An answer to this question is by no means evident at this point. Neither is an answer altogether clear when we ask how long the Communists can go without developing a presence in the Basque country and Galicia. Moreover, as the Communists battle it out with the Socialists for the political space of democratic socialism in Spain, what of the ultraleft and particularly of the *Partido del Trabajo* and the *Organización Revolucionaria de Trabajadores?* Will these parties (now in the process of fusion) develop a presence in

Andalucía and Madrid sufficient to cause the PCE damage? There is, more-over, no guarantee that the Communists will be successful in wearing down the PSOE. The practice of *compromesso storico* politics, as the Italian Communists have recently found out, does not always bring a favorable outcome. Failure to make headway against the Socialists could cause serious debates within the PCE on the subject of alternative alliance strategies and partners and these in turn could become enmeshed in the struggle for leadership in the post–Carrillo PCE.

Socialists and Communists have taken important steps in the first years of the post–Franco era to establish their organizations and to develop a presence in important sectors of Spanish society. Those efforts have had mixed results and, as a result, no definite assessment is possible today as to their individual prospects, their relationship with each other, or the likelihood that they will in the end emerge as the only viable methods for the Spanish Left. Regional parties and sentiment are strong in areas like Andalucía, the Basque country and Cataluña, and both the PSOE and PCE will have to find ways of dealing with that reality even as they battle it out for influence at the national level. The patterns of competition and coexistence between Socialists and Communists which will develop in Spain over the next decade will have many similarities with those of the left in other Latin European countries, but they will also be distinct and draw from very specific sources in Spanish history and tradition.

Notes

1. Provisional results for the June 1977 elections may be found in *Informaciones* (Madrid), June 14, 1978. The parties of the extreme Left had not been legalized in time for the election and thus had to campaign under fictitious names as parts of umbrella coalitions. Under these circumstances, it could be argued that they ran at something of a disadvantage. A good case can be made for the opposite point of view however. It was far easier for the Spanish voter to vote for a coalition called the *Alianza Electoral de los Trabajadores* or the *Candidatura de Unidad Popular* than for movements like the *Organización Revolucionaria de Trabajadores* or the *Movimiento Comunista* which stood behind them. The unofficial but rather complete results of the March 1979 election may be found in *Nuestra Bandera*, 99 (May 1979): 35–40.

2. For an assessment of these changes, see the author's chapter entitled "The Domestic and International Evolution of the Spanish Communist Party" in Rudolf L. Tökés, ed., *Eurocommunism and Détente* (New York: New York Univ. Press, 1978).

3. *Cambio 16* (Madrid), January 8, 1978.

4. See the *Manifiesto de Reconciliación Nacional* in *Mundo Obrero*, third week of April 1975, which stated that "the democratic evolution of the state by way of legal reforms [is] objectively and subjectively impossible."

5. At the Madrid provincial conference in March 1978 in remarks to the delegates.

6. For a detailed analysis of the strike and the circumstances leading up to it, see Félix Fanés, *La Vaga de Tramvies del 1951* (Barcelona: Editorial Laia, 1977)

7. Jon Amsden, *Collective Bargaining and Class Struggle in Spain* (London: Weidenfeld & Nicholson, 1972), p. 150.

8. Victor Manuel Arbeloa, "Posiciones Políticas ante el Cristianismo y la Iglesia," *Pastoral Misionera* XI: 8 (November–December 1975): 725–741.

9. On the PSOE, see Felipe González and Antonio Guerra, *Socialismo es Libertad y Notas para una Biografía* (Barcelona: Edicions Galba, 1978); Jose Manuel Arija, *Nicolás Redondo* (Madrid: Editorial Cambio 16, 1977); Ramon Chao, *Después de Franco, España* (Madrid: Ediciones Felmar, 1976), pp. 211–232; and Sergio Vilar, *La Oposición a la Dictadura* (Barcelona: Editorial Aymá, 1976), pp. 165–181.

10. The effort was widely publicized in early 1978 as the result of reporting done on the polemics caused by the publication of the book *Autobiografía de Federico Sánchez* in late 1977. The author of the book, Jorge Semprun, was a former member of the PCE Executive Committee and had been responsible with Carrillo for the decision. See *Cambio 16*, January 22, 1978.

11. See, for example, the remarks by Santiago Carrillo in *Demain l'Espagne* (Paris: Editions du Seuil, 1974), p. 175.

12. Santiago Carrillo in an interview with *La Nouvelle Critique* (Paris), October–November 1971, p. 24, remarked that at the dawn of the post-Franco era the Communist party was in a position analogous to that of the PSOE in 1930. The PSOE won 105 out of 470 seats in the Constituent Assembly election of June 1931 and was the hegemonic party on the left in the *Cortes* or parliament.

13. *Saida* (Barcelona), March 21, 1978.

14. Santiago Carrillo, *"Eurocomunismo" y Estado* (Barcelona: Editorial Grijalbo, 1977), p. 212.

15. See "Contrary to the Interests of Peace and Socialism in Europe—Concerning the Book '*Eurocommunism*' and the State by Santiago Carrillo, General Secretary of the Communist Party of Spain," *New Times* (Moscow) 26 (June 1977): 11.

16. The analysis which follows in the next five paragraphs was first published in the *Washington Quarterly*, II, 2 (Spring 1979): 105–109.

17. *Cambio 16*, February 26, 1979.

18. For a discussion of the PSOE congress, see the coverage in *El Pais, Triunfo,* and *La Calle* of the last two weeks in May 1979.

5

The Views of the Left in Italy and France on International and Domestic Economic Issues

Giuseppe Sacco

International Economic Issues

The Oil Price Increase and the Trend toward Cartelization in Other Raw Materials Markets

The increase in the price of crude oil that the OPEC cartel managed to impose in 1973–74 highlighted a problem which the West European left has been unable to solve: conflict of interests among the working class of the developed countries and the so-called *nations prolétaires* of the Third World. There was indeed little doubt that the increase in the price of oil was going to affect the standard of living of the working class in Europe. But it also dramatically interrupted the secular downward trend of the price of oil relative to the price of the main imports of the oil-producing countries. And the downward trend of the terms of trade of raw materials—although its existence is not universally considered as proven—has long been one of the main elements on which the left, Marxist and non-Marxist, has based its critique of capitalist "imperialism."

The dramatic nature of the increase in the price of oil during the winter of 1973–74 and the politically motivated embargoes imposed by most Arab producers, have made the oil issue seem to world public opinion to be a special one, with features quite different from the general issue of raw-materials supply to the industrialized countries. In fact, however, logically the two issues are quite similar and, at least theoretically, there is a possibility that producers' cartels for other raw materials might repeat the OPEC coup and thereby permanently change the terms of trade with manufactured goods. Indeed, the political problems posed by these two issues for the left in the industrialized countries are quite similar, since it is clear that low and generally declining prices, as well as safe and easy supply of other raw materials, no less than the low cost and easy availability of oil, had contributed to the great improvements in the standard of living that the working classes have enjoyed in the postwar period in the neocapitalist countries of the industrialized West. In the end, writes an Italian Socialist economist:

The problem that neo-capitalism has failed to solve, and one which represents one of its main contradictions, the problem of disequilibria between developed and underdeveloped countries, has to find a solution, sooner or later. Either this solution is found in a positive way with a gradual diffusion of economic development, or it might be found in a negative manner, with a redistribution that will reduce the wealth of the industrial countries.

It is quite obvious that the political forces that represent, or pretend to represent, the working classes of the industrial countries look with some discomfort at this second possibility, which would strongly affect the standard of living in the neocapitalist countries. These forces therefore cannot but worry about a crisis triggered by the first successful drive to increase substantially the price of an essential primary commodity. According to the same Socialist economist, the meaning of the present crisis "is that—at a moment that coincided with the Arab-Israeli war, but in circumstances that could have been triggered by any other event—this redistribution of wealth has been demanded with irresistible force by a group of underdeveloped countries."[2]

Notwithstanding these concerns, the political parties of the left recognize on purely political grounds that Third World aspirations are well founded. They generally also recognize the justification of the OPEC decision to increase the price of oil, and look with a benevolent eye on the possibility of a general increase in raw-material prices. This second attitude is of course the easier and less costly in popularity since the possibility of an actual repetition of the OPEC strategy in other commodity markets appears unlikely, and since the impact on the everyday life of European workers in any case would be less direct and less immediately visible than in the case of oil.

It is the French Socialists who dare to put the issue in quite clear terms. In the view of the PS, with the December 1973 OPEC decision to quadruple the price of oil, "the old economic order, based as it is on the postulate of an unlimited supply of cheap natural resources from the Third World, is shaken. A new balance of power is appearing. Dependence is no longer one-way and the affluence of the Western economies is directly endangered by OPEC's action."[3] The point, therefore, "is not to state that whatever is good for the Third World is, in itself, also good for the French workers. We—the Socialists—know that today's general economic trends, steered by the multinational corporations (MNCs), that try to perpetuate the crisis and to manage it according to their own interests—set the workers of the world one against the other."[4]

Even if the traditional scapegoat—the MNCs—is in an unclear manner accused of being responsible for present economic trends, the unspeakable truth is uttered: the interests of the workers of the world are in conflict, and a choice has to be made among them by the left. The awakening of the Third World and its economic demands therefore become a central issue for the West European left, one very difficult to deal with but almost impossible to avoid, especially after an episode such as the increase of oil prices of 1973–74.

Confronted with trends that set the workers of the developed and of the developing countries "one against the other," the PS has made a remarkable effort to set forth a clear and politically acceptable position. The attitude of the Socialists toward the Third World, writes the PS official responsible for Third World questions, "is based essentially on two refusals."[5] They concern "two illusions: an old one, *Eurocentrism*, and a new one, *Third-Worldism*.

Eurocentrism is a well-known temptation of the workers' movement in the developed countries. It consists in believing that the destiny of human civilization depends only on the evolution of European countries (which nowadays means all the advanced countries) and that only what happens in this area is really important.

Third-Worldism had its first adherents in the 1960s. Inspired by the analysis of economists from the developing world, and appropriated by an extremist faction in France, this theory states that the main changes from now on will come from the Third World. In this "area of hurricanes," far from the middle–class–like working class of the affluent countries, the "proletarian nations" prepare the revolutions necessary in our times. The duty of today's militant Socialists is therefore a systematic support of the demands of Third World countries. A socialist has to reject both these temptations for one and only one reason: they tend to replace the analysis of reality based on class struggle (that is, the approach of Socialist theory) with an analysis in terms of nations' struggle.

The Socialists sympathize with the global demands presented by the countries of the Third World: improvement in their terms of trade, more transfer of capital and technology, and so on, "but, of course, as the PS is the party that represents the interests of the popular masses of a developed country, we should certainly insist—if we were in power—on the delay of certain changes (in the industrial structure, for instance) and on a careful management of the transition process."[6]

Supporting (although with some precautions) the positions of the "Group of 77," the French Socialists stress the "inequity" of the existing order but also the drawbacks in the tendency of producers to create commodity cartels. "The reaction to the present system has brought about a trend to cartelization. . . .This policy has obtained non–negligible results. . . but still has some limits: it cannot be applied to all products, and not all raw materials producers are in the Third World. Moreover, this policy is not without danger: it can replace a relationship based on force with another, similar relationship, with no improvement in justice. The poorest LDC's had the opportunity to learn this during the oil crisis. . ."

If producers' cooperation has been a positive step, because it has disturbed the capitalist organization of the petroleum market, the real goal to be sought is to base trade on really equitable cooperation rules. This implies a reduction of price fluctuations, the maintenance of prices at levels both equitable to the consumers and remunerative to the producers, and the establishment of mechanisms for long-term adjustment of supply and demand. These objectives have to be pursued with a global approach, involving a number of commodities large enough to really influence the whole raw materials market, and aiming at a form of international planning, as the market mechanism is clearly unable to stabilize the prices at a satisfactory level. Only the creation of international buffer stocks for an adequate number of commodities will make this possible.[7]

The French Socialist program[8] therefore proposes "world agreement on basic raw materials, long-term purchasing agreements, and the organization and financing of buffer stocks." But neither the program nor the official program of the French Socialist party,[9] which states in more detail this support for the creation of a pool of buffer stocks for raw materials, mentions the request by the "Group of 77" for a "second window," which aims to introduce structural changes in the world markets and in the economy of the producing countries. This request is indeed one of major specific points that make up the difference between the positions of the developed and developing countries in the international forums where the reorganization of world commodity markets is being negotiated. "It would be desirable," state the French Socialists, "to create a single financing mechanism for these multi-product stocks in order to escape the logic of individual commodity agreements. This would make possible a certain compensation for price changes among different products and, if necessary, the enlargement of the operation of the common financing fund to include other products."[10] The position of the French Socialists on this specific issue thus coincides, in spite of their assertions of support to the Third World, with the attitude of the OECD countries, which is fiercely under attack by the "Group of 77." However, one may assume that this is probably due more to lack of knowledge of the technicalities under discussion in the international forums than to deliberate choice.

Moreover, the French Socialists seem to believe that "apart from market stabilization, the creation of a network of buffer stocks would create the conditions necessary to support the price level" of raw materials exported from the LDCs.[11] No explanation is given about the connection between these two things, apart from a reference to "medium-term purchasing and selling agreements attached to the functioning of the stocking system" which would be the "normal prolongation" of the negotiations in which the price level would be decided. For any reader aware of the power-lessness of buffer stocks vis-à-vis long-term price trends, the meaning of this proposal is obscure.

The French Communist Party has adopted a clear-cut position in support of terms of trade more favorable to the producers of all raw materials. Already in the Twentieth Congress (1973) of the PCF Marchais stated that "the national liberation movement has entered in a new phase, a phase of struggle against neo-colonialism, for economic independence and for real sovereignty. . .in a difficult struggle for the development of a national economic system whose first precondition is free control of their national resources" by the governments of the developing countries.

At the subsequent PCF Twenty-first Congress, which met at the end of October 1974, Marchais repeated the same line. He said in his main report: "By taking legitimate measures to compensate for the deterioration of the terms of trade, and to recuperate their national riches, the oil-producing countries do not affect the interests of the working class and the people of the advanced countries." Indeed, "it is perfectly possible to make the great oil trusts bear the new costs with no impact for the people."

The French Communists therefore try to escape the dilemma which the conflict of interest between the Third World and the working classes of the advanced countries poses to the European left by flatly denying that this conflict of interests exists. As far as the oil price is concerned, the PCF affirms that it is only the fault of the great oil companies if the average Frenchman is affected by the change in ther terms of trade between oil pro-ducers and oil consumers. To maintain this point, Marchais was obliged, a few months after the oil crisis, to engage in a campaign—to which he tried to give the appearance of an all-out war—against the oil companies. The pretext was the so-called "Schwartz report," from the name of the non-Communist member of the National Assembly who chaired the parliamen-tary commission of inquiry on the behavior of the French oil companies during and after the crisis. The entire party machinery was engaged on this occasion in a colossal propaganda effort, called *opération vérité,* in which the proof of the obvious fact that oil importers had profited from the price increase was distorted in order to convince PCF followers that the energy crisis itself was a result of the speculative activities of the oil companies.

Some further light on the attitude of the PCF on these problems has been cast by Paul Boccara, a member of the Central Committee and a spe-cialist in international economic problems. According to this representative of the PCF, "one would fail to perceive the real problem [of the prices of raw materials] . . . if only the stabilization of export earnings, or the price of exports, were taken into account. What has to be considered is the *relation-ship* between export earnings and the cost of imports into these [commodity-exporting] countries (imports whose quantities and prices are both growing), the relationship between export earnings and the conditions of their real, non-dependent development."[12] In order to establish a fair price, "based on productivity conditions as well as on long-term decline of raw material prices," a radical departure from the present organization of world markets is envisaged, much more radical than the one the LDCs themselves advocate. For the PCF, "government to government agreements are necessary, and a France ruled by the *Union de la Gauche* could start operating in this direction with our partners of the underdeveloped countries, and maybe with certain developed countries as well."[13]

In other words, while the French Socialists propose a reorganization of the world market for raw materials in order to improve its functioning, very much along the line of the OECD government proposals, the PCF advocates a total politicization and bilateralization of raw-material trade, on the model of the trading systems presently existing in the Communist countries of Eastern Europe. But it is worth pointing out that, while "state trade" countries allow—up to a certain point—bilateral disequilibria (which are indispensable in order to ensure rational specialization of the different countries), the French Communists do not miss an opportunity to point out the benefits that the French economy would receive from government agreements for *bilaterally balanced trade* with the Eastern bloc or some pro-Soviet Third World countries.

According to the scheme proposed by the French Communists, increases in the earnings of exporting countries would not affect production costs in France, since government-to-government agreements would eliminate the monpolistic rent presently received by the MNCs, guaranteeing at the same time "stable and remunerative prices [that] would increase the earnings of the LDCs concerned, and would therefore enlarge the market they provide [for French exports], with no negative impact on our costs."

The best example of this substitution of the world market for raw materials with a network of bilateral government-to-government agreements is provided in regard to oil itself and by the policy of PCF proposes in order to guarantee the French economy the necessary oil supplies and to cover France's serious oil deficit. "The deficit with Saudi Arabia is more than half, almost two-thirds of the total oil deficit in 1976. . . . On the contrary, our trade balance with another oil producer, Algeria, is in surplus. We could buy much more gas and oil from Algeria . . . and sell her more, so that our relations would be stronger and more balanced. Instead, we have scaled down our imports from Algeria, pushing her into deficit, and this does not favor our exports."[14]

The general problem of ensuring a supply of adequate and cheap raw materials to the French economy is approached in the same way: government-to-government agreements with Communist countries and "progressive" LDCs, coupled with a strong self-sufficiency drive. Indeed, a leftist government would "enlarge international trade" mainly through "agreements with the Socialist countries, which can provide minerals and take French exports in exchange."[15] But strong criticism also has to be directed—in the Communist view—at both national and multinational mining corporations for not devoting enough exploration efforts to French territory, where a number of mines (mostly coal) that have been closed in the recent past should be reopened. At the Twenty-first Party Congress, Augustin Laurent, a prominent PCF member, pointed out that "if national coal production had been kept at its normal level, 20 million tons of oil imports could have been saved. . . . Life is indeed proving that we have been right in the 1950s when we fought the Schuman plan, in 1960, when we fought the Jeanneney plan, and in 1968, when we fought against the closing down of coal mines."[16]

The attitude of the PCF on these issues is quite coherent; it can be criticized and rejected in toto, but—unlike the PS position—offers little ground for criticism of a technical nature.

In comparing the position of the French PS and PCF on the issue of raw materials prices, one should emphasize that, if the Communist position appears less exposed to criticism on logical and technical grounds, this is due in the first place to the fact that the PCF, unlike the PS, has given no really comprehensive and detailed explanation of the party's position on North-South relations.[17]

The attitude of the Italian Socialists is, in this respect, quite anomalous. The issue of the conflict of interests between the working classes of the advanced countries and the Third World does not seem to deserve much attention[18] beyond general sympathy for the "exploited countries." In the Socialists' view, at the origin of the present crisis there are two main factors. The first consists of "the efforts of exploited countries that try to put an end to their total submission to the wealthy countries," so that "international tension, today totally located in the Third World, represents a class struggle phenomenon that is bound to become more relevant in the future, together with an increased awareness of the present exploitation." The second main factor, according to the Italian Socialists, consists in "short term speculative activities of capitalist multinational corporations—one could just say of American multinationals—that take advantage of the demands of raw materials producers and especially of the oil producers in order to create artificial bottlenecks in the market, and therefore increase their profit margins."[19]

According to an important Socialist figure,[20] "there is no conflict of interests between the oil producers and the European countries, [since] both

are the victims of the same manipulations of the multinational corporations." In the OECD "there is no coincidence of interests at all, because the
dependency of Europe (a greater importer of raw materials) is very different
from the condition of the U.S., which imports only a minimal fraction of its
supply."[21]

The positions of the Italian Communists on the question of the price of oil
and raw materials are somewhat different from what we have seen until
now. The PCI does not try to convince its followers of the fact that the
workers of Italy and of the developed countries in general had nothing to
fear or to lose because of the tremendous 1973-74 increases in oil prices.
This PCI line, which contrasts with the position of the PCF, seems similar
to that of the French Socialists. Indeed, *Politica ed Economia,* the monthly
journal of the Italian Communist party's Center for Economic Studies
(CESPE) approaches the problem in a slightly different and more sophisticated way than the French Communists but still maintains the allegiance of
the Italian Communists to the cause of the Third World. "Some observers
see the recent increase in the prices of raw materials[22] as a part of a process
leading to a change in the terms of trade between developed and developing
countries. The 'unequal exchange'. . .would then be in the process of
becoming less unjust. . . . Whatever the case, simplistic generalization
should be avoided. . . . The raw materials whose prices have increased most
noticeably in the last year are the ones whose market is controlled by the
multinational corporations; or the ones on which there has been a strong
concentration of international speculation, aimed at making supply more
difficult and more costly to competing enterprices. A typical example is the
Japanese hoarding of Australian wool." Oil is not mentioned, but it is
implied that the price increases has nothing to do with a reversal of the
"unequal exchange."
     The long-term evolution of oil prices is explained by the PCI by the
interplay of a variety of forces: the oil-producing companies, the oil-con-
suming manufacturing companies, the nationalized enterprises (such as ENI
and Elf-Erap), and the USSR as an oil exporter. "Views differ on the question of which forces brought about the decline in oil prices (between 1955
and 1970). Authors such as Peter Odell attribute it to the pressure of manufacturing industry in a phase of trade liberalization," but "it has to be
added" that 1955 was also the year when the "optimistic forecasts for the
nuclear sector were announced."[23]
     As far as the causes of the "changes—that could have been, but were
not foreseen—of the 1971-73 period. . .it would be too simplistic. . .to
explain everything by a deliberate action, autonomously decided by the
producing countries" reacting against the so-called "unequal exchange."
Indeed, "the slow decline of the oil prices in the preceding fifteen years had

been much smaller than the decline in other raw material prices, so that it was not even mentioned"[24] by the "Group of 77" in their complaints about declining terms of trade. "The majority of oil producing countries never had a militant attitude on prices, and the ones that had claims to advance, normally demanded an increase in their market share, a typical case being Iraq."[25]

This rather cool attitude toward the OPEC countries and their successful action does not mean that the PCI has no sympathy or does not support the request of raw material producers for a change in the terms of trade, even at the expense of living standards in the advanced countries. The PCI is no doubt aware of the fact that "easy access to petroleum and other raw materials, under declining prices, has made it possible to enlarge the domestic market through an increase in wages with no impact on costs,"[26] but considers it morally and politically unacceptable that the prices of raw materials and manufactured goods have no connection with their labor content. "The developed countries are certainly bound to suffer in the future an inflation of prices due to a long-overdue world redistribution of revenue, based on the recognition of the labor values produced in the LDCs. FAO experts believe, for instance, that—if the work of a peasant in Ceylon has to be paid as much as it is in Europe—the price of the tea he produces should be 10 to 15 times higher than it is now. At the present moment, however, the main causes of raw material price increases are quite different."[27]

The obvious conclusion for the PCI is that a negotiated solution has to be found, in which the interests of both parties should be taken into account and common sense prevail. Such a negotiation should "take into account all the global aspects of the crisis." The negotiating parties, for their part, should avoid "the risks that are inevitable in such a case," that is, "that the producers try to pull too much on their side, causing a recession in the advanced countries which would affect both these countries and the Third World. The developed countries, on the other hand, refuse to acknowledge that for too many years they have reduced or prevented the growth of the LDCs, which should have a different role and weight in the international community."[28]

Free Trade, Protection, and the Politicization of
International Economic Relations

As we have seen repeatedly in the previous pages of this chapter, protectionism against imports from the LDCs and the bilateralization and politicization of trade are recurrent temptations to the left in both France and Italy.

The French Communists go furthest in this direction. Of all possible economic policy objectives, national independence heads their list of priorities. They are normally very critical of other countries' protectionism and of U.S. protectionist tendencies in particular. It is quite significant, though, that in order to prove the existence of American protectionism, they always cite the difficulties put in the way of utilization of the *Concorde* on the Atlantic route. The reasons that the PCF gives to explain why it is favorable to the *Concorde,* however, are typical of the most classic economic nationalism.

The official summary of the debates of the Twenty-first Party Congress[29] reports wide criticism of "the considerable waste due to non-utilization of the human and technical potential" of the French aerospace industry. "At a time when our country enjoys—thanks to the quality of our workers—a position of undisputed leadership, inside the so-called western world, in supersonic transportation, and when it clearly appears that the future of long range transport is in the supersonic plane, the government decides to stop both production and the development of improved models. Will in the future our airline, Air France, be obliged to buy American supersonic aircraft?"[30]

The French Communists openly propose a complete reorganization of the foreign economic relations of France. Indeed, at the Twentieth Congress of the PCF, Paul Boccara pleaded for a "complete control[31] of external economic relations (including capital transfers) by the public industrial sector, the (nationalized) banking system and, most important, by democratic planning."[32] This *encadrement* would have a twofold impact, first on the organization of foreign trade in order to control its direction, and second on the specialization of France in the international division of labor, in order to control its content.

As far as control of choice of trade partners is concerned, the same Boccara, in an interview with the official Communist journal *France Nouvelle,* asserts that France should buy "less oil from Saudi Arabia, which does not buy enough from us and lets us go into deficit with her, and more oil from Algeria, Libya and Iraq, to which we can sell much more, and with which we can increase our cooperation." Similarly, he adds, France has to buy "less capital equipment from the United States and the Federal Republic of Germany, through a stimulation of national production, but also through the establishment of new trade relationship in the field of plants and equipments and development of technological relations and co-production in Europe, with Italy—for instance—as well as with the socialist countries."[33]

This view can be considered representative of the official position of the PCF. Indeed, the theoretical and political journal of the Central Committee of the French Communist party elaborates on it, and even tries to define it in ideological tems. A new concept is formuated: the concept of "economic exchanges," which, in contrast to "commercial exchanges," are exchanges based on government–to–government agreements with state–trading countries, above all the USSR. According to the French Communist journal, the present crisis has made is indispensable for the West to move from commercial to economic exchanges. "The reality that appears more and more clearly" therefore is that governments of the western countries, and especially that of the United States, have "to reconsider their economic policy" and take "the road to Moscow."[34]

Illustrative of the historical and ideological perceptions of the French Communist leadership is the following quotation: "The internationalization of economic life is represented mainly by a rapid development, on a new basis, of international trade. Without a doubt, trade among peoples and among countries goes far back in the history of mankind, but in the last few decades it has taken a completely new form. The existence, first of all, of the USSR, and later of a world system of socialist countries, has changed the very basis of international trade."[35]

From this perspective, the trade policy of the French government is judged severely. The French government has tried, since 1969 (that is, after the departure of de Gaulle from power), to reduce Franco–Russian trade, on the "pretext" of the mediocre quality of Soviet–made goods. But the PCF argues, refuting this "pretext," that "for a long time now American and other capitalist businessmen have shown their interest for the very advanced technology [of the USSR] in fields such as metals transformation, machine tool building, electronics, optics, aluminum production, and the mining of useful minerals."[36] The main responsibility for the failure, on the part of the French government, to grasp the opportunities for trading with the USSR is laid to Common Market commitments (which represent "a serious abdication from national sovereignty").[37] "To escape the limitations created by EEC rules, the agreement signed by France and the USSR in July 1973 presents absolutely innovative terms, called by economists 'compensation deals,' on the basis of which France ships to the USSR capital equipment that will be paid for with the goods produced with their equipment."[38] Despite the risks that this type of agreement creates for the capital equipment supplier, and the widespread damage that this dangerous form of new competition from the East has done—and is doing—to the western working class, the PCF regards such a new conception of international trade as "absolutely desirable," since it is "based on the principle of mutual advantage." Indeed, "bilateral commercial agreements are absolutely in the interest of our country."[39]

Of course, the generalization of such practices would create a drastic shift in the geographic pattern of French trade, with a reduction of commercial relations with the western countries where these trading practices are uncommon, and a development of "economic exchanges" with the eastern bloc. But the PCF thinks that it is also "in the interest of the great foreign capitalist corporations to expand international relations, even if the partner refuses to be dominated, on the condition that a stable and reciprocally profitable relationship is guaranteed."[40] This would mean nothing less than establishing with the multinational corporations (MNCs) the same type of relationship they presently have with eastern bloc countries. The fact that this type of relationship is in the interest of both parties "is shown by the recent developments—that are bound to continue in the future, because of the crisis of [western] monopolistic state capitalism—of the economic relationships between the advanced capitalist economies and the socialist countries."[41]

France should therefore not only become a state trading country, where trade would be bureaucratically regulated on the basis of government-to-government or government-to-foreign company agreements, but should also restrict the choice of her trading partners to those countries (that is, the eastern bloc countries) or MNCs that accept this type of "economic exchange"; not only should she have a bilaterally balanced trade, but should have the *content* of trade regulated by long-term "compensation agreements." Apart from the fact that the very nature of these agreements demonstrates the technological backwardness of the eastern economies, one might wonder how it could be in the interest of the French working class to generalize the job-destroying practice of creating in eastern bloc countries (that is, in cheap-labor countries) high-level technology plants to be paid for with the products of these same plants.

The tendency to politicize trade relations is evident in parties other than the PCF, although the Communists alone propose a coherent and detailed program to bring about the conversion of France into a semiautarkic state-trading country, similar to a CMEA member. At least, one has to respect the coherence of the PCF attitude, which contrasts dramatically with the chaotic mixture of unrealistic views advanced by the Socialists. Were a Communist government to implement its program, transforming the French economy and society would cost France much of the prosperity the French have acquired in the half-century since World War I. On purely logical grounds, however, their policy appears feasible. A coherent and consistent Socialist attitude, on the other hand, is difficult to identify, or even to summarize. Indeed, one can distinguish a wide array of Socialist positions on these matters, ranging from views very similar to those of the PCF (for example, Jean-P. Chevènement) to those of the official economic advisor of PS General Secretary Jacques Attali, to whom the main problem of France—in the last analysis—is its insufficiently capitalistic nature[42] and its insufficient participation in today's economic phenomena, an inefficiency stemming from the lack of French-based MNCs comparable in size and strength to the United States multinational. But the picture of the variety of approaches to world economic problems inside the French PS is further complicated by the fact that it is impossible to identify clearly "radical" and "moderate" positions that would correspond respectively with a government-controlled, self-reliant economy versus an open decentralized one. Certain recognizable differences in attitudes toward international economic affairs often turn out to have unexpected roots. "Social democrats" with Catholic backgrounds, such as Jacques Delors, sometimes show autarkic attitudes: "The anarchy of world trade enables the strong to become stronger and makes the weak weaker. . . . We cannot found growth on a continuous increase of exports: there are more disadvantages than advantages in being dependent on the world economy."[43] On the other hand, one finds Michel Rocard, formerly one of the leaders of the extremist PSU, and now considered a "planning technocrat," saying, as he did at the 1977 Congress of the PS, that "without an aggressive political and economic design we will slide into protectionism. France has to export in order to be independent."[44]

Moreover, some Socialist personalities that are normally considered to be "moderates" or even "social democrats" seem to find protectionism quite appealing. "The socialists wish to keep the French economy open," affirms Jacques Delors[45] —the Délégué National of the PS for international economic relations—but he immediately undercuts his assertion by adding that this pledge to keep the French economy open does not mean "making exports a dogma, and not even the main engine for expansion." Moreover, since "competition exists in the French market as well as in the world market, we should reduce the imports that our industry can substitute in normal competitive conditions."[46]

It is understandable that the Socialists tend to pass over the question of their policy toward foreign investments. The official documents of the PS are quite vague on this issue: "The attitude of the PS on foreign investments should not be dogmatic. . . . Movements of investment capital between France and foreign countries have to take place in a controlled framework and reflect equitable reciprocity."[47] To avoid what has happened in the past, when too often the internationalization of investments brought about a limitation of French sovereignty, the left will manage to make foreign investment part of cooperation and codevelopment agreements that France will conclude with other partners.

As far as the new competition in manufactures from LDCs is concerned, a socialist France should—again in Delors's view—accept imports, and restructure the threatened French industry to produce those goods for which it is still competitive, and produce the capital goods necessary for the industrializing countries. But not everybody in the PS, not even among the

Socialist "moderates," shares this view. It was indeed Mitterrand's most influential advisor, Jacques Attali, who invented the concept of "implosive nongrowth"[48] (that is, changes in production that coincide with politically determined changes in demand structure). "Implosive nongrowth naturally implies a smaller degree of external openness, because the gains from trade. . .become negative after a certain threshold, a threshold which was passed with the increase in the price of energy."[49]

The successes of the "export-led" development model (that is, the reverse of Attali's "implosive nongrowth") in a number of developing countries appear to these "friends of Mitterrand's" as the "reproduction one and a half centuries later of the excesses of early capitalism." This reproduction of history is taking place "in some totalitarian third world countries" where the governments "exert a merciless repression of any efforts toward social progress." The competition of these countries is therefore "illegal and unfair, since it is based on exploitation."[50]

This complex variety of views explains why the official stand of the PS very seldom appears clear-cut, sometimes as the result of a compromise among, and quite often as the simple adding up of the economic proposals related to, conflicting political policies.

In general, a "strategy to reduce dependence" and to give a "higher degree of autonomy to national economy policy" is considered by the Socialists as the natural aim of the policy of the left in international economic relations. This autonomy is limited today by physical scarcities (in energy and raw materials) as well as by "a past development based on the opening of borders and on international trade."[51] This is therefore considered a drawback as bad as the insufficiency of mineral resources.

This "strategy to reduce dependence" includes steps such as "a larger autonomy in the field of energy, a diversification of supplies" as well as "long-term agreements with raw materials producers" and "an appropriate exchange-rate policy." This in any case would be "not a strategy of isolation, but a dynamic strategy in the international framework." For the French Socialists, the EEC remains "a reference framework and a preferred field for cooperation," since it has contributed, together with "the development of international trade," to "the growth of living standards." But today the stiffening of competition can sometimes endanger the very survival of some industries because of "underpaid manpower" or because of "more efficient technology."[52] In these cases, the resort to "higher tariffs on these products or to restricting imports by decree is very appealing," although, the PS cautions, such a policy can be adopted only if the utmost attention is given to the international balance of forces. Indeed, protectionist measures taken by France could bring about retaliatory measures in foreign countries against French products. And such an escalation could be extremely dangerous for the country. Protectionism, therefore, is not bad in itself, but only in cases in which France is not strong enough to resort to it with no risk of retaliation. According to the PS, French "economic policy has to act in favor of endangered industries in order to protect the workers" but "cannot take measures that could trigger a reaction capable of endangering the export sectors."[53] In any case, "as stop-gap measures, an efficient protection of French production will be necessary. But the resort to quantitative restrictions and to strengthened tariff protection will be reserved to the situations that require urgent measures to defend employment and protect production plants."[54]

A government of the left, according to the Socialists, should on the one hand correct the present policy, which "does not pay enough attention to the possibility of substituting national products for foreign goods," and, on the other, should improve the situation in exports. "A too-large fraction of our exports is made up of raw agricultural products, low value-added intermediate products, and manufactured goods (such as the automobile) exposed to increased competition and to the business cycles of foreign countries. Moreover, our sales abroad are made by a small number of firms, while it should be possible to increase the exports of many small and medium-sized enterprises."[55] What is necessary, together with protection of the domestic market, bilateral agreements with raw materials producers,[56] import substitution, exchange control,[57] and purchase or regulation of foreign firms operating in France[58] is "the development of the activity of French firms abroad: creation of new enterprises, improvement of their operating environment (that is, the action of the diplomatic and commercial services abroad)."[59] In other words, the French Socialists want the best of both worlds, the world of economic nationalism and the world of free trade and competition.

Quite similar, although much less detailed and never officially presented in a comprehensive text, is the position of the Italian Socialists. As far as protectionism is concerned, on several occasions the belief that it was indispensable to the Italian economy has been expressed by Antonio Giolitti, the man to whom the PSI—when it has been in government—has entrusted the greatest responsibility for economic policy (the Ministry for Budget and Economic Planning). It was also Giolitti who represented Italy at the VI Special Assembly of the United Nations (where north-south economic relations were being discussed), and who was the Socialist candidate for the Presidency of the Republic as recently as 1978. In 1975, Giolitti indeed declared that "it seems very difficult to me to avoid [in order to find a way out of the present crisis for Italy] resorting to protectionist measures. Irrespective of the technical means through which the protectionist effect is obtained. . .I believe that such a line of action cannot be ruled out."[60]

One year later, at a seminar organized by the Italian Communist party to discuss "Economic Crisis and International Constraints on Italy," Antonio Giolitti seized the opportunity to plead for import controls. "I understand the importance of the profession of faith made by the leaders of the Communist party in favor of the liberalization of international trade. But let me add a plea against the full application of this principle, because I am convinced that the situations we have to face do not allow ruling out the possibility of resorting to import controls."[61]

An explanation of the political line underlying these statements can be found in an article on "Economic Policy and International Choices" published in the theoretical journal of the PSI by a prominent Socialist economist. "Beyond our present economic and political difficulties," he wrote in 1974, "a great opportunity is appearing in the field of international economic policy. The oil crisis (and the ensuing balance of payments problems) could be faced through. . .an agreement with France,[62] that would lead to bilateral agreements with the oil-producing countries, . . . [to] a different equilibrium inside the EEC, less tied to American policy. With such a choice, oil policy, by isolating Italy at least partially from the cartel, would reacquire the elasticity it lost after Mattei's death. . . . In short, this would be a policy founded on a higher degree of isolation[63]—or a lesser degree of openness—to international trade. . .a [commercial] policy open only to a few of our partners in international trade."[64]

The limits to such a policy, in the Socialists' view, are similar to those indicated by the French Socialists: the danger of accelerating protectionist trends in the United States. But the advantages—similar to those expected by the French Communists from their proposed policies—would be that, while in a pro-American and pro-German strategy "deflation is one of the objectives, in the pro-French case the balance of payments is reequilibrated through purely political measures (increase in the gold price, bilateral agreements for petroleum). . . . In addition, this policy is the only one compatible with an economic policy directed by the public sector, instead of one directed by the private."[65]

The establishment of bilateral relationships with "a few" of Italy's partners was actually attempted by Socialist Undersecretary of State for Foreign Affairs Cesare Bensi, who, during a journey to Syria and Iraq, claimed to have found the "proof" of the belief that "a direct approach to the Arab world is the best therapy to 'heal' the relations of our country with the countries of that region. We should pursue [Bensi concluded] a form of partnership with the oil producing countries that have a substantial development potential, such as Iraq. . .[through] general agreements involving not only [the creation in Iraq of] the oil-related industries, such as refining, petrochemicals and marketing, but also the construction of a fleet specialized in oil transportation."[66]

In the opinion of the Italian Socialists the arguments for and against bilateralism "should not be encouraged" because they are "nominalistic."[67] The only real problem the PSI seems to have with bilateralism is the political "decency" of the partner. The argument on bilateralism, said Pietro Nenni, the founding father of the PSI—and still president of the party—"is artificial and byzantine, . . .because the Europeans eventually deal, in these bilateral negotiations, with U.S.-owned multinationals."[68] To the Socialists, the main problem appears to be the question of whether it is a scandal or not to enter into bilateral negotiations with "reactionary" oil producing countries. "I believe," says Nenni, "that [these agreements] can be useful from a commercial point of view, if they work to solve supply problems for a few months or a few years. There is no scandal in a commercial agreement with Saudi Arabia, or with Iran, or a Persian Gulf Sheikdom or Emirate, if it is a good deal. . .but I do not think that one can give a political Third-Worldist[69] interpretation to such commercial operations, especially when they involve, as one of the partners, corporations with mostly American capital, such as Aramco. . . . In sum, no objections from our side to commercial agreements, but all political theorizations should be avoided."[70]

Much more cautious, and remarkably different from the position of both the French Communists and the Italian and French Socialists, is the position of the Italian Communists. "We believe," writes Eugenio Peggio in his official capacity as secretary of the PCI's Center for Economic Studies, "that Italy, because of the trading system to which she belongs. . . , because of the ideals of peace and cooperation she nurtures—cannot look for a solution to her problems through choices inspired by narrow-minded conceptions that would lead to nationalistic and isolationistic trends." He goes on to say:

> The pressures, coming from many sides, to revert to protectionist or even autarkic economic policies cannot and must not be encouraged. The very history of Italy shows that the periods marked by protectionist and nationalistic policies are the ones during which national economic development has been extremely weak, or even nonexistent. On the contrary, the periods in which our country, thanks to a policy of openness to world markets has strongly developed its foreign trade, are also the periods marked by the most significant progress of the Italian economy and society.

> Protectionist trends do not exist in Italy alone. Indeed, it is mostly in other countries—such as the United States, France and other EEC and non-EEC industrialized countries—that strong pressure is building up for the adoption of protectionist measures, that would have, and are already having, very negative consequences for the Italian economy, as well as for international trade.

The PCI's position on these issues is clearly stated: "Italy has no interest at all in a further deterioration of international economic relations, a deterioration that might lead to an undoing of one of the main factors in the great postwar expansion of the world economy—the liberalization of trade. From this very point of view, the undoing of the Bretton Woods system has already had extremely bad consequences. . . . Presently, a few protectionist initiatives may trigger a trade-war that would be ruinous to everybody."[72]

Elaborating on the same line, Luciano Barca[73] goes even further: "I think it is useful to repeat—but neither as an act of faith nor with the extremism of the recently converted—that we are against protectionism. I think is is useful because [in Italy] we have a system that has survived for too long just because of protection (the protection of low wages, of low raw materials prices and Third World exploitation), which is now looking for new protection through devaluation and inflation."[74] According to Barca, the discussion on external constraints is largely useless: "The problem is not to be for or against international constraints, especially for a country to which the choice to stay in open international markets is a compulsory one, today as well as in the future. . . . International constraints, indeed, are just the other face of international cooperation and of the international division of labor, without which there would be no progress." The only problem is therefore "to find out in which position Italy may stay—as she has to stay— in the network of reciprocal constraints"—and in which way she might "have more weight in the decision-making process in the various systems to which Italy belongs: the monetary system, NATO and the EEC."[75]

The PCI's view of the position Italy should have in the international economic system can be summarized in the following way: "The present structure of Italy's foreign trade has been formed, in the last thirty years, in the framework of the Bretton Woods system, that is, in a climate of certainty and strong commitment to free-trade, on the basis of spontaneous international market mechanisms. . . . This has had positive results, one of which is the rather high degree of competitiveness of the Italian industrial system. But is has also brought about disequilibria, inequalities, distortions and limits to growth." A policy of industrial restructuring is therefore necessary, and "for a country like Italy. . .there should be no doubt about the type of changes to be introduced. They should tend. . .to increase the number of domestically produced goods, mostly in the agricultural sector, to expand and drastically strengthen the industrial sector, especially in the South: and all this adds up to a policy that implies. . .a higher degree of international openness of our country, and a larger and more conscious participation to the trends towards increased interdependence in Europe and in the world."[76]

If the views of the PCI are compared with the approach of the PCF on one hand, and of the Socialists of both countries on the other, the least one can say is that the stands of the two Communist parties have the merit of being clear. But this is almost all they have in common, at least on the specific issue of free trade versus politicization of commercial relations. The

PCI's position is miles away from the views of the PCF, and could indeed be accepted by any American liberal. This was confirmed when MIT Professor Franco Modigliani expressed his "agreement with the point of view—put forward by Mr. Peggio in his very interesting report—that self-reliance and autarky (a word that makes me remember the times of the fascist dictatorship), offer no solutions to present problems."[77] On the other hand, the PCI's stand comes as a shock to many well-established ideas of the West European left. One should not be surprised, therefore, if it has been sharply criticized for being too favorable to free trade by the well-known Cambridge (England) economist Bob Rowthorn: "Free trade is a luxury Italy cannot afford," he declared in response to Peggio, "because the free trade system presently existing means freedom only for the capitalists."[78]

Domestic Economic Issues

In the economic systems of Western European countries, a close interrelation exists between international and domestic issues. This is due not only to the obvious fact that, inside the EEC, the boundary between what is domestic and what is international has become progressively blurred, but also to the existence of some very relevant transnational economic phenomena, such as (1) the obstacles encountered by some European countries to stay in (or to enter) the market for advanced industrial products (such as aircrafts and space, atomic energy, and armaments); (2) the internationalization of production processes due to multinational firms, foreign investments, and national investments abroad; (3) the decline of certain traditional industries in Europe because of intra–OECD competition (such as in the case of steel and ship-building, where the main problem has been until now mostly Japanese competition), or of the competition of cheap–labor LDCs (such as in the case of clothing and consumer electronics).

The political forces under study in this chapter do not approach all these issues in the same way. Indeed, some of them concentrate their attention on some issues, and sometimes on one issue only. In all cases, differences in emphasis are such as to make their positions not exactly comparable.

The position of the French Communists on economic questions appears indeed to be quite clear and to cover all these aspects. Moreover, the PCF has helped to make industrial policy, a subject that used to be restricted to only a small circle of specialists, a subject of everyday discussion. "Our factories close down; our capital is invested abroad. Let's produce French!" proclaimed PCF posters on the walls of Paris at the end of 1977. A few weeks later, the orthodox Gaullists opened their campaign with enormous pictures of the *Concorde*, coupled with the slogan, "Yes, to an innovation-oriented France." "Industrial policy," comments one perceptive observer, "has entered not only the policy debate, where it has been for a long time, but the electoral debate, and this is quite new."[79]

Criticism of French industrialists, and of Giscard's government, for "preferring foreign beauties"[80]—that is, for investing abroad, for accepting the presence of MNCs in France, for entering joint ventures with foreign partners, for purchasing foreign technologies—is a permanent element of the PCF's arguments and propaganda. At the Twentieth Congress of the PCF strong condemnation was expressed for the abandonment of the *filière française,* the French technology for natural uranium atomic power plants, for the "sellout" of Citroën to Fiat,[81] for the merging of Creusot-Loire (a steam turbine maker) "into the Westinghouse orbit," for the allowing of a joint venture between Creusot-Pechiney and Westinghouse (production of nuclear fuel). "In an industry of the utmost importance for the future, the government has chosen to abandon national independence, and to offer to U.S. trusts the possibility of doing what they like with our national riches."[82]

On a few occasions, however, the PCF has gone beyond this petty nationalistic attitude and has shown a deeper and more sophisticated approach to the problems of the so-called process of capital internationalization. In the face of this phenomenon, the main problem for the Communists is how they propose to adapt their main tool in industrial policy (nationalization) to the transnationalism of today's industrial phenomena, and to the multinational nature of the modern industrial enterprise. According to the PCF,[83] when "the MNC is a conglomerate of different activities" there are "no problems." Things are different when the production processes of individual goods have themselves become multinational; in this case one-way dependence can be avoided "not with autarky and isolation, but with a diversified system of trade and cooperation agreements established with the maximum number of other actors operating in the same field, irrespective of their nationality or the social regime in which they live." However, the "most advanced" example of such coproduction agreements is still "the *Concorde* experience." Totally ignored are the radical differences between the nature of the French-British division of labor in the *Concorde* project and the type of division of labor that, thanks to the MNCs, is spreading between some developed and some developing countries. The same Communist author does recognize the existence of these differences, however, when he writes that "coproduction has to be based on complex, long-term contracts, while in the MNCs everything is speculation and instability."[84] It is therefore not surprising that the attitude of the PCF on industrial questions is always a conservative one, aimed at preserving jobs at home at any cost.

The PCF points out that "the so-called industrial redeployment has, in recent years, brought about a wild competition with the manufactured products of developed countries, by making use of cheap labor of Southeast Asian and Latin American countries, but with *capital provided by the great capitalist groups*. . . . This *monopolistic* redeployment has already led to overproduction and unemployment. It is based on. . .a contradictory and intolerable association of material waste and low wages. . . . It goes without saying that we cannot accept—under the pretext that this allows more industrial development in the LDCs—this savage competition, organized to the advantage of the big industrial multinationals."[85] Sometimes, the multinationals disappear from the picture, and the French Communists' rationale for explaining why they are opposed to imports of manufacturers from the Third World takes on almost racist undertones. "New factories have been opened in Southeast Asia, where transistor radios are produced with underpaid and underqualified manpower, competing with workers in industrialized countries, thus creating unemployment and downward pressure on wages. It is sometimes observed that, when a new factory is opened (in an LDC) it creates jobs and purchasing power. In such a way, we are told, a country can take off. This is false, because when 2,000 workers are necessary, 5,000 starving peasants gather in shantytowns around the cities. What is first needed is not transistor radios, but other goods suitable to national needs. What these countries need is a developing agriculture, adapted to soil and climate, in order to reduce hunger."[86]

Nationalization in the industrial sector was the point of open disagreement that brought about the PS–PCF rift on the common program before the last French general elections. But it has also been the main area in which the relations between the Communists and the "renewed" PS[87] were difficult all through the 1970s. As early as 1972, Marchais declared to the PCF Central Committee that "the nationalization of the steel industry was the toughest point in the negotiation" with the PS.[88] The 1972 Common Program devotes four pages to this problem. In it the nine groups to be nationalized are named, plus three others where government participation is foreseen. On every other aspect of the nationalization issue, disagreements were large. "We could not find an agreement," one reads in the official Socialist edition of the program, "on the content of nationalization since the PC refuses all direct participation of the workers in management." When the Common Program was revised five years later, in the summer of 1977, the disagreement was even wider, involving not only the number of firms to be nationalized, but the very aim to be sought through public property in the industrial sector.

For the Communist party, this is the modern way to make the means of production collective property and the "basis on which workers' power will

be established, the starting point for social progress."[89] The orthodoxy of
this approach is indisputable. Indeed the same simplified Marxist theory of
history is applied by the PCF to 1936 as to 1977. The result is an identical
analysis of the social and political situation.

In 1936, the division of the French society into two halves "—the two
hundred families and the popular masses led by the working class—was
already similar to today's monopolistic state capitalism."[90] Four decades
after the *Front Populaire* the French Communists still regard nationalization the best solution to present problems.

The public sector is considered the "cornerstone" of a process of
change leading to a Socialist society. The question of the number of firms to
be nationalized is critical. Indeed, there is "a threshold [which must be
crossed in order] to seriously weaken, in one blow, monopolistic domination. Moreover, democracy has to be pushed far enough to make irreversible. . .[these] conquests."[91]

Self-management, as proposed by the PS, is rejected by the Communists, who propose a "global national self-management." Indeed, "when
socialism exists, workers will decide and the state will manage."[92] The
destruction of the bourgeois state therefore does not mean the disappearance either of its bureaucratic structure or of the social function it per-
forms; only its class character is changed.

Although at the time of the final PS–PCF conflict, just before the general election of 1978, it appeared that the disagreement was almost exclusively on the number of private companies to be nationalized, in reality
there was a more fundamental disagreement—at least with some of the
Socialists nearer to Mitterrand's position—on the very purpose of the
nationalizations. In some instances, such as in the case of the steel industry,
the conflict of views was almost paradoxical. The PCF insisted on total
nationalization, while the Socialists opposed it, because—as J. Attali
wrote—"this would in effect compensate the great capitalist groups for
their poor past management,"[93] and would help private capitalists get rid of
a sector with no future. In general, while the PCF seeks public ownership as
a tool to preserve the endangered industries and fight against capitalist
"waste" that tends to reduce capacity, the Socialists consider it a precondition for structural change in "the many sectors (steelmaking, aviation, ship-
building, etc.) where reductions in employment appear inevitable."[94]

It has to be noted, though, that the differences among the French
Socialists and Communists are not always so wide and so clear-cut. Indeed,
of all the different groups that comprise the PS the one that has the most
detailed and coherent industrial policy program is also the one that is near-
est to the Communists—the CERES. In the view of J.P. Chevènement, the
leader of CERES, the necessity of restructuring the French industrial sector
goes without saying, although "a long-term socialist [industrial policy] pro-

gram cannot exist without a program for independence from the world capitalist market."[95] The French industrial sector should therefore be divided into four main subsectors, of which three would be almost completely government-owned or controlled: the first, "totally isolated from the world market" in order to preserve national independence, would include armaments, energy (including the nuclear industry), basic research, and possibly agriculture; a second, ("an area of encouraged economy") would include industries to be subsidized because they form, for reasons related to value-added, jobs provided, balance of payments effects, what is regarded as the desirable international specialization of France (steel, aircraft, and so on); a third, comprised of industries that produce for French public consumption (building, mass transportation, health, social services, and so on); and a fourth, comprising a "market sector, open to international competition" where "many firms, but not all, will stay private."[96]

But the CERES is only a minority, although a strong one, inside the Socialist party. The large majority of the PS, however, offers *autogestion* (self-management) as its economic program. "Self-management" has no theoretical basis, and is not conceived of as a natural result of an historical succession of "production relationships." The concept, indeed, is quite vague, and its success is largely due to the fact that the traditional labels—socialism, democracy—seem to have lost their appeal. What is important for the *autogestionnaires* is not the size of the nationalized sector, but the "quality" of the nationalization. "Neither centralism, nor productivism, nor technocracy, but a redefinition and a new sharing of power: in short this is our position."[97]

It is obvious that the disappointment with the role performed in French society by the government-owned sector created after World War II is basic to this search for a new form of social ownership for a socialist society that would make human need, instead of profit, the rationale for work. A very ambitious search, it would seem, but a challenging task: "France can be the birthplace of this form of socialism, a spark of hope for the whole world."[98]

In comparison to the French left with its views on problems of industrial policy, the Italian Communist and Socialist parties seem to live in a different world. Indeed, the area of domestic economic policy appears the very one in which the identification of differences and similarities among French and Italian political forces is most difficult and, on the whole, practically useless. Not only are the main themes of the political debate radically different in Italy (because the order of priority and importance attributed to problems is not the same), but the Italian left seems to have different constituencies, divergent strategies, and incompatible and actually opposed aims.

The nationalization issue that agitates the French left, one which is normally considered a qualifying banner for any European labor or Socialist party, disappeared long ago from the programs of the Italian Socialists and Communists. Historically, it is indeed the right that has created and inflated the government-owned industrial sector. Apart from the nationalization of electricity (which was imposed by the PSI when it first joined the Christian Democrats in government and had essentially political objectives since the "electric barons" were very active and influential in the political arena), no major enlargement of the public sector has been demanded since by the left. Even the PCI declares, and has been declaring for years, that "no expansion of the public sector is desirable."[99] First of all, say the Italian Communists, "we do not have an *étatist* view of power; in our view, alongside the public sector—which, we insist, is already large enough in Italy and should not be enlarged further—the private enterprise sector must exist, and indeed has to be encouraged."[100]

In reality, the difficulties which many enterprises have encountered in recent years have obliged the government to intervene repeatedly with large subsidies. But even in these cases, the political forces on the left—including the Communists—have supported the preservation of a ficticious private majority in the voting stocks, as well as a real concentration of managerial power in the hands of the private partners.

According to some observers of the Italian scene, four different phases can be distinguished over the last ten years in the attitude of the PCI on economic matters. Around 1969 the traditional idea of an alliance of workers and peasants to bring about a "Socialist revolution" begins to fade away, along with the "kind of neo-Keynesianism geared only to an undifferentiated enlargement of individual wages and consumption."[101] Gradually, a Ricardian element appears, with the PCI identifying "parasitic rent," and not profit, as the main enemy of the Italian working class. Simultaneously, the new stand of the PCI against the nationalization of economic activities was announced. At the end of 1972, when Berlinguer became Secretary-General of the PCI, the importance of profit was acknowledged, and it was explained that the task of the Italian working class was essentially to struggle for increased productivity, and to make all classes—including the working class itself—accept sacrifices. The fourth phase, finally, began in 1975, when "supranational economic planning" at the European level was advocated, with the qualification that planning should "not prevail in an automatic and authoritarian way over market rules."[102]

More recently, however, the unpleasant experience of the PCI in sharing Andreotti's responsibility but not his power, as well as the repeated hints of voters' dissatisfactions with government inefficiency, helped to push the Communists toward a harder line. What Communist militants saw as "one-way sacrifices" came under heavier fire and contributed to the PCI decision to topple the Andreotti government in January 1979.

In the view of the Italian Communists, industrial policy has to pursue "the aim of a substantial improvement of the position of Italy in the international division of labor, and to make this position more consistent with the potentialities and the needs of Italy."[103]

Technologically and/or economically obsolete plants have to be "radically transformed," but at the same time government purchases geared to the satisfaction of public needs in housing, mass transportation, schooling, health, and so on have to be rationally planned to help "the Italian industrial system cover the gaps existing in its structure." A policy geared to push Italian industry in the direction of technologically advanced sectors (such as aircraft, computers, nuclear power plants) "would be an illusion." What is to be preferred are quality improvements "in intermediate technology sectors, where possible increases in employment are the largest."[104]

But these are the very sectors in which competition is stiffening, inside the OECD and even more dangerously with industrializing cheap-labor countries. The PCI seems perfectly aware of this fact and of the consequences it implies for the Italian working class, should the "illusion" of a substantial change in the international specialization be rejected. Italy, say the Communists,

> is constrained by the divergent ways in which trade union struggle develops in the different countries. . . . In all capitalist countries, the crisis has brought about a serious attack on the popular masses. Unemployment has grown. . . . Everywhere, the dominant economic and political forces try to make the workers pay. . . .the cost of the decision taken by firms and by government in order to find an end to the crisis.
>
> From this point of view, the situation in Italy *cannot be substantially different* from that in the other industrialized capitalist countries. But it is well known that, since the late 1960s, the Italian unions have become very strong, and have been able to achieve great successes [emphasis added].

In the other capitalist countries, therefore, where the unions have shown "inferior capacity to defend and affirm workers' rights," their struggle "has had a smaller impact than in Italy." They have presented "very moderate demands," and "have proved ready to accept large reorganizations of production activities," while "this openness is almost nonexistent in Italy." And this, "for a country like ours, open to the international market, and having to face the challenge of international competition, *creates problems that should not be underestimated.*"[106] Through the smokescreen of cautious wording, the meaning is nonetheless very clear: one of the factors that prevents Italian industry from consolidating and improving its position in the international division of labor is the excessively high cost of labor, linked to inflation by automatic adjustment clauses. This does not mean, of course, that the PCI favors more "reasonable" union behavior; it only sug-

gests that unions should not concentrate their combativeness on wages but
on other objectives more important in the long term to the workers themselves. "The line that the unions have chosen many years ago gives first priority to full employment and to investment, and subordinates to these aims
their behavior on matters such as wages. Following this line, the unions
fight with all the working-class strength that can be mobilized."[107]

In the present situation of Italy, the PCI can entertain no illusions
about a "preferential treatment" for the unions by a coalition government
with Communist participation, such as occurs in Britain under Labour governments. The Secretary-General of the CGIL, Luciano Lama, himself a
member of the PCI, makes this very clear: "Trade union autonomy is a
condition that cannot be forfeited, no matter what type of government, or
what type of parliamentary arrangements."[108] It is therefore as a Communist that Lama is in favor of trade-union moderation. "A line of moderation is not a self-defeating line, if the unions set qualitatively more important objectives, objectives worth more than a nominal increase in wages;
objectives such as a development policy for the South, a policy to restructure our industrial system into one more modern and more complete, a policy for the full employment of the resources of our agricultural sector."[109]

If we now move to examine the role the PCI sees for the MNCs in the
future of Italian industry, we again have to quote Peggio:[110] "In the framework of the policy for industrial restructuring and for an enlargement [to
sectors and products presently missing] of Italian industry that we are proposing, MNCs can certainly find a place. We do not indeed think that
MNCs should be banned from Italy. . . , although these companies cannot
be left outside of any control." For this purpose, "a good example for
Italy" can be provided by "the countries that have studied the problem
most seriously. . .such as Canada, France, or Japan." It is worth pointing
out that the Italian Communists regard "as an example" the behavior of
that very French government which the French Communists continuously
accuse (because of its tolerance for foreign investments) of "selling out
France" and of "giving up national independence."

The attitude of the PCI toward the MNCs is in fact rather complex. As
has been pointed out by an Italian economist[111] "in the party press, among
party members and among trade unionists, a strongly negative attitude is
widespread. . .[but] the attitude of the party leadership is quite different,
and there is an evident effort to find a pragmatic line."

In an interview in *Business Week,*[112] Giorgio Napolitano, member of
the PCI *Direzione,* summarized the PCI attitude in the following way: "We
are not against the presence of MNCs in Italy. We only oppose certain
habits of the MNCs, such as moving rapidly from one country to another.
But this is not a problem for Italy alone, which is why a code of conduct is
being discussed in the EEC." And if Napolitano is worried because the

MNCs might leave Italy, Peggio worries because the MNCs do not invest enough in Italy. "It cannot be accepted that foreign enterprises come to Italy only to take a share of the market"[113] from production plants located in other Common Market countries.

This pragmatic attitude can sometimes create paradoxical situations, such as the one related by Peggio: in Milan, at the general assembly of the workers of the pharmaceutical firm Lepetit (owned by Dow Chemical), "the official spokesman for the Socialist party said that the Lepetit case showed how necessary it was to expel the multinationals from Italy. For my part, I said clearly that the PCI does not believe that the multinationals have to leave Italy: on the contrary, we have to encourage them to stay."[114]

The judgment of the PCI leaders on radically anti-MNC positions is extremely severe: "In the ritual condemnations of the multinationals, moralism has replaced the analysis of the hard laws of the economy; these condemnations were therefore of no use either in correcting the negative elements in the growth [of the MNCs], or in identifying the positive ones [growing world interdependence, diffusion of technology and management skills, and so on]. . . . An interpretation [of world problems] where a satanic role is attributed to the multinationals (considered the cause of all evils, from pollution to Chile) might be satisfactory for moralistic populism, but explains nothing, and proposes even less."[115]

Given this pragmatic position on the issue of the MNCs, one may wonder what the PCI's attitude would be on the question—much more serious for Italy than for any other OECD country, given the specialization of the Italian industry—of the new competition from Third World manufactured exports. Indeed, it is through the loophole of the MNCs that the European left normally finds the pretext for a protectionist attitude against the exports of industrializing cheap-labor countries.

According to the PCI,[116] the "maturity of the Italian working class" can be seen from this attitude in the face of the competition from the newly industrializing countries on both the domestic and the world markets. Indeed, "from the rank and file of the Italian working class, neither a mood of intolerance has risen against the LDCs, nor the protectionist demands that can be seen in the present attitude of large sections of the working class of the West."[117]

But such moderation is not sufficient: "Just because of the very difficult times ahead, this maturity has to be coupled with a serious effort to understand the global nature of the present crisis." The analysis of the left on international realities has been—according to some Communist leaders—terribly poor. Its support for the struggle of the Third World was "large and passionate," but it has been forgotten that the people of these countries "could die for independence, but not live on independence"; that, after political freedom, these countries were bound to demand a different role in the international division of labor. The support for their struggle "has not been accompanied by a theoretical effort and by a political initiative, common to the LDCs and the working class of the West, to stage a battle for new economic structures, new economic relations, for global development."[118]

The problem created by the emergence of a number of new competitors in the LDCs has been underestimated by the left: "We were looking at Vietnam, but we could not see what was going on at the same time in Hong Kong and in Seoul."[119] Now, the only way out appears to be "a consultation among the social partners in Europe and in the LDC, as a step to the opening of the European market to Third World products and to the simultaneous restructuring of the industrial and agricultural systems in the EEC countries." A new division of labor has to be the ultimate target of this transformation, but not a new distribution conceived of only as the "dislocation" to the LDCs of some of Europe's activities, assumed to be "an abstractly fixed amount": the real "challenge is an international division of labor that would increase employment, useful production, and world development."[120]

Notes

1. See Giorgio Ruffolo et al., "Crisi energetica e modello di sviluppo," *Mondo Operaio* 1(1974): 10. Although they cannot be considered as representing the official stand of the PSI—that does not seem to exist—Ruffolo's views have a wide and acknowledged influence.

2. Ibid.

3. Parti Socialiste, *Les Socialistes et le Tiers-Monde* (Paris: Flammarion, 1977), p. 122. This book, after a foreword by Lionel Jospin, "Secrétaire National du PS chargé des questions du Tiers-Monde," states that "the content has been examined by the Executive Bureau of the Socialist Party and approved for publication."

4. Lucien Praire, "Requiem pour Nord-Sud," *L'Unité,* November 18-24, 1977. Praire works with Jospin in the "Third World Secretariat" of the French Socialist party.

5. Lionel Jospin, "Les socialistes et le Tiers-Monde," *Nouvelle Revue Socialiste,* April 1976.

6. Ibid.

7. Jospin, "Les socialistes et le Tiers-Monde," p. 156.

8. PS, *Programme Socialiste,* p. 196.

9. Jospin, "Les socialistes et le Tiers-Monde."

10. Ibid., p. 158.

11. Ibid.

12. Paul Boccara, "De nouvelles relations économiques internationales," in L. Blanquart, ed., *Changer l'Economie* (Paris: Editions Sociales, 1977), p. 105.

13. Ibid., pp. 106–107.

14. This approach was related to the central issue of the Communist program for the 1978 general election nationalizations. As Boccara writes: "Such a change is, of course, possible only under the condition of national control of the petroleum industry in France; that is why we have proposed the nationalization of the Compagnie Française des Pétroles-Total." See *Changer l'Economie,* p. 96.

15. Yves Fuchs in *Cahiers du Communisme.*

16. See the proceedings of the Twenty-first Congress of the PCF in *Cahiers du Communisme.*

17. The opposite is true, as we shall see further on, in the case of the Italian Communist and Socialist parties.

18. Indeed, the PSI has very seldom felt that these questions deserved any attention at all. Quite paradoxically, if one goes through the theoretical journal of the PSI, *Mondo Operaio,* from 1973 on, the only two systematic treatments of these questions one can find are by such authors as Harold Wilson and John Pinder, who are certainly Socialists but whose opinions can hardly be considered as representing the views of the Italian Socialist party.

19. Cesare Bensi, "Dalla guerra dei prezzi alla cooperazione economica," *Mondo Operaio,* February 74, p. 11. Bensi was at the time Undersecretary of State for Foreign Affairs in the Italian government.

20. Although it is impossible to identify an official position of the PSI on these matters, Bensi seems to represent in foreign relations the most authoritative voice of the party in 1974.

21. Bensi, "Dalla guerra...."

22. Eugenio Peggio, "Crisi energetica, inflazione e crisi econimica," *Politica ed Economia,* October 1973. Peggio was at the time Secretary General of CESPE, Member of Parliament, and Minister of Economics in the PCI's "shadow cabinet."

23. Francesco Pistolese, "La cooperazione internazionale in campo energetico," *Crisi economica a condizionamenti internazionali dell' Italia,* pp. 97–98. Pistolese was at the time the PCI's expert on energy questions.

24. Ibid., p. 100.

25. Ibid.

26. Ibid., p. 99.

27. Peggio, "Crisi energetica."

28. Giancarlo Olmeda in *Politica ed Economia* 5:4, p. 69.

29. This manipulated version of the proceedings is the only one that has been published in *Cahiers du Communisme.* It can be considered very

"official," since the authors of the "summary" are four prominent members of the Central Committee.

30. In "summary," *Cahiers du Communisme.*

31. The very French word *encadrement* (literally, "framing") has absolutely no corresponding concept in any other language known to the author; it is used in the meaning of the English expression "officering" not only for an army, but also for the civilian population and activities, in the sense of subjecting it to the control of nonlelected government officials.

32. Proceedings of the Twentieth Congress of the French CP.

33. P. Boccara, interview by J.L. Gombeaud in *France Nouvelle,* January 9, 1978, p. 47.

34. L.Baillot, "Relations économiques internationales: nécessités et possibilités," in *Cahiers du Communisme* 50:7-8 (1974).

35. Ibid.

36. Ibid. The reader should not be surprised by these assertions. The PCF has indeed an extraordinary capacity to present very seriously the most bewildering assertions: at a meeting of the Communist Parties of Western Europe, for instance, the PCF presented a document in which it was said that "the successes obtained by the agriculture of the Socialist countries show the incapacity of capitalism to solve its problems." On that occasion, the Italian Communist daily *l'Unità* reported that "there was no consensus" among the PCs. See *L'Humanité* and *l'Unità* of May 24, 1975.

37. See G. Marchais, *Report to the Twentieth Congress of the PCF,* 1972.

38. L. Baillot, "Relations économiques..."

39. Ibid.

40. P. Boccara, in *Proceedings of the Twentieth Congress of the PCF.*

41. Ibid.

42. See, for instance, J. Attali, *La nouvelle économie française* (Paris: Flammarion, 1978).

43. Interview with the *Quotidien de Paris,* November 25, 1977, quoted in Christian Stoffaes, *La grande menace industrielle* (Paris: Calmann–Levy, 1978), p. 11.

44. Quoted in Christian Stoffaes, *La grande menace...,* p. 12.

45. At the same seminar. Ibid., p. 20.

46. Ibid.

47. Parti Socialiste, *89 réponses aux problemés économiques* (Paris: Flammarion, 1977), p. 69-70.

48. See in J. Attali, *La parole et l'outil* (Paris: PUF, 1975).

49. Alain Boubil, *Le socialisme industriel,* introduction by J. Attali (Paris: PUF, 1977), p. 64.

50. Ibid. p. 68.

51. Parti Socialiste, *89 réponses ...,* p. 101.

52. Ibid., p. 103. The idea of protecting an economic system against "more efficient technology" would deserve some comments of its own.

53. Ibid.

54. PS, *Programme Commun de Gouvernement de la Gauche: propositions socialistes pour l'Actualisation* (Paris: Flammarion, 1977).

55. Ibid., p. 107.

56. Ibid., p. 108.

57. See also in *Programme Commun...*, pp. 88–89.

58. Ibid., p. 102.

59. Ibid., p. 108.

60. Antonio Giolitti et al., "Uscire dalla crisi," *Politica ed Economia* 1-2 (1975): 54.

61. Antonio Giolitti, "Crisi economica e condizionamenti...."

62. This Socialist author does not explain why France, assumed to follow a policy of bilateral agreements with the oil producers, should be interested in finding "allies" on this line, since any "ally" would be a competitor.

63. Literally, "una politica di maggior chiusura (o di minor apertura) al commercio internazionale."

64. Paolo Leon, "Politica economica e scelte internazionali," *Mondo Operaio* 3 (1974): 13.

65. Ibid.

66. Cesare Bensi et al., "Dalla guerra dei prezzi alla cooperazione economica," *Mondo Operaio* 2(1974): 13.

67. Ibid., p. 11.

68. "L'Europa e il Terzo Mondo," interview with Pietro Nenni, *Mondo Operaio,* February 1974, p. 5.

69. In Italian, *terzomondista.*

70. Pietro Nenni, "L'Europa...," p. 6.

71. Eugenio Peggio, report to the seminar on "Crisi economica e condizionamenti internazionali dell' Italia," p. 24.

72. Ibid., pp. 24–25.

73. Member of Parliament, member of the Direction, and the head of the Section for Economic Planning Reforms of the PCI.

74. In "Crisi economica e condizionamenti...," p. 167.

75. Ibid.

76. Umberto Cardia, "La nuova politica italiana degli scambi," *Cooperazione* 3(1977): 40. Signor Cardia, member of the Foreign Affairs Commission of the House of Deputies, is the head of the Commission for International Cooperation of the Italian Communist party.

77. Franco Modigliani, Proceedings of the CESPE Seminar, p. 244.

78. Bob Rowthorn, in Proceedings of the Seminar on "Condizionamenti...," p. 248.

79. Christian Stoffaes, *La grande menace industrielle* (Paris: Calmann-Levy, 1977).

80. See Michéle Dominique, "Ils preférent les belles étrangères," in *Economie et Politique,* January 1978, p. 24.

81. The cooperation agreement between the two firms, announced in October 1968, was terminated in June 1973.

82. René Guyard, in Proceedings of the Twentieth Congress of the PCF, in *Cahiers du Communisme.*

83. See J.P. Delilez in *Cahiers du Communisme* 50:10 (October 1974).

84. Ibid.

85. Paul Boccara, *Changer l'Economie,* pp. 108–109.

86. André Lajoinie, member of the Bureau Politique of the PCF, in *France Nouvelle* (weekly for PCF party officials), January 2, 1978, p. 45.

87. The "renewed PS" can be defined as the result of a process started around 1970 with the abandonment of the "social democratic compromises" of Guy Mollet's times, and the adoption of a new political line whose most salient feature is the belief that a break with capitalism is inevitable.

88. Reported in *Economie et Politique,* February 1973.

89. Quoted in Victorri and Stoffaes, *Nationalisation* (Paris: Flammarion, 1977), p. 18.

90. PCF, *Les Communistes et l'Etat* (Paris: Editions Sociales, 1977), p. 81.

91. Ibid., p. 49.

92. Ibid., p. 167.

93. *Nouvel Observateur,* August 28, 1971.

94. Report to the Comité Directeur of the PS of its meeting of March 22, 1977.

95. J.P. Chevènement (member of the Bureau Politique of the PS), Report to the seminar on Socialist Industrial Policy, Paris, January 12–13, 1977, in *Cahiers du Nouvel Observateur* 10 (April 1977).

96. Ibid., p. 10.

97. Edmond Maire, in *Syndicalisme Hebdo,* November 4, 1976, p. 16.

98. Jacques Attali, in *Faire,* no. 17, p. 48.

99. See the main report by Giorgio Amendola at the seminar on "Impresa pubblica e participazione democratica," in *Quaderni di Politica ed Economia* 7(1973).

100. Enrico Berlinguer, declaration at a TV press conference, June 16, 1976.

101. R. Chiaberge and G.P. Vitale, "Il compromesso economico," *Il Mondo,* January 5, 1979, p. 47.

102. Report to the PCI Central Committee, May 14–15, 1976.

103. See Eugenio Peggio, main report to the PCI's seminar on *Crisi*

economica e condizionamenti internazionali dell' Italia, March 15–17, 1976, in *Proceedings* (Rome: Editori Riuniti, 1977).

104. Ibid., pp. 20–21.

105. Ibid.

106. Ibid.

107. Luciano Lama, in *Crisi economica e condizionamenti...,* vol. 1, p. 239.

108. Ibid., p. 244.

109. Ibid., p. 243.

110. E. Peggio, main report to the seminar on *Crisi economica e condizionamenti...,* p. 35.

111. Giacomo Luciani, *Il PCI e il capitalismo occidentale* (Milan: Longanesi, 1977), pp. 59–60.

112. May 3, 1976, pp. 121–122.

113. E. Peggio, report to the seminar on *Crisi economica...,* p. 36.

114. In an interview with the international consulting firm Hill and Knowlton; *Lettera Finanziaria dell' Espresso* (Milan) 25 (June 14, 1976): 11–12.

115. Renato Sandri, *La Sfida del Terzo Mondo* (Rome: Editori Riuniti, 1978), p. 96. Signor Sandri is a member of the Italian and European Parliaments, vice-president of the Development and Cooperation Commission of the European Parliament, and vice-president of IPALMO (Institute for Latin American, Africa, and the Middle East). In this institute Christian Democrats, Communists, and Socialists, in their official political capacities, work together.

116. See G. Napolitano, in *Proceedings* of the Meeting of the Central Committee of the PCI, October 27, 1977.

117. R. Sandri, *La sfida...,* p. 101.

118. Ibid., p. 99.

119. Ibid., p. 98.

120. Ibid., p. 99.

6
The Left and Security Problems in Italy, France, and Spain

Stefano Silvestri

Italy, France, and Spain are the hinterland of the Atlantic Alliance. The biggest American and/or NATO bases in Southern Europe are in Italy and Spain, and France provides the vital depth necessary for the defense of Central Europe.

Today, however, none of those three countries is fully integrated into the Atlantic Alliance. Spain does not belong to it (even though she has bilateral treaties with the United States, France, and Portugal, all three of which are alliance members). France is not a member of the NATO integrated command, although she has stayed in the alliance and although she has shown clear signs of once again gradually closing the gap between her strategic and operational choices and NATO's. Italy is, formally speaking, fully integrated within NATO, but it is geographically separated and traditionally has restricted herself to the role of defending her national territory from a direct attack (which if it were by land would cross a band of neutral countries) and of playing host to the American air force and navy strike forces.

The decision as to whether to participate in the alliance or in NATO and whether to sign important bilateral defense treaties with western countries has been and continues to be the subject of debate in all three of these countries. None of these three countries, however (with the possible exception of Italy immediately after the war), has ever felt itself to be on "the front line" in the East–West confrontation.

France, the only country of the three which has had the ambitions and the potential of a great power in recent times, has played its cards in the Third World and within the Western Alliance. The change in de Gaulle's attitude toward the Soviet Union was more a function of France's special position in the West than an attempt to develop an alternative to American policy.

The first problem which we must therefore deal with is that of the *perception of threat*. It is no coincidence that all three countries have a powerful "pacifist," "Third World," "Mediterranean," "African," "pro-Arab" lobby (the precise label depends on the particular moment in time and on differences between national cultures and traditions). This lobby has always attempted to provide an alternative to East–West polarization. Such an alternative would give the country a particular position which would not necessarily be neutral or anti-European (anti–West or anti–East). At the same time, however, the lobby usually takes little notice of the limits and obligations which spring from the division of Europe into two blocs.

Partly, of course, we are dealing with a nationalist tradition. In the countries where nationalism is strongest (France and Spain) this tradition takes on a revanchist or nuclear "strike force" coloring. In Italy, where the nationalist tradition after the Second World War is not as strong, it every now and then assumes Catholic/humanitarian tones, becomes a campaign in defense of the disinherited, or claims socioeconomic justification. Whatever form it takes, the tradition of the "third road" is present in a wide spectrum of sociopolitical forces from left to right. Thus it is useful to bear in mind that in Italy in 1948–49 the opposition to the Atlantic Alliance did not only come from the left but that an important section of Christian Democrat politicians (Dossetti, La Pira, Fanfani) was also opposed to the idea. In France it was a conservative government which took the decision to leave NATO. Franco's Spain for a long time kept up an independent pro-Arab stance which was only reduced by the progressive internal weakening of the regime. While it may perhaps seem somewhat paradoxical, all the serious problems and the internal dissent which have weakened NATO in these years have been started by conservative (or at most, center) governments.

Naturally, though, the left in these three countries suffers from the same problems. Thus we have a populist, "Third Worldist," Mediterranean left as well as the more traditional pro–Soviet left. Despite the fact that the PCI, the PCF, and the PCE were in general quite happy uncritically to follow the strategic convolutions of the Soviet Communist party, they have always made a point of emphasizing the "originality" of their line of thought. They were of course limited in this by their "tactical" situations; the least independent of the three was the Spanish Communist party in exile. Nonetheless, once it had regained its freedom of action, the PCE exploded, revealing the strong hidden pressures on it. The PCF preferred to emphasize the themes inherent in the French nationalist tradition rather than ideological characteristics. The PCI on the other hand has carefully used Gramsci's writings to restate the (greater, lesser, or minimal) degree to which it differs from the Soviet Communist party.

In my opinion, the problem lies in a different "perception of threat" which is not clearly matched with the perception of the bigger allies. This produces different conclusions as to what is the best model for international stability and security.

Nonetheless, in spite of these reservations (which, incidentally, are only present in part of public opinion), it is still true that these countries are allied to the western powers and that the Marxist left has for a number of years and in a number of ways supported the rationale and the policies of the Soviet Union. This division has taken on all the connotations of a choice of one model of civilization or society against another and is thus more than simply a question of international political or military alliances. At no time since the end of the wars of religion has international politics been so highly ideological, and for so long.

Inevitably this situation has led to the technical side of defense problems being put to one side; security policies tend to be rejected or accepted on a priori grounds. Options in defense and foreign policy have taken on crucial domestic political significance. The government, with its western option, distinguishes itself from the antiwestern opposition. Every debate on the substance of these policies (parliamentary control, cost-efficieny, strategic or tactical deployments, technical requirements or performance of weapons, and so on) is sliced down the middle with this ideological razor.

This is particularly true for Italy and Spain. France, on the other hand, has gone through de Gaulle's nationalist experience which, on the hypothesis that France could adopt an independent role (that is, the more traditional role for a European power), took the country out of the logic of the East-West dilemma. Nonetheless here too defense options have taken the "absolute" tones of decisions for or against national independence, for or against "une certaine idée de la France." This has led to a less concrete debate.

Today this situation has changed due to the simultaneous working of two factors. First, the old government coalitions have either broken down (as in Spain) or are opening to the left rather decidedly in Italy, more timidly in France. This makes it necessary to adopt less ideological, more flexible attitudes even on international and security problems. Second, it has been difficult to maintain a clear distinction in a period of East-West détente and of growing contacts between Communist and western government leaders.

Today the French, Italian, and Spanish left has made substantial modifications in its analysis of the international system as far as the Communist bloc and the relationship between the Soviet Communist party and the three Communist parties, which we are considering here. Relationships between the Socialist and Communist parties have also changed; this has forced the left to make some important ideological revisions on the basic problem of the "choice of sides." It has also brought about a deep change as far as security policy is concerned, and it is this change we intend to analyze in the following pages.

Nonetheless the idea has remained that the division of the world into two blocs and the security policy which derives from that fact does not fully correspond to national requirements. Moreover, the evolution of "Eurocommunism" has weakened the links of the three Communist parties with Moscow while at same time increasing the importance of internal perceptions over international requirements. This has produced a tendency for the further isolation of national political discussion within the three countries from the "perceptions" of the political classes in the other allied countries. Since an alliance can only function if there is a sufficient number of common denominators and common perceptions of the threat, of the ways in which it is necessary to face it, and of priorities, we must continually seek to evaluate the motivations and reservations present in these political parties. We must also attempt to determine whether these motivations and reservations (and not just actual decisions) are evolving, and if so in which direction.

Italy

Italian security policy has always been highly influenced by the ideological debate. After a brief period of national unity following the war and the resistance struggle (in which all the parties participated from the Communists to the Christian Democrats and the Liberals, with the single exception of the extreme right) the division between government and opposition was translated into a division between pro-Atlantic and pro-Soviet forces.

Italy's strategic position in this period was influenced by her proximity to Yugoslavia and Albania. Frontier problems with Yugoslavia (Trieste and the Istrian peninsula) were added to the problems arising from the peace treaty and gave these a nationalist hue. On this occasion the left parties, while wishing to avoid a break with Belgrade, attempted not to appear to be antinational. At the same time the fact that the British and Americans were fundamentally favorable to the Yugoslav position (except on Trieste) prevented the question from worsening divisions within Italy.

In practice, Socialist Pietro Nenni's work as foreign minister in the various "governments of national unity" and the policy followed by Palmiro Togliatti, the PCI leader, aimed at a compromise not very dissimilar to the agreement reached by a Christian Democrat government in 1955 and finally ratified in 1975 by a broad-based coalition government backed by left-wing as well as centrist forces.[1]

In the early years of the postwar period the antifascist parties helped to draw up a new constitution and participated in the first coalition governments. It was from this experience that the concept of the *arco costituzionale* (constitutional arc) was derived, referring to that group of parties which despite all ideological and political differences, accept the values of the republican constitution as their own. Right from the beginning this guaranteed the political legitimacy of the PCI, at the same time preventing the splitting of the country and the kind of civil war between prowestern and pro-Communist forces which occurred in Greece.

For this reason and despite ideological differences the PCI has always been regarded as one of the Republic's founding fathers, perhaps more as an estranged brother than as a complete enemy. The Italian political system has never completely broken off political contacts with the left.

Meanwhile the PCI, too, has confirmed this, opting decisively for democratic parliamentary methods and dismantling the clandestine apparatus built up during the antifascist period and the resistance. One illustrious victim was the PCI's own organizational secretary, Pietro Secchia, who favored the maintenance of a tougher, more militant party.

The acceptance of constitutional legality, even on security questions, has had important consequences. The Italian constitution considers defense as a policy involving the general, that is, the national interest, one which should thus be isolated as fas as possible from political controversy. The chief of the armed forces is the President of the Republic, who does not have to answer to Parliament. This, as we will see, has a series of far from insignificant consequences concerning party and parliamentary influence over defense policy. For the moment it is sufficient to note the way in which in Italy the ideological division between East and West is counterbalanced by this "constitutional unity," which is anything but revolutionary and which has proved the most important factor working toward the integration of the left into the "government area."

The principal and decisive choice, for or against the Atlantic Alliance, came after the 1948 elections. These elections confirmed the existence of a majority government (as opposed to the Socialist–Communist minority), and the Atlantic decision was seen by the majority as a useful means of bolstering its identity and confirming its separation from the opposition parties. In this way it is possible to maintain that it was not only international reasons which were responsible for the decision to join the Atlantic Alliance but also reasons of internal policy.

Twenty years later, Giulio Andreotti (the present prime minister) wrote about the De Gasperi governments, in which he was closely involved, that foreign policy was considered as having priority over internal Italian choices.[2] Andreotti considered the international picture as a positive element which allowed the "parliamentary line-ups" to be kept under control. Luckily, he wrote, "At the crucial moments, principles of international coexistence always end up being the factor determining the final decision."

Within this framework, the policy of the left had no genuine counterproposals: Andreotti's interpretation of foreign policy as a type of "norm" which can be used to regulate a coalition on internal policy was in practice accepted by the left. This explains for the most part the progressive pro-West evolution first of the PSI and then of the PCI.

As the PSI moved closer to government (between 1958 and 1964), the party's "pacifist" or "Third World" line met with difficulties. This line had been supported in those years, for example, by the Christian Democrat

Amintore Fanfani, who as foreign minister during the Arab–Israeli war of 1956 had tried to work out a "third way" for Italy which would have been pro–Arab and thus distinct from the pro–Israeli line taken by the West. The PSI, on the other hand, found itself faced with the problem of how to integrate itself further into the West. As it found it difficult to base itself directly on NATO, it preferred to publicize the merits of European integration (the EEC and in the final analysis also European defense). As for NATO, the Socialist party stated that it accepted the organization only inasmuch as it was a "defensive alliance which is geographically limited" and insisted on the necessity of positively activating Article 2 of the North Atlantic Treaty with regard to European totalitarian regimes (primarily Portugal). Nonetheless, two "souls" coexisted in the reunified Socialist party; there was a pro–Atlantic wing and a more neutralist, previously pro–Communist, section of the party. Thus, for example, there were those who stated[3] that the "purpose of the Atlantic Treaty ought to be discussed," even though they finished up by saying that "to ask for the giving up of the treaty is a political mistake because it is necessary to let time pass so that the prospects which will appear after the dissolution of the blocs can be seen." At the same time the Social Democratic wing insisted on sticking to the Atlantic Treaty because it was a "choice of civilization" providing a secure link between Italy and American democracy.[4]

The meeting point of these opposing views was limited to the common pro–European outlook which they held. They favored Community integration, and it was this point which was coherently developed.

The road which the PCI took tells a remarkably similar story. Basically it also had internal and international motivations. The starting point can be taken as 1967–69, when the "Prague Spring" and the student movements in Italy (with their criticism of the PCI "from the left"), together with the obvious crisis in the center–left government coalition formula (and the new split between the Socialists into the old groupings of PSI and PSDI), forced the PCI to rethink its strategy. Already in 1967 the PCI had taken the political decision not to fight a campaign against the renewal of the Atlantic Treaty, twenty years after it had been signed (in 1969), and proclaimed the necessity of facing "the delicate problem of Italy's international relations with a new spirit."[5] From these small beginnings came the PCI December 1974 statement, in which Enrico Berlinguer made clear that in the opinion of the PCI Italy should not start by taking unilateral action which might alter the military and strategic equilibrium which exists between NATO and the Warsaw Pact and that as a result, for the moment, she should stay in NATO. It was in this period that the PCI had considered the Chilean episode (1973) very carefully and had come to the conclusion that it was necessary to go into government in some sort of wide coalition formula which would not disturb the international balance. It was from this point that the party's transformation gathered momentum.

But as in the case of the PSI, it is the "European" outlook that shows itself to be the new touchstone of the international policy of the left. And it is in the same direction and toward contacts with the European Social Democrats, the EEC, and so on, that the efforts of the PCI have been directed, much more than toward a real security policy.

This has isolated the "pacifist" and "Third World" tendencies in Italy even more. They have been left without any big parties to support them and they have been somewhat dispersed through all the parties from the PCI to the PSI to the Christian Democrats. These forces are now trying to regroup.

Thus, for the first time since the war, the Italian foreign policy and security debate is once again beginning to return to the traditional lines of Italian political history after these had tended to be abandoned over the last thirty years. Once the 1948-49 rift between pro–Americans and pro–Soviets has been resolved, at least in principle, with the conclusion that Italy should stay in the zone of western influence, the old contrast between a pro–European and a "Mediterranean" line reemerged, which had already set Giolitti and Crispi against each other at the end of the nineteenth century and the beginning of the twentieth and later provided a bone of contention between the democratic parties and the Fascist regime.

Given these premises, what is the Italian left's security policy? As we have already seen, the Italian left has not been very original in the field of wider choices and general policy on defense. First the Socialists (in 1960) and then the Communists (in 1974) accepted the fact that Italy should stay in the Atlantic Alliance and NATO. Both emphasized the *defensive* role of the Alliance and the geographical limits of the Treaty.

The point about the geographical limits is probably the more confused of the two. It is intended to make clear (1) the fact that although these parties are prepared to take part in the alliance they do not wish to commit themselves to the support of American policy in the rest of the world; and (2) in particular they want to preserve freedom of choice with regard to what happens in the Middle East and North Africa.

This second position is not only held by the Communists, rather, it is common to the whole of the Italian political line-up (as, by the way, it is also in France and Spain). It partly derives from the "pacifist" tradition which is also present in the Catholic sector of the Italian political elite. In traditional terms, the section of Italian political groupings most favorable to Israel has been the lay-Liberal-Socialist line-up. (In 1967, the Socialist party still supported Israeli government policy, while the Communists had a number of reservations; they defended the survival of the state of Israel but supported many Arab and Palestinian demands.) The situation changed over the period between 1967 and 1973: there was growing criticism of continued Israeli occupation of the territory which had been taken in the Six Day War. This tendency reached its peak during the 1973 war, when the majority of Italian political groupings both in and out of government

(Christian Democrats, PSI, PCI) worked out a common position opposed to the use of Italian territory as a base for the American airlift to Israel and to the use of the American and allied supplies in the war in the Middle East.

The fact remains that the extraterritorial waters of the Mediterranean are an integral part of the area covered by the Atlantic Treaty and the Sixth Fleet. This is an important margin of ambiguity which the formula referring to the "geographical limits" of the treaty does not resolve.

The position which has been taken about allied and American bases in Italy is less ambiguous. In this case it has been clearly stated on more than one occasion that it is intended to maintain the agreement without modifications. Every now and again there is a more critical demand in the Italian press to have greater Italian control over the "nuclear components" on the bases. But in none of these cases has the issue been taken up officially by any of the major parties.

In this case the ambiguity of the situation is due, at least in part, to the secrecy surrounding the government's role in decision-making on and control over nuclear weapons. This internal debate does not, however, affect the maintenance of these weapons in Italy.

The general strategic question of theater nuclear weapons is more complex. Italy was only just touched by the great debate during the 1960s on the multilateral force (MLF) and on independent nuclear deterrents. Some rather unimportant traces were left in certain sectors of the administration, particularly in the Ministry of Foreign Affairs, in the Ministry of Defense, and in the body responsible for nuclear energy, the National Committee for Nuclear Energy (CNEN), where a number of bureaucrats have more or less openly supported the idea of a national nuclear deterrent under a "European" cover. These survivals of nationalism were, however, politically defeated with Italy's ratification of the Non-Proliferation Treaty in 1975 and afterwards more or less disappeared. The left, while remaining vaguely in favor of nuclear nonproliferation and disarmament, tended not to be involved in the debate. Once more concrete decisions had to be taken and the left began to participate in the real strategic debate, this lack of preparation began to make itself felt.

This was seen during the debate on the "neutron bomb" in the second half of 1977. The entire debate was heavily influenced by "moral" considerations (it was no coincidence that it opened with an article by the pro-Communist Catholic moralist Senator La Valle)[6] without any discussion of the military issues. Even in the calmer, better-informed articles, such as those by Senator Calamandrei and by G. L. Devoto,[7] the military expert, these were only touched upon. In fact these questions were set aside in favor of political arguments about détente.

However, this is not to underestimate the importance the PCI attributed to the critical position expressed, for example, by some sectors of the German SPD, which already in July 1977, before the PCI had made its position known, had taken a strongly negative stance.

Nonetheless, if we compare the PCI's position on this particular question with the party's general political evolution, we find it to be particularly backward and still in line with Soviet attitudes and tactics. This lack of a deeper approach to strategic and military problems can be seen from an analysis of the Italian debate on these problems.

In this field, the debate has been limited to vague suggestions. The discussion always accepts the view that Italy should stay in NATO, though every now and again there is an emphasis on a certain margin of "autonomy." Among the main spokesmen for this point of view are the Communist Senator Pecchioli, the independent who was elected with Communist support, Senator Pasti (who is also an ex-air marshal), and the Socialist deputy Accame (an ex-navy officer who was chairman of the Chamber of Deputies Committee on Defense from 1976 to 1978 and is now the Socialist party defense spokesman).

None of these has committed either the PSI or the PCI in the defense of their positions, so they can therefore be considered at most as an indication of opinions which exist in the two parties.

In various ways these members of Parliament have criticized the present direction of Italian defense policy as too heavily based on the northeastern sector (the border with Austria and Yugoslavia). In particular, Accame and Pasti have critized the apparently "offensive" tendency in Italian armaments (the new Tornado fighter bomber, the new helicopter carrier which has been laid down in the navy yards, and so on).

The two politicians seem to be generally in favor of territorial defense together with a lesser offensive component. Pasti, for example, has proposed aircraft with shorter range and less sophisticated technology; Accame has proposed a reduction in the number of large naval units and the greater use of an integrated system of mines in the Mediterranean in order to limit the movement of the two superpowers' fleets.

In particular, Accame has developed his own theory of the territorial defense of Italy. It is based on a functional division of the armed forces, which has been partly taken from the French model and partly from the more recent theories of the Austrian and Yugoslav defense forces: one element which is mobile and for attack and mainly made up of professionals, and another component consisting of conscripts who would be armed to carry on widespread resistance throughout the whole territory.[8]

These ideas are more or less in agreement with the Socialists' political proposals, which tend to give more weight to the value of agreements such as Helsinki. These agreements stand for "dynamic evolution within the blocs" and the beginning of a process which will stop "the reduction of forces in the heart of Europe producing an increase of military pressure on Europe's southern flank.'' Measures of the type that Accame proposes tend to reduce the role played by the superpowers and to play down the tension on the frontier with Yugoslavia in such a way as to allow a "symmetrical lessening" of East-West military pressure.

Nonetheless, the major Italian politico-strategic problem is still, as in the past, Yugoslavia. On the left there do not seem to be political problems in this respect: both the Communists and the Socialists have repeatedly declared their support for Yugoslav independence and nonalignment. The PCI in particular has a long history of good relations with Tito and with the Yugoslav League of Communists. The Treaty of Osimo provided a definitive solution to the Italo-Yugoslav border question and was judged positively by the Italian left as a strengthening of Yugoslavia's international position and of ties between the Italian government and the regime in Belgrade.

Nevertheless, if we move from the political to the military level the question becomes more confused. Yugoslavia is a "gray zone" not only for NATO but also for Italy. In particular, there is the question of whether or not to "lighten" the Italian military presence in the northeast of the country on the Yugoslav frontier. This could be consistent with a new analysis of the threat according greater importance to the sea than to the land theater. At the same time, however, with the change in Italo-Yugoslav relations and the definitive solution of the border dispute, Italian land forces, criticized in the past by the Yugoslavs as being too threatening, could help to deter threats to use force against Yugoslavia herself.

In general, PCI leaders, when asked how they would react to a crisis in Yugoslavia avoid answering, arguing exactly like their Yugoslav colleagues that it is neither possible nor wise to try to analyze a crisis which is still purely hypothetical.

Meanwhile, they fear that increased emphasis on the navy and air force over the army would tend to "professionalize" the Italian armed forces as well as be an excessive budget burden. All the same, on the highly delicate problem of Italy's strategic and military role in a Yugoslav crisis there seems to be a degree of rethinking, not yet explicit, which has perhaps been discussed with the Yugoslavs. It is no coincidence that *l'Unità*'s answer to Accame's proposals implying a reduction in Italian forces in the northeast was written by Arnaldo Baracetti, who is normally the Communist expert on relations with Yugoslavia. In his article[9] Baracetti emphasized the need for Italy and her western allies to share a kind of "Mediterranean sensitivity." "This kind of geo-strategical modification has yet to occur and there is still a lot of work to be done before it comes to positive fruition in Italy and in the Atlantic Alliance." The conclusion from these comments seems to be that the Communists would favor a general rethinking of the strategic situation involving NATO as well as just Italy. As long as this re-thinking has not taken place, they would prefer not to make specific commitments but rather to maintain Italy's present strategic–military posture so as not to suggest any change in Italian policy or commitments.

The left is much more sure of itself when it comes to dealing with the social, budgeting, and industrial problems linked to defense. Thus the PCI, for example, has launched a clear–cut policy whereby the party interests itself not only in soldiers and noncommissioned officers but also in officers. Although the PCI has declared itself against enrolling military personnel in unions (its position is different when it comes to the police, which it considers a civil, not a military body) it supports the idea of nominating "representatives" and the creation of a structure in which social and economic problems can be discussed within the military environment.

Positions taken with regard to arms production are also often linked to economic or social considerations (such as maintaining a given level of employment) rather than to a military evaluation. Thus the PCI has supported the MRCA–Tornado program (although it has criticized the aircraft), giving as its reason the employment it produces. This same attitude explains the lack of enthusiasm shown in the criticism of arms sales abroad. There are reactions in the Communist press to obviously scandalous cases, for example, the very considerable sales to South Africa. Nonetheless, Accame has stood alone in sponsoring a bill placing the arms trade under more rigorous parliamentary supervision; to date the bill has made no progress.

On a more general political level we must, however, point out a gradual change in the Communist attitude toward armaments production. This change can be seen mainly in the European Parliament. In this regard, on June 16, 1978, during the discussion of the Klepsch Report,[10] the Italian Communists made a very clear distinction between their position and that of the French Socialists, Communists, and Gaullists, who all voted (with different motivations) against the measure. They also distinguished themselves from the Dutch Socialist Dankert, who had shown some reservations. Spinelli, on behalf of the Italian Communists, gave the following reasons for their positive vote: (1) It is important to open our market to goods from the European arms industry, given the considerable role that this sector has in the Italian and European economies. (2) Such an objective does not conflict with either détente or disarmament. (3) Europe must reduce its dependence on the United States as much as possible and at the same time it must stimulate its own industries. The relationship with the United States must be one of equality among allies.

We see, then, that the Italian left is still looking for its own defense and security policy. Its influence is limited for the moment by political uncertainty and little understanding of specific security and defense problems. However, the left's ability to influence the specific choices made by the Italian government is limited. This limitation is likely to remain in the future.

The most effective channel which the left has for increasing its influence is usually parliamentary control. Nonetheless, in Italy this control is limited both de facto and de jure. As a matter of fact, twenty years of cold war have encouraged a separation between government activity in this field and parliamentary control, for it was maintained by the government that the parliamentarians were not "trustworthy" enough to be let into important military secrets. This has encouraged the separation of the defense decision–making process from normal parliamentary control. The situation is now beginning to change under the influence of the big scandals which have broken over aircraft orders and because of the diminishing of the cold war climate within the country.

Nevertheless, the Italian constitution itself gives the possibility of keeping defense and national security decision–making separate from normal government activity and therefore from parliamentary control. The constitution provides for the setting up of a Supreme Defense Council (constituted under a law passed in 1950) directly dependent on the President of the Republic, thus escaping parliamentary control. This council is responsible for the general lines of defense policy. It is made up of ministers, the chiefs of general staff, and anyone else nominated by the president. It has already deliberated on a number of important questions, such as agreements on nuclear defense and the restructuring of the armed forces, some of which were not strictly within its competence. Apparently at one time the council discussed normative, financial, and budgetary questions. The main feature of the council is its secrecy and its lack of responsibility to Parliament. This allows the possibility of a compromise solution to the problem of the left getting closer to government and the management of the more delicate problems of national security, for in this way the immediate impact of direct Communist participation in these decisions would be avoided, as would their access to particularly sensitive information. At the same time the participation of some ministers and of the prime minister in this body, together with the chairmanship of the head of state, ought to guarantee a certain coordination between the council and the internal political picture.

France

In France the premises are different: (1) France has the heritage of having been a great power and it nowadays still claims the right to play a major international role. Furthermore, it has its own independent nuclear weapons. (This leads to a lively discussion within the country on nuclear questions.) (2) The French left has a long tradition of being involved in deciding important issues which the country has to face, including matters relating to defense and national security.

We thus see on the one hand that the French left feels that it must have an established national security policy, and on the other that such a policy very often takes on the tone and coloring of French nationalism.

There is a heritage received by the left from the great bourgeois revolutionary tradition, exemplified by figures like Jaurès or in episodes like the Popular Front in the 1930s. It is from this tradition that the French left has taken its attachment to institutions such as conscription, and institutionalized notions such as the country in arms, the citizen–soldier, and other rhetorical images. France's love of her *Armée* is nowadays perhaps on the wane, but whatever of it remains is just as much on the left as on the right of the political spectrum.

On top of all this we have the recent Gaullist experience. De Gaulle created a major "national" (and nationalist) force. The left could not remain unmoved in front of the new lease on life which the French nationalist tradition had taken, and so it assumed some of its characteristics.

Today, now that the Gaullist experience seems to be subsiding, we can see how there is a potential return to the politico–parliamentary equilibria of the past. France is moving toward a reconstruction of the center with oscillation and alliances to the left and right. Notwithstanding this tendency, especially in the field of defense and national security, the Gaullist experience is still fundamental and influences the French left's whole policy.

France's withdrawal from NATO in 1966 and her decision to maintain and develop her own nuclear strike force have created a very special situation. France is still a member of the Atlantic Alliance. The effectiveness as a deterrent of her nuclear *force de frappe* still depends on the allies for intelligence, warning systems, and to some extent for logistic support. The maintenance of the alliance and the withdrawal from NATO have created a very comfortable situation, the benefits of which do not involve an equivalent cost. It is very hard for the left to criticize this kind of situation. Its only real concern from this quarter is that there should be no gradual return to NATO and that the situation should not deteriorate so far as to threaten French security. Despite a degree of opposition, defense policy is thus a unifying factor on the French scene. Differences tend to concern general political questions rather than matters of technical, military, or strategic substance.

In the Italian and Spanish cases, apart from the "choice of sides" there is also the very useful point of the "European" option (integration into Europe). So far, this has been the principal motive of the left's evolution toward a western outlook. This does not work in the French case:

1.   The French left has a long history of national policy which gives an a priori legitimacy to its ambitions on government without the absolute necessity (which there is in the other two countries) of looking for international legitimacy.
2.   In Italy and Spain, the "center," which is in government, is European as well as Atlanticist. This is further stimulus for the left to convert to Europeanism. In France the "European" center has, on the contrary, been pushed out of the government or has been heavily conditioned by nationalist forces which are substantially anti-European.
3.   The "European way" is seen in France above all as a growing process of integration with West Germany. This produces problems for the left as well as for nationalist elements.
5.   The independent development of the French left with respect to international "models" (Soviet communism and European Social Democracy) has always meant the defense of French sovereignty and national peculiarity with respect to the rest of Europe.

The Socialist and Communist *Programme commun* discusses defense problems in a very general way. Moreover, the gradual change in the balance of power between the Socialists and Communists in favor of the Socialists has pushed the PCF into accentuating its ideological characteristics so that it can regain its politico-cultural identity and compete with the Socialist party for the leadership of the left. Among the Socialists themselves, the left-wing group CERES has also accentuated its own ideological self-identification vis-à-vis the pragmatism of the majority of the party, because of its fear that participation in government would make the Socialists forget their ideological anti-Social Democratic positions.

All this has produced an ambivalent situation. On the one hand we have a French left which is more interested and competent in problems of defense and international security than the left in Italy and Spain; on the other, especially recently, the whole debate has been increasingly centered on ideological themes and has moved farther and farther away from an examination of concrete problems.

France has a serious problem of redefining her defense and national security policy. She has consistently refused to integrate her defense into a European system, in 1954 when she refused to ratify the EDC treaty and in 1966 when de Gaulle took France out of NATO, but she has not maintained sufficient military power to guarantee her own security.

The *force de frappe* was modified in order to adapt it to a flexible strategy when it became clear that a total *tous azimuts* strategy risked leaving the country completely isolated from its allies, thus aggravating French security problems. Nonetheless the tactical weapons planned to give a new "flexibility" to the French deterrent continue to pose insoluble problems of definition. When should they be used? And above all, where? In West Germany, on the borders with France, on French territory or on the eastern borders of the NATO area? Even strategic flexibility is anything but assured; among other things, the French triad (bombers, IRBMs, and SLBMs) has in practice lost one of its components: the bombers are at best usable only on tactical missions. (This is being more and more admitted even by government source.) The triad is now in danger of losing a second component if the French IRBMs remain as they are today, vulnerable and inaccurate. On the other hand, invulnerable systems involve costs which are anything by negligible. (If mobile solutions are chosen, on U.S. lines, then there will also be very serious ecological problems.) So the French deterrent runs the risk of basing its whole future on SLBMs and tactical nuclear weapons. (This is a choice which the British made long ago, but it implies considerable reduction in the independence of the national deterrent.) With this type of weaponry it is not really possible to elaborate a credible and flexible strategy unless it is integrated with that of the United States.

The very concept of a French national defense system has been shown to be too restricted even from a purely operational point of view. From the moment when Giscard and General Méry (Chief of General Staff) began to reelaborate and extend it ot the point of covering the security of France's allies, in particular West Germany, the limits of a purely national deterrent and defense strategy came even more clearly to light, and the operational justification for rejecting the integration of the French forces into NATO was seriously weakened.

To date, the French government has taken all the steps necessary as preconditions for a change in the basic direction of French defense policy but has then decided not to change it. Thus the policy continues after having lost its basic justification. This offers plenty of room for polemics and recriminations, and it explains how the *force de frappe* problem emerged seemingly from nowhere as one of the principal bones of contention between the French Socialists and Communists in 1977–78.

What sort of concept of defense does the French left have? Communist views tends to be dominated by rigid nationalism. Thus on June 11, 1977, the Central Committee of the PCF recognized that nuclear weapons are the only effective deterrent the country possesses and will continue to posess for some time to come. This marked a move away from the *Programme commun,* previously signed with the Socialists, in which the PCF took a more traditional, cautiously positive line on nuclear weapons (taken up at this point by the PS with a call for a referendum on the question). On this basis Jean Marrane[11] defended the concept of an *independent* as opposed to a merely *autonomous* deterrent, which he believed to be insufficient. Jean

Kanapa[12] defending the *tous azimut* strategy, called for an independent French warning system as well as the retargeting of French IRBMs in line with a strategy of massive retaliation. Meanwhile, the proposal for an agreement with the USSR on "no first use of nuclear weapons" seems to have been mainly determined by political considerations. At the same time there is still an obsessive fear of giving the Germans a *droit de regard* on French policy.

The Socialist position is hazier and more confused. It demonstrates above all the large number of opinions existing within the party.[13] In the beginning, the Socialist party was antinuclear and, all things considered, it was for the Atlantic Alliance. After de Gaulle left the NATO integrated command, however, the Socialist party certainly did not go so far as to propose a return by France to it. Rather, it restricted itself to continuing to propose a complete renunciation of nuclear weapons. During the recent Socialist conference on defense in January 1978, a minority amendment once again showed the Socialist party's "traditional" way of reasoning: in the Socialist view, France, for real defense and for strategic flexibility, ought to rely on the Atlantic Alliance, whose threat to the Soviet Union "is infinitely more dissuasive than a purely French one."

But today this proposition is, generally speaking, unpopular. The PS national convention passed a motion of whose main points were   (1) the continuing political objective of France giving up her nuclear weapons; (2) total world disarmament through suitable convened conferences; (3) in the meantime, the operative maintenance of the autonomous French nuclear system; and (4) the referring of the final decisión ot the French people by referendum.

Mitterrand clarified his point of view even further when he criticized both those who put all their trust in nuclear weapons and those who want to give them up immediately, thus risking the destruction of the present French defense system. He declared himself willing to collaborate with the United States not only on disarmament but also on nuclear nonproliferation and he made an elegant if not very explicit distinction when he gave the assurance that France would be *une alliée loyale* but would not be *une alliée integrée*. The same Mitterrand wrote[15] that "a policy of alliances is today a necessary but no longer a sufficient condition to safeguard our national independence." On the one hand this statement serves as a justification for alliances but on the other it serves as a proposal for France's "own role" in a disarmament policy through which she might reach security. Such a disarmament policy would not of course have France once again lining itself up with the countries which have already been going down that road for some time. Instead, France would try an original method which Mitterrand then indicated. Its main characteristic would be above all an all–embracingness both as far as the negotiators are concerned and as far as the subjects which the negotiators are to deal with.

The most striking characteristic of this program is that there is a great similarity between Mitterrand's proposals and Giscard d'Estaing's as far as French role in disarmament strategy is concerned. In both cases the common concern seems to be that of putting an end to France's isolation, of avoiding a direct bilateral agreement between the United States and the Soviet Union, and above all preventing the West Europeans from becoming the "object" of the negotiations. On the contrary, both leaders seek to use France's atomic trump card so that even if nothing else happens the "nuclear" countries are reinstated into the negotiations on an equal footing.

In sum, if progress is to be made in integrating France into the rest of Europe, it has to be functional and must not seem to be a challenge to the sacred principle of national independence.

French policy cannot of course be reduced to its simple nuclear aspect. On the contrary, if we want to be realistic, we have to admit that although the nuclear aspect receives the most attention, other issues such as policy on conventional weapons, arms production, the arms trade, and the French presence in the Third World are much less obvious but more important in their practical consequences.

From this point of view there are also considerable ambiguities and differences. Thus, for example, in the report which we have already quoted, Kanapa (PCF) suggested strengthening conventional weapons, maintaining conscription, and substantial improvements in the economic conditions of conscripts. Jean Marrane took the same position in the book which we have quoted and specifies his dislike of European "standardization" measures. It is curious that his argument is diametrically opposed to that presented by Spinelli on behalf of the Italian Communist party at the European Parliament.

The Socialists are also in favor of maintaining conscription. Thus Jean Marceau, for example [16] complained about a system of unjust exemptions and dispensations which make military service no longer egalitarian and obligatory.

When it comes to arms sales, though, the stances taken by the Socialists and the Communists are decidedly contradictory. At the same time that it criticizes the sale of arms to certain reactionary countries, the PCF hopes that there will be development in this sector as a guarantee of French independence and initiative in the Third World. (The party is only worried about changing customers.) On the other hand, although Mitterrand [17] remembered that the *Programme commun* had merely planned for "la cessation de toute vente d'armes et matériel de guerre aux gouvernements colonialistes, racistes ou fascistes" (the position also accepted the PCF), and although he emphasized the economic importance of a sector which employs 275,000 workers in France, he was nonetheless worried about giving any specific policy indications. Thus he talked for example about the necessity of industry redeploying "ses exportations par des contrats de coopération avec les pays européens" (this is the opposite of what the Communists suggested and is more advanced than present French policy); he also proposed public control which would take the form of "information obligatoire des commissions de défense compétentes de l'Assemblée et du Senat sur toute signature de contrats de vente d'armes" (a similar proposal has been put forward in Italy by the Socialist Accame).

We must finally note that the Socialist and Communist reactions to the French government's African policy have been different. Mitterrand has preferred to limit himself to noting a degree of contradiction and incompleteness in France's African initiatives and to a search for the international political logic underlying them. Marchais on the other hand has taken refuge in rhetoric with the accusation that these actions show a slavish French subordination to the United States.

We have already pointed out on a number of occasions how Mitterrand's positions seemed to be reconcilable with Giscard's while Marchais's are generally closer to the nationalist right and the Gaullists, at least as far as international politics is concerned. For example, not only Marchais but also the Gaullist Alexandre Sanguinetti complained about French African policy, saying that it could seriously damage France's relations with certain African countries.

But this schematization is insufficient. The reality of the situation is that all French political groups from left to right seem to a greater or lesser extent to be fascinated by the same mirage of national power "autonomous" or "independent" according to the speaker's modesty.

The fact is that there does not seem to be an alternative international position for France as far as the left is concerned. Everyone seems to be convinced of the necessity and of the usefulness of keeping the country outside close integration, be it Atlantic or European. The recent "independent" evolution of the PCF with respect to the Soviet Union has added a new element to the discussion of national independenc but has not led to the search for a new international context for French policy.

Taken as a whole and especially if we look at the problem in terms of security, we have seen that despite concepts such as "Eurosocialism" and "Eurocommunism" the French left is firmly anchored in France and leaves the whole burden and prospect of European integration to the forces in the center of the political spectrum.

From this point of view, France's strategic position and her defense strategy seem after all to be based on a rather large and general consensus. Even though each party has different criticisms or preferences, taken together they seem to agree on the "eccentricity" of France's position, so much so that even Giscard's modest European or western initiatives are unanimously criticized by both left and right because they seem to risk bringing about a "change" in France's international position.

Until now it is the Socialist party which seems to be the most aware of this situation. The PS is also the party which has paid most attention and reflected most on defense problems. It has even reached the point of trying to formulate an "alternative policy." But the weakness of the reforms proposed is such that the President of the Republic seems to have largely taken the wind out of the sails of the "alternative," thanks to a number of initiatives of a similar type which have been already taken.

Is all this reassuring for the West? What it is today is certainly not enough to guarantee NATO or to allow a more integrated development of European defense. Nor is it a sufficient guarantee in the case of political upheavals in Southern Europe. This France or the France of the left cannot represent a pole of stability and it certainly cannot have ambitions of replacing the United States or even Western Germany in this role. It is possible that it will not add its own instability to the instability elsewhere but even that possibility is based more on the contingent characteristics of the present political circumstances than on permanent structures.

Spain

The Spanish left has only recently become legal again. In the past it had been linked to alliances and program which turned out later to have little value. It is enough to consider the rapid evolution of the Spanish Communist party, which went from alignment with Moscow to the drastic attitude taken against eastern socialism and Leninism. Without doubt the PCE is today the party farthest along the road to reformism. The Socialists themselves have undergone a rapid evolution. Initially they were divided into a large number of subgroups. Under Franco's regime these groups were characterized by the declarations of leaders whose real electoral weight was unknown. Among these, for example, Enrique Tierno Galván was first a European and then became more and more anti–American. When it came to the elections he took a small fraction of the vote and later moved into González's much more successful PSOE, which is moderate and prowestern.

The Spanish left also carries with it the weight of its country's history. Thus for example it feels the colonial commitments which Spain still keeps up. However, the independence which has been guaranteed to the ex–Spanish Sahara has for the most part taken the sting out of the polemics and reduced Spain's African commitments. It is certainly true that the "Plazas de Soberania" (the two ports of Ceuta and Melilli, which are in Morocco), are still in existence, but even in this case the prevalent view seems to favor a bilateral Spanish–Moroccan agreement giving the two cities back to Rabat.

Another problem of a certain importance is that of the Canary Islands.

Africans consider these to be African territory. Both Algeria and the OAU call for their independence. Hence Spain's African policy, while facing less dramatic problems than in the past, still presents a general problem for foreign and alliance strategy. To some extent this problem is due to inter–African conflicts (for example, the conflict among Morocco, Algeria and the Polisario) which cannot be resolved from Madrid. In part it is due to Spain's uncertainty over her role in the Mediterranean and in the West. She has enjoyed in the past a degree of political isolation which has naturally led to an increase in the influence of "Third–Worldist" and "pro–Arab" schools of thought, which were strong even in the Franco period. Today the supporters of these ideas find it difficult to decide whether to align themselves with the radical or with the moderate Arabs and appear to contradict to some extent the pro–European line of the new leadership of the Spanish centrist and left–wing parties.

Present Spanish relations with the United States are highly complex, for predominantly ideological reasons, but they probably are not a real problem. On the contrary, Spain's Mediterranean line could create problems for its growing ties with Europe and the possibility of participating in foreign policy cooperation among the EEC member states, for example over recognition for Israel.

The problem of Gibraltar and that of American bases on Spanish territory is still probably the biggest bone of contention between Spain and the West. But here, too, the differences between center and left do not seem to be very important. As a matter of fact all the Spanish parties claim sovereignty over the Rock of Gibraltar, but they do not seem to be inclined to bring on an international crisis in order to get it. As far as the American bases are concerned, they do not seem to be in any great danger. The center has called for bringing Spain into NATO. The bases would then be absorbed into NATO's multinational arrangements. The Communists and the Socialists, on the other hand, would like to avoid joining NATO. They are against the hegemony of the two blocs over the European system, but they also favor freezing the present situation. That would mean extending the treaty with the United States (which expires in 1981), although in principle the two parties continue to oppose foreign bases on Spanish soil. The Socialists, who by now have 30 percent of the votes, seem also to oppose joining NATO, although some of them favor a possible "European agreement" on defense. Thus the problem of alliance membership is posed extremely ambigously. The Socialists seem favorably disposed toward continuing the present set–up, that is, an agreement with the US for a fixed period of time; nonetheless, they are influenced by pressures from their European allies. What is more, the debate ends up by involving broad questions of international politics such as whether Spanish membership in the alliance would complicate Yugoslavia's position.

Nonetheless, these hesitations are balanced by the positive view taken by the PSOE on European arms production. The arguments used are not dissimilar to those coming from sections of the PS in France and the PSI in Italy (technological development, maintenance of existing levels of employment, further European integration, and so on).

Taken as a whole, the Spanish left seems to be quite close to the French left in regard to opposition to the Americans and closer to the Italian left on European integration. This could influence the attitude of the Spanish government toward NATO. It is in the government's interest not to oppose the Socialists too forcefully on this issue. The government is equally interested in playing host in Madrid in 1980 to the new round of the Conference on Security and Cooperation in Europe (CSCE). For this reason, it might be pushed into looking for a sui generis solution for the NATO issue, which would be halfway between complete adhesion and refusal of integration.

There is, however, also the old problem of American nuclear warheads in Spain. According to the latest Spanish–American agreement, the warheads ought to be withdrawn by 1979. It is likely that this deadline will be met, in part because of the gradual change in the technical characteristics of the American strategic deterrent. But the problem could be posed once again in a more complicated fashion if there were a political evolution in Italy which forced the American government to withdraw its warheads there. It is very unlikely, however, that in such circumstances Spain could take the weapons without creating serious internal political problems.

The problem of the relationship between the political parties and armed forces in Spain is much more complex. In this case the Franco heritage and the possibility of the military's being used for internal political ends is the left's biggest worry. The tragic experience of the civil war has certainly not been forgotten. However, up till now this does not seem to have persuaded the left to push for a substantial change or a different type of institutional control over the armed forces. It seems, rather, that the left is trying to dilute such a risk by linking Spanish defense as far as possible to that of democratic Europe and by showing itself to be in favor of any possible form of integration between Spanish and European forces. This would certainly diminish Spain's independence from Europe (and from the West), but on the other hand it could guarantee the political neutrality of the Spanish military in internal political questions.

Conclusion

This analysis of left–wing positions with respect to defense and security problems seems to make clear several points:

1. The policies taken by the left in the three countries examined here are heavily influenced by the historical characteristics of the countries themselves. This often brings about an accentuation of a "perception of threat" which differs from traditional NATO and Atlantic Alliance perceptions. This is not peculiar to the left, for it is also present to a certain extent in the center and the right.

2. Not one left-wing party in these three countries seriously wants to rock the boat. In different ways and with different formulae they all seem to be rather in favor of maintaining the status quo.

3. The main road to integration for the left in the West, and this also applies to the field of the national security, seems to be not so much the Atlantic Alliance, even though in practice nobody fights it, as the European Community and the prospect of European integration.

4. The real threat to the prospect of integration does not come from forces which are tied to the Soviet Union so much as *nationalist* forces in the most traditional sense of the word. The latter are also willing to arrive at compromises acceptable to the United States, the alliance, and even NATO; but they intend to go ahead only insofar as these are *temporary* and *tactical*. They therefore operate effectively *against* the prospect of western integration.

5. None of the left-wing parties in these countries seems to have a clear, complete, and coherent picture of the security policy and commitments of its country, let alone its future prospects.

6. None of these parties has worked out a contingency plan to deal with a serious military crisis. They all prefer to hope that such an event will not happen. However, this does not mean in any way that they will react negatively if the situation should present itself. As a general rule, all the parties have a strong tradition of fighting for national independence. It is therefore likely that in the case of a *direct* attack on their country, and probably an attack on the other European countries, they would react positively by gathering around NATO. What is more difficult to predict is how they would react in the face of an *indirect* crisis which might come from a more ambiguous route or from outside allied territory. In these cases the position taken by the other European countries and by the United States would probably be decisive. This was the case in the Middle East crisis in 1973. The left kept up a critical attitude toward Israel (and as a consequence also toward the United States) which was not substantially different from that of their governments.

The attitude taken by the left with respect to defense and security problems seems to be strongly influenced by outside events, be they initiatives of the government or of allies. There is no reason to believe that this attitude will be changed easily.

If this is true, then the greatest part of the problem, as far as Spain, France, and Italy are concerned, consists in working out with the present governments what degree and what type of integration these countries should have in the alliance, NATO, or the Common Market.

We are dealing with a problem which is also important for American policy. There are strong nationalist forces within all of these countries which at any given moment can seem to be more or less in favor of improving the relationship with the United States, for tactical reasons. In times of crisis and if there is no integrated security system which works, then nationalist forces can seem to be the lesser evil. This is especially true if such forces seem to be anti–Communist or anti–Soviet.

This type of policy has its weak point, however, in its fragility and in the rapidity with which it can disintegrate. The nationalist evolution in Italy, France, and Spain cannot but accentuate the *centrifugal* peculiarities of these three countries with respect to the West and accentuate the differences in the perception of threat which we mentioned at the beginning of this chapter. The same type of evolution for the left, if it became deprived of its European referent, could not but send it once again in the direction of formulae which would be pacifist, neutralist, Third Worldist, or even tend once again toward linking up with the eastern bloc. Since it is by now clear that the left is going to play an important role in the future of these countries, it should be apparent what the stakes are in avoiding such a turn of events.

On the other hand, the development of the "European" outlook is not only linked to the good will and the cooperation of the other partners (and in the first place the Federal Republic of Germany) but also to a gradual change in the relationship between Europe and the United States within the alliance.

We can therefore postulate the possibility of a conflict between the prospect of greater stability in the long term and the defense of particular interests in the short term. It is upon the solution of such a conflict that will depend the kind of influence that the Socialist and Communist left will have, in the final analysis, over the future of security in this part of Europe.

Notes

1. P. Quaroni, "Le Trattative per la Pace," in *La Costituzione e la Democrazia Italiana* (Florence, 1969), vol. I, pp. 733–734.
2. G. Andreotti, leading article in *La Discussione* II (November 1967).
3. Riccardo Lombardi, "Una scelta internazionale," *L'Astrolabia* 38 (September 1967).
4. A. Occhetto, "Attualità di Yalta," *Rinascita,* August 25, 1967.

5. A. Garosci, "L'Italia e il Patto Atlantico," in M. Bonanni, ed., *La Politica Estera della Repubblica Italiana* (Milano, 1967) vol. II, pp. 545-560.

6. R. La Valle, "Bomba N e destino dell'uomo," *l'Unità,* July 31, 1977.

7. F. Calamandrei, "Sulle obiezioni alla campagna contro la bomba N," *l'Unità,* September 7, 1977.

8. F. Accame, "Come si difende la democrazia di un popolo," *Avanti!,* August 13-14, 1978.

9. A. Baracetti, "Un no fermo all'esercito di mestiere," *l'Unità,* May 12, 1978.

10. Paper presented by the Political Commission on *The European Cooperation in the Armament Supply Sector,* by Egon Klepsch, European Parliament, doc. 83/78, Strasbourg, May 8, 1978.

11. J. Marrane, *L'Armée de la France democratique* (Paris, 1977).

12. J. Kanapa, "La défense nationale, action pour l'indépendence, la Paix," report to the CC of the PCF, Paris, 1977.

13. Prof. Stanley Hoffman, discussing this paper during a conference in Bologna, September 1978, said that there are really four PS voices on defense: (1) "the ultra-Gaullist": independence, neutralism, and nuclear defense; (2) "the new Europeanist": a European nuclear force with France as the nucleus; (3) "the orthodox": a greater French conventional contribution to European defense in NATO; (4) "the pacifist": everyone should disarm and blocs should be ended. The final position taken by the PS will be the result of a mixture of these four.

14. K. Evin, "Une bombe à la carte," *Le Nouvel Observateur,* November 28, 1977; and "La Convention Nationale du PS sur la Défense," *Le Monde,* January 10, 1978.

15. F. Mitterrand, "Une stratégie pour le désarmement," *Le Monde,* part I, December 14, 1977; part II, December 15, 1977.

16. J. Marceau, "Pour une défense populaire," *Le Monde,* December 8, 1977.

17. F. Mitterrand, "Une Strategie...."

7 Democratic Socialists, Eurocommunists, and the West

Heinz Timmermann

The Western European Left: The Beginnings of a Transnational Dialogue?

In recent years, a number of factors have given rise to increased cooperation at the Western European level, and particularly at the European Community (EC) level, between parties of the same or similar basic orientation.

In 1976, the parties of Conservative and Christian character united at EC level to form the "European People's party." Some of its more right-of-center constituents, in particular the parties of the Christian Union in West Germany, the British Conservatives, and the French Gaullists, have also been at pains to supplement this exclusive circle by constituting a Western Europe-wide "European Democratic Union." The Liberal parties, for their part, joined in forming the "Federation of European Liberal Democrats" in 1976. And the Social Democratic and Socialist parties can look back on a long tradition of transnational cooperation in the Socialist International. As early as 1957, they formed a "Liaison Bureau of the Socialist Parties of the Member States of the European Communities"; in 1974 they resolved to adopt the title "Confederation of Socialist Parties of the EC." In so doing they created, even at this early stage, an instrument whereby they could coordinate their actions and evolve joint conceptions at the level of the European Community.

Only the Western European Communists have refrained to date from creating a Western European regional center of coordination, basically for two reasons: on the one hand, their bitter experiences during the Comintern and Cominform periods, during which the CPSU set the line in practice despite the theoretical equality of the member parties, have made them skeptical toward coordination and decision-making centers in any form. On the other hand, it is questionable whether, in the light of the fundamental differences in their respective conceptions, they would be in any position at all to agree even on the most basic common program. Even the Communist party group in the European Parliament in Strasbourg, which is made up essentially of delegates from the Communist parties of Italy (PCI) and France (PCF), is unable, because of fundamental differences of principle on central questions—among them problems of Western European integration—to agree on any common denominator.

There are various reasons for this rapid intensification in transnational cooperation among the non–Communist parties of Western Europe. Without doubt, one of the most essential reasons is the fact that, since it entered into the phase of "positive" integration in the early 1970s, the EC has come to be regarded as the framework within which many questions of general political importance are discussed and resolved. Here the non–Communist parties' main aim is to coordinate their approaches in the light of the direct elections to the European Parliament, which were held for the first time in June 1979, and for each group of parties to find its own common line for its dealings with its political opponents.

From the point of view of the Social Democrats and Socialists (the "Democratic Socialists"[1]), who have always regarded international solidarity as an integral aspect of their operations, the European level has come to be particularly important. This is due in part to the widely shared desire to develop an autonomous European line on important international questions. Furthermore, Western European integration, which at times revealed pronounced tendencies toward the setting up of a "Europe of banks and businesses" (Willy Brandt, 1973) rather than of a Europe of the workers, affords, in the opinion of the Democratic Socialists, numerous hitherto unexploited opportunities for improving the situation of the workers. The internationalization of production and the growth of supranational institutions provide the material basis for augmenting the international solidarity and cooperation of the labor force as organized in the trade unions and political parties and for increasing and consolidating its influence in organizational and institutional terms.

At the same time, the Democratic Socialists are widely agreed that *all* relevant political forces must join together in building up Western Europe—including those referred to as the "Eurocommunists" (that is, the Communist parties of Italy, France, and Spain). In many cases, this line of thought goes even further. It is true that Democratic Socialists have—in the words of (West German) SPD official Horst Ehmke—"reason enough to be cautious and skeptical in their approach to Eurocommunism, because of their experience with the Communists." However, neither should they "reject out of hand the possibility that the historical rift in the labor movement in Western Europe may one day be healed."[2]

The present study can give only tentative, contradictory, and often hypothetical answers about relations between the Democratic Socialists and the Eurocommunists and their prospects for the future. The process of dialogue has as yet hardly proceeded past its initial stage. It must, however, be borne in mind that conditions *within* these parties also differ widely from country to country and from party to party, so the desire for closer transnational contacts between the two groupings, clearly discernible here and there, comes up against a number of reservations.

Nevertheless, recent years have seen a series of bilateral contacts between Democratic Socialist parties and Eurocommunist parties, even across national boundaries. In many fields, one of them policy on Western Europe, there are even signs of a certain convergence *on specific questions.* The aim of the present study is to cast light on these tendencies, for example, by examining the Eurocommunists' attitudes on the traditional values of the Western European democracies and by analyzing the attitudes of both sides concerning the unification of Western Europe and to foreign relations (NATO, United States, Eastern Europe). It then attempts to summarize these analyses and to formulate a few theses on prospects for future development.

The Left after 1945

The Third Road Concept and Its Collapse

In the wake of the Second World War, the left exercised considerable influence upon state and society in many countries of Western Europe. Not only was it represented in the national governments, in most cases in coalition with parties of the bourgeois center—but it was also firmly established in society by way of its close connections with the unified trades unions. The Social-Democratic/Socialist wing of the Western European labor movement, and possibly also *some* sections of the Communist parties (cf. the "own road to Socialism" concept), were at that time searching for new alternatives to capitalism and Soviet socialism. In the wake of the world economic crisis of 1929 and fascism in Germany, capitalism appeared to have been discredited for all time, and Soviet socialism did not appear to be a model to be imitated, at least not to the Social Democrats and Socialists. In the final analysis, these prevailing concepts, reflected in a number of constitutions (for example, in the constitutions of Italy and France and those of several Federal *Länder* in West Germany), boiled down to a "third road" somewhere between capitalism and Soviet socialism. In these concepts, *political* democracy, which had been won back by great sacrifice in the war against fascism, was to be consolidated and supplemented by *economic* democracy (nationalization of the key sectors of productive and commercial capital, extension of workers' rights of participation in management). On the one hand, so ran the reasoning, private economic power must be prevented from ever again being translated into political power; on the other the state had to be given the means of dismantling traditional privileges and of better fulfilling its social duties by means of democratically coordinated and controlled economic planning.

The Social Democrats and Socialists saw the *foreign policy* counterpart to this domestic policy orientation, with its emphasis on the welfare state and "democratic socialism," in a concept which envisioned that Western Europe (including Great Britain) would acquire an identity of its own, a democratic-socialist "Third Force" between the two superpowers, the United States and the USSR.

However, with the outbreak of the cold war, hopes of a "Third Road" between capitalism and Soviet socialism had to be buried after only a few years of life. The suppression of Social Democracy which went hand in hand with Moscow's bringing into line of Eastern Europe; the Soviet attempts to prevent the democratic reconstruction of Western Europe under the Marshall Plan; the revived total orientation of the Western European Communists toward the Moscow line via the Soviet-controlled Cominform bureau—all these were factors which compelled the Democratic Socialists to amend their concept: "They were able to assert their independence and their changes for the future not as a third force but only as the left wing of a Western counter-front under the leadership of the United States."[3]

After a more or less prolonged phase of hesitation and opposition—for which, at times, the most varied of motives were responsible—the Social Democrats and Socialists of what became the six-member Community decided to participate actively in the economic and political integration of Western Europe, which up to then had been promoted by the Conservative-Liberal forces in those countries in close consultation with the United States. The first to play an active part were the Socialists of France and the Benelux countries. They were followed by the German Social Democrats, whose main reason for holding back had been the irreconcilability of integration in a European Community and the reunification of Germany. Later, after the dissolution of their unity of action with the Communists, the Italian Socialists also began to follow this line.

All links with the Communists were severed. From this point onward, the Communists were once again looked upon as Russian parties with which it was not only not possible to defend democracy, much less build up a democratic Europe, but which were likely to smother any party foolish enough to have dealings with them. "Anybody who did not wish to see the Prague coup d'état of February 1948 repeated in Western Europe now had to face up to the Communists as enemies of liberty."[4]

Factors of Change

This systematic observation of a demarcation line between Social Democracy and the Communists, which had its counterpart in the Communists' view of the Social Democrats as pillars of the bourgeois-capitalist restoration, was relaxed at a national level in some cases as early as in the early

1960s. A process gradually got under way which eventually led to dialogue and informational contacts between Democratic Socialists and Eurocommunists across national boundaries. What are the factors which induced this change and in what context is the change to be seen?

Without any doubt, fundamental importance must be attributed to the crisis in the international Communist movement, in the wake of which a number of parties were able to disentangle themselves from Moscow's politico-ideological embrace and to develop their own policies. In the case of the PCI, for example, the party's present approaches can be traced back as far as 1956, the year in which the party leadership took advantage of the de-Stalinization process under Khrushchev to evolve the ideological and political foundations for its "Italian road to Socialism." In its "elements for a program declaration," dating from 1956 but from which the party continues to quote even today, the PCI, referring to the progressive obligations imposed by the Constitution, advocated a strategy of far-reaching structural reforms. The essence of this strategy was to transform the democratically and pluralistically constituted bourgeois state gradually, by way of consensus and without disrupting the continuity of the Constitution or demolishing the state apparatus, into a Socialist one.

In the case of the Communist party of Spain (PCE), it was the shock induced by the intervention of the five Warsaw Pact powers in Czechoslovakia in August 1968 which, more than anything else, motivated the party to take a critical look at the theory and practice of Soviet socialism and to start to "think with its own head" (Carrillo). The PCE no longer measures the internationalism of any party by its attitude to the Soviet Union but rather "principally by its ability to carry out the revolution in its own country."[5]

In the case of the PCF, finally, it was the preferential relations of the Soviet Union to Gaullist France which were instrumental in the party's emancipation from the CPSU: the French Communists were bound to gain the impression that Moscow gave greater priority to stabilizing its relations with a bourgeois regime than to the legitimate interests of a sister party in bringing about far-reaching social change. The conclusion drawn by the PCF was that it should work toward socialism "in French colors"—a socialism, naturally, which, in contrast to the concepts of the Italian and Spanish Communists, is of a more pronounced national character and which—as will be shown—does not accept for its purposes some of the essential elements of the "philosophy" of the western community.

This rethinking process on the part of the Eurocommunists, sparked off by the crisis within the Communist movement, was intensified by the consequences of the policy of détente. Furthermore, the policy of détente went a long way toward scaling down domestic political polarization in Italy, France, and, eventually, also in Spain and toward rehabilitating the

Eurocommunist parties as national forces in the eyes of broad sections of the population—a development which, by the same token, induced the Eurocommunists to rethink their traditional positions and to relate more closely to the conditions and traditions of their national and Western European regional milieus.

Finally, this adaptation process among the ranks of the Eurocommunists was accelerated by the fact that—particularly in the countries of Southern Europe—the Socialists themselves were undergoing profound change. For against the background of the general economic recession, coupled with high inflation, mass unemployment, and severe shortages in infrastructure (housing construction, transportation, education, and so on), the Socialists of Southern Europe had been calling since the late 1960s for drastic reforms in the economic structure of their countries, accompanied by large-scale worker participation in management, whether these reforms take the form of more pronounced economic planning for society (PSI, PSOE) or of the expansion of the nationalized sector of the economy (PSF). The Social Democrats in Northern and Central Europe, too, intend to pay more attention than they have done in the past to augmenting political with social democracy. This, however, is where similarities emerge between Democratic Socialists and Eurocommunists, ones which have given rise in Italy to the formulation of the PSI's long-range program for a Socialist-Communist "alternative of the left" and in France even to the elaboration of a "Common Program." For a short time in 1975–76 it even looked as though a specific southern axis of Latin European Socialism might emerge with the prospect of close cooperation between the Socialists and Eurocommunists of this region and with the aim of building a "Mediterranean Socialism."

Finally, the Democratic Socialists and the Eurocommunists were equally concerned with concrete problems which were already emerging as a result of the integration process itself. Thus, for example, the multinational corporations had gained an organizational lead, and not only over the labor movement as organized in the trades unions and political parties. They were also in a position of strength in their dealings with individual countries—by virtue of their ability to exercise considerable influence on the economic and social policies of those countries by transferring production, redirecting flows of capital, and so on as part of their own investment policy.

Under these circumstances, the policy of Western European unification took on a new dimension for the Italian and Spanish Communists, especially since, in the 1960s, first the PCI and later the PCE also had come to regard the internationalization of production as an irreversible and fundamentally positive process. In their opinion, the EC could, if the powers of its institutions were extended and their democratic legitimation emphasized, exert greater influence on economic processes in Europe, for example by enforcing stricter controls on the labor organization of the multinational corporations and by determining the location, nature, and size of their investments. This reasoning has numerous points of contact with the concepts held by Social Democratic and Socialist parties.

From Confrontation to Dialogue: The Pattern of Relations within the Western European Left

Clear as it is that it was external factors which triggered and/or accelerated processes of change within the Western European left, so it is also clear that the reverse is now happening, that this left is on the point of exercising greater influence in the shaping of its environment, and particularly that of Western Europe.

The Achievement of Trade Union Unity under ETUC Auspices

In this context, certain processes at the trade-union level merit special attention. True, pronounced ideological, political, and organizational differences remain. In recent years, however, the formation of multinationally organized capital on an increasingly large scale has heightened in the majority of trade unions the awareness of the need for action and organic unity at all levels, especially the more it became evident that without it the rights and opportunities for influence which the trade unions had struggled so hard to achieve, such as the right to strike, worker participation, and so on, were in danger of being undermined and effectively whittled away.

Since the early 1970s, trade unions have, irrespective of their political orientation, started to regard their historical differences not as an impediment but as an opportunity to present a united front to the latest challenges in accordance with the national background conditions of each. On the basis of the experience gained at the level of corporation-wide trade-union committees, as a basis organization, and as a follow-up to the transnational organizations of the occupational secretariats (metalworking, chemicals, foodstuffs, and so on), the trade unions joined in 1973 to form the European Trade Union Confederation (ETUC) with the aim of formulating global sociopolitical and social demands on behalf of the working population and of exerting pressure on the national governments and the organs of the EC in support of these demands. Thus in 1974 the ETUC forwarded to the EC Commission a list of proposals for effective control of multinational corporations. In April 1978 it even organized the first Western Europe-wide token strike as a protest against the high unemployment rate (about 6 mil-

lion throughout the EC as of mid-1978) and to induce the national governments to take vigorous countermeasures.

Since July 1974, Italy's Communist-Socialist CGIL has been a full
active member of the ETUC, having decided to relax its ties to the Moscow-
controlled World Federation of Trade Unions (WFTU) in order to be able
to work in the region in which it has its roots and in which it is faced with
problems and challenges similar to those of the other EC trade unions. In
March 1978, the CGIL canceled its associate membership and officially left
the WFTU. Similarly, the CGT, a union with close connection to the PCF,
voiced criticism on questions of principle prior to and during the April 1978
WFTU Congress in Prague, particularly with reference to the lack of political and social (right-to-strike) freedoms in Eastern Europe.

The Left-Wing Parties

It is important to distinguish among three dimensions in which the mutual
relations of the Western European left are carried on: relations among the
Communists, relations among the Democratic Socialists, and relations
among the two categories (or between parts thereof).

The Western European Communists: Widening Divergencies. As far as the
Western European *Communists* are concerned, the differences among them
have become so pronounced that similarities do not go beyond extremely
vaguely worded general declarations such as were last formulated at their
Brussels Conference of January-February 1974. A number of common
viewpoints did emerge at the bilateral meetings of the PCI/PCE (July 1975)
and the PCI/PCF (November 1975) and at the March 1977 Eurocommunist
Summit Conference in Madrid. It was agreed that political democracy is to
be attributed fundamental importance in Socialist society and the necessity
of the complete independence of each and every Communist party was also
emphasized.

In central questions, however, such as those of relations with the bourgeois state and its institutions, the economy, the strategy to be employed in
changing society, policy toward alliances and attitudes toward the EC,
NATO, and the United States, concepts were so divergent that the Italian
and Spanish Communists appeared to be nearer to the Latin European
Socialists in many respects than to the French *Communists* (or, of course,
to the Western European Communist parties loyal to Moscow).

The Western European Democratic Socialists: Unity in Diversity. By way
of contrast, the Socialist International and the Social Democratic and
Socialist parties of Western Europe which dominate it have moved in the

other direction. After a long phase of relative stagnation and insignificance in their multilateral cooperation, 1974–75 saw the beginning of a development in the wake of which the Democratic Socialist movement in Western Europe displayed new dynamism. At the same time, however, the movement appeared to divide into two separate tendencies: one of Social Democratic character in Northern and Central Europe, followed by the German, Austrian, and Scandinavian Social Democrats and the British Labour party and another of Socialist character in Southern Europe, followed by the French, Spanish, Portuguese, Italian, and Greek (PASOK) Socialists. While the "Social Democrats" accused the adherents of the "Socialist" course, and Francois Mitterrand's Socialist party (PSF) in particular, of what they considered to be too wide an opening toward the Communists, the latter polemicized against "Social Democrats" who, in their eyes, were content merely to manage the capitalist crisis and to modernize the existing system.

In the end, Mitterrand took the initiative and embarked upon the formation of an informal southern axis among the Socialists. At two meetings, in May 1975 at Mitterrand's country seat in Latche (South of France) and in January 1976 in Paris, the French, Belgian, Spanish, Portuguese, Italian, and Greek Socialists exchanged experiences and resolved to cooperate more closely in the future.

However, it became clear even at the Paris meeting that, with the exception of the PASOK, nobody was seriously interested in the formation of a clearly defined axis among the Socialists of the South. The Spanish Socialist Workers' party (PSOE) and the Portuguese Socialist party (PSP), in particular, came out against such a prospect, the more so since their attitude to the related question of cooperation with the Communists in their respective countries, by contrast with that of the French and Italian Socialists, is also negative.

PSF executive Claude Estier, a close confidant of Mitterrand, thereupon pointed out that the Paris Conference had neither been intended to "work out a joint strategy for the various Socialist Parties" nor to "create a new organization in order to consolidate them within or outside of the Socialist International."[6] Mitterrand might, furthermore, have achieved his *tactical* objective, that of persuading the "Social Democratic" tendency, particularly the West German SPD, to accept a formula which would leave every member party of the SI free to decide upon its policy on entering alliances on the basis of its own national conditions. In actual fact, the principle of "Unity in Diversity" prevailed among the European Social Democrats and Socialists in 1976, a principle which no longer denies the national and regional differences between the various parties but makes precisely these differences the prerequisite for the cooperation to which they aspire. For "every Socialist (Social Democratic) Party has its own identity, but all

together are prepared to cooperate and in a position to realize this cooperation."[7]

The situation in Europe, SPD politician Karsten Voigt had written as
early as in 1975, compels Social Democrats in different countries

> to go along different roads in order to reach the same or similar destina-
> tions. The pursuit of goals which may well be identical in the long term or
> of orientations on the basis of the same basic values and fundamental prin-
> ciples of Democratic Socialism calls for a practice which is not identical but
> which differs, which is mutually complementary and promotive, in various
> Western European states. Anybody who accuses other parties of following
> an aberrant social practice, foreign and security policy or policy of parlia-
> mentary alliance, or short- or medium-term program formulations,
> although these are necessitated by dissimilar national circumstances and
> traditions or by specific relationships of parliamentary or social forces, has
> not yet understood the principle of "unity in diversity" as the politico-
> organizational principle and objective of international Democratic Social-
> ism.[8]

That this principle now enjoys general recognition and observation in practice was due to no mean extent to the approach of the direct elections to the
European Parliament, which made the problem of concerted action more
and more urgent, at least for the member parties of the "Confederation of
Socialist Parties of the EC." Against this background, the fact that the SPD
and PSF, the two most important Democratic Socialist parties of Western
Europe, were able to improve their mutual relations was of decisive importance. They have met at irregular intervals in bilateral working parties
(economy and society, European Community, Third World) to consolidate
their mutual understanding. In June 1977 the eleven member parties of the
"Confederation" even succeeded, after difficult negotiations, in preparing
a detailed draft for a joint electoral platform for the European Parliament
election, which had as its main themes "Democracy and Institutions,"
"Economic and Social Policy," and "Foreign Policy."[9]

Moreover, the important special interests on the part of individual parties, different as they were in each case, converged in the desire for closer
cooperation among Democratic Socialists. In the case of the SPD, for
example, a governing party in a country heavily dependent upon economic
and political cooperation in Western Europe, this special interest was the
intention not to allow any gap between itself and the countries of Latin
Europe, in whose politics Socialists are already playing a decisive part (Portugal, Italy) or may in the future (France, Spain). With Western Europe
constantly growing closer together, the Democratic Socialists also had to be
interested in seeing the Socialists grow in strength and in intensifying their
relations with them.

For their part, the Socialists of Southern Europe hoped for twofold support from the SPD. On the one hand, they expected support from the most influential party of the SI in their national competition with other parties, including the Communists. On many occasions the SPD has granted such support, in conjunction with other parties, whether in the form of material aid (for example, the aid granted to the Portuguese and Spanish Socialists via the Friedrich Ebert Foundation, which has close ties to the SPD[10]) or in the form of political solidarity (cf. the committee formed by Brandt, Mitterrand, and Palme in support of Mario Soares in 1975 or their attendance at the PSOE Congress of December 1976). Furthermore, the Latin European Socialists count on the ability of the SPD to exert its influence in the West German government and in multilateral organizations such as the European Community in order to help Socialist-led governments out of economic difficulties (Portugal) or to give the Socialists economic and—for example, vis-à-vis the United States—a certain degree of political cover on their flanks in the event that they should assume power (France, Spain).

Information Contacts between Democratic Socialists and Eurocommunists. As unequivocally as the Democratic Socialists of Western Europe give priority to their mutual relations over their contacts with parties of different politico-ideological orientation, they also make clear just as unmistakably that they are not prepared to forgo at least informational contacts with Eurocommunist parties. Here, however, the attitudes of the various Democratic Socialist parties vary greatly, both as regards their view of the Eurocommunists and with respect to the nature and extent of the contacts which have taken place.

The most cautious party in this respect has been the SPD, a fact to which that party's adverse experience in its dealings with the East German Communists no doubt made a decisive contribution: the suppression of the Social Democrats in what was at the time the Soviet Zone of Occupation (and in Eastern Europe in general), the trauma of national division, for which the Communists are generally considered to be responsible by West German public opinion, and finally the continued strained and conflict-ridden relations between West and East Germany, even after the signature of a body of treaties on the basis of Ostpolitik.

Nevertheless, in early 1977, having engaged in talks with prominent representatives of the PCI before the SPD-FDP Ostpolitik, the SPD also started to relax its position of not engaging in informational contacts with the Eurocommunists, and to warm up particularly toward the PCI. The SPD was following attentively the course of development in the Communist parties of the member countries of the EC, as a resolution on policy toward Europe passed by the SPD Party Congress in Hamburg in November 1977 stated. The resolution continued:

> Important European Communist parties have started to dissociate them-
> selves in some ways from the ideology of the Communist countries of East-
> ern Europe and from the constitutional practice of those countries. This is
> particularly true with respect to the questions of the dictatorship of the
> proletariat, of commitments to national constitutions, and of whether or
> not the multi-party system should be respected.... The process of adapta-
> tion to the changing conditions of European society on the part of the
> Communist parties must be considered seriously and discriminatingly. The
> outcome of this development is at present wide open.[11]

In contrast, the positions not only of the Southern European Socialists but
also of the Social Democrats of Scandinavia, Great Britain, and the Benelux
countries are much more open. Since 1977 all of them have established official party contacts with the Italian (and some of them with the French) Communists. According to the joint communiqués, these contacts involved not
only clarifications of the domestic situations in their respective countries
but also, and above all, discussions on possible procedures for surmounting
the economic crisis, on the integration of the EC, and on problems of
détente and of relations to the Third World.

These efforts by the PCI to develop better relations with the Social
Democrats of Central and Northern Europe have been to a considerable
extent a deliberate PCI attempt to court the confidence of parties or those
of the governments which they lead or influence, on whose solidarity or
benevolent neutrality, the PCI may very soon have to depend if, as it hopes,
it continues to make progress toward assuming government responsibility.
Similar considerations, indeed, have induced the Latin European Socialists
to seek contacts with the West German SPD.

This does not imply, however, that those Democratic Socialist parties
which have established formal relations with Eurocommunists aim for
transnational alliances or parliamentary ties with them. Their relations, like
those of the SPD, hardly amount to more than informational contacts; and
insofar as there are any farther-reaching forms of agreement at the national
level (France, Spain, Italy), the relationship is rather one of "loyal competition in pluralism"[12] or even one of *inherent conflict* in which one of the
aims of the Socialists is to accelerate the evolution of the Eurocommunists
and to change the balance of power among the parties of the Left in their
own favor. The French Socialists in particular and recently the Italian and
Spanish Socialists have stressed this again and again.

Democratic Socialist reservations in principle with respect to the Eurocommunists persist. On the one hand, their insistence on "democratic centralism"—a principle which it is difficult to reconcile with the acceptance of
pluralism and political democracy for state and society—gives cause for
misgivings. The Eurocommunists' still extremely solicitous attitude toward
the Soviet Union and their support of Soviet foreign policy also keep alive
the skepticism of the Democratic Socialists.

These are problems which it behooves the Eurocommunists themselves to settle. It was with this in mind that the Democratic Socialists, at the levels of the SI and the EC, eventually reduced their position to a common denominator. Chairman Willy Brandt, speaking on behalf of the SI, said that as far as he was concerned it was not yet possible to determine where the transition on the part of the Eurocommunists was attributable to "tactics in the interest of power and where to developments born of recognition." It must be taken seriously that the representatives of these parties wanted to remain Communists. However, it must also be appreciated that "some of them appear to be willing to enter upon the venture of democracy."[13]

As far as the European Parliament is concerned, the Democratic Socialists will not, to use Ehmke's words, "form any parliamentary association with Communists." At the same time, however, they would not permit any situation which would "isolate certain political groups a priori and thus exclude them in practice from the construction of a democratic and Socialist Europe. . . . The basic consensus on the construction and on the unification of Europe must incorporate *all* relevant political forces which are qualified and prepared to participate, including Eurocommunist parties." Thus, Ehmke concluded, "the European Parliament could indeed become a place of meeting, of discussion, and of a new, wider European consensus."[14]

Stances of the Left-Wing Parties on Western Europe: Convergences and Divergences

Political Democracy and Gradual Social Change

The incipient discussion among the left-wing parties in Western Europe focuses around the reappraisal of political democracy on the part of the Eurocommunists and around the question as to whether the latter regard social change as a gradual process of stage-by-stage reforms or whether they intend to bring about this change by means of a radical break with the existing system. In the years following the First World War, one of the reasons for the disintegration of the labor movement was the diversity of attitudes toward political democracy and its basic rights and freedoms and toward the problem of social transformation.

It would go beyond the bounds of the present study if we were to analyze these two aspects in greater detail. It is, however, the author's opinion that the Eurocommunists' answer to the question as to which attitude they assume on this point in theory and in practice is of supreme importance in order to be able to assess the substance of their "turn toward Europe" and also to detect any convergences with the Democratic Socialists. For the

Democratic Socialists have always defended political democracy as an indispensable element of their conception of socialism and are of the opinion that the changes which are necessary with a view to increasing economic democracy can only be brought about step by step and not by a radical break with the capitalist system.

In both these points there are pronounced differences between the French Communists on the one hand and the Italian and Spanish Communists on the other. With its retreat into its politico–ideological "bunker" (Althusser) which became evident in 1977–78 in its polemics against the Socialists, the PCF isolated itself, for all practical purposes, within the left wing of Western Europe and once more assumed traits, at both national and international level, of an "antisociety" which had been considered to have been for the most part superseded. As long as it maintains its present strategy of consummating an irreversible break with the existing system and of assuming the leading role in this process, the PCF can be disregarded as far as a common approach toward a Democratic Socialist Western Europe is concerned.

The Italian Communists (and, to a certain degree, the Spanish Communists, also), on the other hand, have in the meantime, as PCI official Napolitano emphasized, unequivocally opted for a "choice of camp [*scelta di campo*] in favor of Western-style democracy" by advocating "the continued development and the preservation of the liberal and democratic traditions of the Old Continent"—traditions "which may be counted among the best that Europe has brought forth."[15] According to their analysis, the state must no longer be looked upon merely as the agent of the big bourgeoisie but rather as reflecting the balance of forces in society. In the case of the Italian Communists, this analysis of the state has given rise to a transformational strategy of a gradualist nature, that is, they are pursuing the step–by–step transformation of society by means of a multitude of far-reaching reforms in the economic, social, and institutional sectors (for example, by supplementing representative democracy with various forms of citizen participation in neighborhood councils, the business sector, education, and so on).

The Issue of Western European Integration

Without any doubt, the Communists of Italy and Spain have already executed a credible "turn toward Europe" in many respects. This is true with regard to prospects for the political, economic, and social shaping of Western Europe just as much as to the potential for long–term cooperation to this end with the Democratic Socialist parties. A comparison of concepts between these Communists and the Democratic Socialists is facilitated with respect to a number of problems by the election platform[16] elaborated by the Democratic Socialists of the EC member countries for the elections to the European Parliament. Admittedly, it is important to point out in this context that the Labour party did not participate in the discussions on the draft for this platform and that the French Socialists retracted their initial approval for primarily tactical reasons (with an eye to competition from the PCF) in June 1978.

Nevertheless, despite all the differences between the Democratic Socialists, even on main themes (for example, with respect to the configuration of the economy or to the character of Western European integration and its institutional organization), the draft contains declarations which in the future could help form a *minimum consensus* among the Western European left. Seen in this light, the election platform is *technically* out of date; in its *substance,* however, it contains statements and concepts which constitute signposts for the future and thus lends itself for use as a criterion for our present purposes.

In this election platform, the Democratic Socialists of the member countries of the EC (accompanied by their Spanish and Portuguese sister parties) proceed from the basic assumption that individual countries are nowadays too small to be able to fulfill the tasks with which they are faced and that even this fact alone is sufficient to make the integration of Western Europe appear both essential and justified. In the preamble, these tasks are linked with the objective of "building a Europe in peace with more freedom, justice and solidarity." The authors of the draft attach particular importance to the "transformation of the economic and social structures," for "up to now the Europe of commodities has been too much in the foreground and the Europe of the worker, of political views, of civil rights, of economic and social rights, and of democratic rights not enough." Of course, as the platform admits in its section on "Democracy and Institutions," "the vesting of European organs with new authorities. . .must not impede the implementation of a Socialist program at the national level." European integration must be carried out in such a way "that Europe can develop toward an independent democratic–socialist model of its own."[17]

Here, too, there are no signs of consensus with the PCF. The French Communists disapprove of integration absolutely, for two main reasons. First, they regard the EC as a capitalist bloc under the domination of Washington and Bonn which affords the labor movement no chance of a gradual Socialist transformation. Second, they have always been opposed to renunciation of national sovereignty in any form, a stance which reflects the basic current of public opinion in France of a pronounced aversion to integration. If in the Joint Program of June 1972 the PCF nevertheless agreed to "participate in the further extension of the EEC and its institutions," it must still be remembered that in so doing the party was referring only to the

economic interrelationships existing at that time and that Marchais emphasized in a speech, not published until 1975, before the Central Committee
that all concessions with respect to the EEC were essentially of a technical
nature only.[18] At any rate, the PCF did not agree to take part in the direct
elections to the European Parliament, of which it had originally disap-
proved, until the French government had given its assurance that it would
not support any move to vest any new powers in the European Parliament.

The Italian and Spanish Communists, on the other hand, accept the
position of the Democratic Socialists insofar as they declare that a democratic Socialist society can only be realized in a West European context and
that the West Europeans can only rise to the new economic and political
challenges by acting in unison and taking as their objective the extension of
the economic and monetary union to a political union with supranational
institutions and jurisdiction. In Italy the PCI was one of the political parties
which came out most strongly in favor of early direct elections to the European Parliament. Furthermore, it let it be known on a number of occasions
that it had no objections to Willy Brandt's proposal that the European Parliament should be considered, as it were, a "constituent" of a political
union.

The PCE, for its part, committed itself strongly to Spain's quest for
membership of the EC. Recently the party even suggested that "by means
of special ad hoc measures, the Spanish electorate should be given the
opportunity of taking part in the elections to the European Parliament next
year."[19]

As far as the further institutional expansion of the EC is concerned, the
Democratic Socialists are of the opinion that any powers lost to the national
parliaments should be transfered to the European Parliament. Furthermore, the competences of the Commission should be extended at the
expense of those of the Council to enable the former "to proceed in its own
right within the framework of the policy of the Community as jointly form-
mulated."[20] Here, too, there are convergences with the views of the PCI,
which in its 1976 electoral program advocated a "substantial extension" of
the competence of the European Parliament and which called in the European Parliament itself for the authority of the Commission to be
extended.[21] The PCE has not yet commented on these topics in such clear
terms.

In the opinion of the PCI, of course, all this must be accompanied by
an extension of the control and decision–making rights of the Economic
and Social Committee of the EC and by more pronounced institutional
incorporation of the trade unions into that committee. The wording of the
electoral platform of the Democratic Socialists reveals similar sentiments:
"The democratization of the Economic and Social Committee presupposes
more equitable representation of the workers and an expansion of its

powers. Half the members of the ESC must be representatives of the labor force.''[22]

Establishing where there are convergences and divergences in the field of economic policy is a more difficult task. Here, too, the French Communists stand on the sidelines. Parties which like the PCF look upon the crisis as largely home-made, and thus draw the conclusion that social transformations can be implemented most effectively by means of restructuring measures in the *national* sector and of economic protectionism and bilateralism, run the risk of isolating themselves at the national and international levels of the labor movement and of weakening the forces of reform.

In addition to the distinct attitude on these questions adopted by the PCF, there are other economic positions competing within the ranks of the Democratic Socialists and among the other Latin Communists. While the Social Democrats of Northern and Central Europe long concentrated on introducing their own national concepts, in most cases with a welfare-state bias, into the transnational discussion and, in the process, assigned to the Community the role of not much more than a social corrective, the Latin European Socialists, like the Italian Communists, were advocating radical, internationally coordinated intervention into the labor organization of multinationally organized capital, coupled with checks on the location, nature, and volume of its investment activities.

In the meantime, these contrasts have become much less sharp. The structurally inherent economic crisis throughout Western Europe, the consequences of which are revealed most distinctly by a relatively high unemployment rate, made the Democratic Socialists join together to think about new instruments for guiding the economy. The draft of the election platform contains the following statement on this point: "For Social Democrats, a policy of full employment means consciously playing a part in shaping inevitable economic change instead of merely reacting to adverse economic trends. This presupposes structural reforms and a forward-looking economic policy flexible enough to adapt itself to technical-economic changes. . . . The task of adapting available capacities to accommodate the requirements of society as a whole can only be fulfilled by using the instruments of a clearly defined and consciously molded policy of economic structure." Besides, planning and democratization "must not be restricted to the public sector alone." It is imperative "to improve the democratic control of the economy as a whole."

On the other hand, the election platform calls for "the creation of a communal instrument with the legal and technical facilities required for controlling the activity of large companies," for "representation of the workers in the decision-making bodies of the dominant companies," and the "obligation of the concerns to prepare and publish consolidated balance-sheets in accordance with uniform regulations and guidelines."

Finally, the Democratic Socialists intend to enlarge the European Regional Fund and to link it "effectively to social, industrial and agricultural policy." Here they are interested primarily in creating jobs in the structurally underdeveloped border and agricultural regions.

All these objectives are shared by the Italian and, insofar as they have made their position explicitly clear at all, by the Spanish Communists. It is particularly noteworthy that the PCI in its 1976 electoral program unequivocally rejected as a matter of principle "any attempt to cordon off Italy by economic policy and to return to protectionist and autarkic concepts." Instead, the PCI advocated "an 'open market' system, that is, as system of free competition at an international level" and a "harmonious development of economic and trade relations among the states of the European Economic Community and the establishment of a new system of world-wide economic cooperation."[25]

With respect to the multinational corporations, the PCI now proceeds on the assumption that these do have a part to play in the economic development of the various countries. Otherwise, there is no way to explain the fact that in November 1977 the leadership of the PCI, in conjunction with the CGIL, with which it has close connections, and together with the other significant Italian political and social forces, was at pains to convince the top managers of multinationals, most of them with parent companies whose headquarters are in the United States, of the expediency of long-term investment in Italy. Of course, there were two preconditions to be met: the multinationals must not lead Italy into a position of technological dependence or regard the country merely as a market for their mass-produced commodities. On the contrary, they must carry on research work in Italy and build production facilities with a high degree of technological sophistication and capable, particularly in the Mezzogiorno, of absorbing manpower on a large scale. Within this framework, they would have to be prepared to coordinate their investment plans with national economic planning on the basis of consultation with the competent political bodies and to agree to appropriate controls and supervision.[24]

It is precisely here that the PCI envisages important functions for the EC: its democratically legitimated organs could play an active part in monitoring international influences, such as the movement of multinationally organized productive and commercial capital, for compliance with the relevant recommendations of the OECD, the ETUC, and the UN commission concerned with this question, a task which is becoming more and more difficult to perform at the national levels. Furthermore, in the opinion of the PCI, the EC must be given more financial resources of its own in order to be able, particularly by way of better utilized and larger regional, social, and development funds, to pursue an active policy on economic structure and to overcome the economic and social disparities within the EC.

The European Community's Identity in Foreign Affairs
and Security Problems

Naturally, the attitude of the left-wing parties toward the integration of the EC goes a long way toward determining their position on the problem of the foreign-policy identity of the Community. Here too the policies of the PCF contrast sharply with those of the Democratic Socialists, the Italian Communists and, in some respects, the Spanish Communists.

The French CP. The French Communists continue to maintain that international politics is government by the mutual antagonism between two camps, which are irreconcilably opposed to one another: the American-led camp of the imperialists on the one hand and the Soviet-led camp of peace, progress, and socialism on the other. They thus identify themselves with the objectives of the Soviet policy of peaceful coexistence and détente, at least to the extent that they hold that any shift in the world balance of power in favor of "socialism" enhances conditions for consolidating détente and provides the Communists with the opportunity of taking the first step along the French road to socialism.

If we call to mind once again the PCF's aversion to any renunciation of national sovereignty, to any curtailment of national independence, then it is almost inevitable that the French Communists should reject outright any move toward evolving a foreign policy identity for the EC, just as they object to France's links with NATO. The fact that they ceased some time ago to *advocate* France's withdrawal from the alliance and are now content to *oppose* its effective reintegration into the NATO military organization is attributable to purely tactical motives. They even forced the Socialists to concede that France must be in a position to stand up to *any* aggressor, obviously a blow directed at unpopular partners in the EC and NATO.

The PCF resorted to similar arguments when it had second thoughts about its earlier opposition to France as a nuclear power and finally explicitly accepted the *force de frappe* in May 1977: the party leadership sees French nuclear capability as an instrument with which to defend national independence and sovereignty and thus to safeguard the French road to socialism, for example, against the Federal Republic of Germany if that country should attempt to misuse its increasing economic weight and its superiority in the conventional military sector as a means of bringing its political influence to bear in France. In the final analysis, the PCF appears to envisage for France a policy which reveals certain analogies to Yugoslavia: a neutralist policy designed to give a government of the left the opportunity of building socialism unhampered by external influences and of playing an active and independent role between East and West.

It would appear at first glance that the line followed by the Spanish left largely coincides with that of the PCF, at least as far as security policy is concerned, for both the PSOE and the PCE reject the idea of Spain's joining NATO. Furthermore, both advocate in principle the closing of the American military bases on Spanish soil (though these could remain in use pending the conclusion of an East–West agreement on the mutual reduction of troops and bases).

Nevertheless, both parties have clearly stated that they would come to terms with Spain's joining NATO if this were what the majority of the population desired. It is also significant that neither the PCE nor the PSOE (in contrast to the PCF) bases its foreign and security policy options on the assumption that any weakening of the West, any shift in the balance of power in favor of "socialism," is to be considered desirable: on the contrary, the PCE takes the view that it cannot be the job of Communists in the West "to increase the power of the military bloc in the East."[25] Most importantly, however, both Socialists and Communists are firmly committed to seeing Spain join the EC with the aim of actively supporting the development of the Community into a political union. The attack against Carrillo in Moscow's *New Times* was primarily directed against precisely this aspect of the PCE's line. This only goes to show that the Spanish Communists' policy on Western Europe is being taken seriously by the CPSU.[26]

The PCI and the Democratic Socialists. As a whole, therefore, the foreign policy positions of the PCE do reveal certain points of agreement with the concepts held by the PCI which, for its own part, is moving toward positions like those laid down by the Democratic Socialists in their election platform. Most important, both parties subscribe to a foreign policy analysis which diverges more and more from the notions held by the PCF. While the latter, as we have seen, sees world politics as no more than a struggle between two camps which are irreconcilably opposed to each other, the PCI and PCE take the view that such an appraisal no longer reflects the situation as it is today.

In their attitudes to the Soviet Union, though they support the main principles of Moscow's foreign policy (for example, in the armaments sector and in their attitudes to the Third World), the Italian and Spanish Communists do not conceal the fact that they see certain expansionist tendencies in the USSR's conduct. This is shown, for example, by the fact that the PCI has on numerous occasions emphatically affirmed its interest in the independence of Yugoslavia—an admonition which under the present circumstances could only be directed at the Soviet Union. Nor does the PCI nowadays consider Soviet–Cuban activities in Africa to be wholly positive, and it even disapproves openly of the part played by Cuban and Soviet elements in Ethiopia's conflict with the liberation movements in Eritrea.

Conversely, the Communist parties of Italy and Spain base their international analysis on the assumption that the West is nowadays no longer a uniform hostile bloc which demonstrates willingness to negotiate only because the growing power of the socialist states is forcing it to do so. There are, in their opinion, powerful forces in the West which have, out of their own conviction, made their contribution toward launching and consolidating the policy of détente. This attitude becomes particularly clear when the PCI calls for a "new internationalism" which is to have no more to do with a "Manichaean division of the world."[27]

Relations with the USA

There are certainly different points of view with respect to relations between the EC and the United States among the Democratic Socialist parties, for example between the German Social Democrats and the French Socialists. While the former considers close relations with the United States indispensable, even if only for reasons of security, the latter's attitude to the United States is considerably more critical: it fears that the United States, as the predominant capitalist power, might thwart not only democratic–Socialist social changes in Europe but also the emergence of a new European power. One of the reasons why Mitterrand considers the unification of Western Europe to be desirable is that "the Community is an obstacle in the way of the strategy of international capitalism."[28]

Nevertheless, the Democratic Socialists have been able to find a common denominator which provides for greater autonomy for Western Europe within the framework of the community of Western nations. In any event, they stated in their election platform, the indispensable development of cooperation between Europe and the United States "presupposes mutual respect for the sovereignty" of the partners, not only with respect to bilateral questions but also in solving the problems of third countries. In this context, "the existence of a European dimension consolidated by direct elections to the European Parliament" was "of great importance."

Relations with NATO

On the topic of security policy, the election platform states: "Europe's security is tied up with the maintenance of military equilibrium. The states of the European Community can do justice to their security interests vis-á-vis the Warsaw Pact only by virtue of their association in the Atlantic Alliance." At present it cannot be foreseen when this situation might change. Nevertheless, the long–term goals remain "the surmounting of the blocs," the "organization of peace" (especially by means of gradual disarmament and troop reduction), and the "deepening of Helsinki," particularly in the field of confidence-building measures.

The views of the PCE differ vastly from those of the Democratic Socialists in that, by virtue of its policy on nonalignment, it focuses its attention on relaxing Western Europe's ties to the United States and would like to see it play an independent role somewhere between the two superpowers. The PCE wants "a Europe which is equally independent both of the United States and of the Soviet Union; a Europe which is neither anti-Soviet nor anti-American, but which is capable of making its own autonomous contribution toward the evolution of international life." Against this background, the party favors the integration of Western Europe, and not only its economic and political integration but "naturally [!] also the military implications which this might involve."[29]

Since the early 1970s the PCI has been pursuing a similar concept which also involved quite a pronounced anti-American accent in its call for autonomy for Europe. The point of departure for this concept may be taken to be Berlinguer's vision of the "world-wide role of a democratic, independent and peaceful Western Europe which is neither anti-Soviet nor anti-American but which establishes relations of friendship and cooperation with these and with other countries."[30] Amendola went one step further and joined the PCE in recognizing that the creation of a common Western European defense policy is an important task—at least to the extent that "the Community strives to consolidate its autonomy vis-à-vis the United States."[31]

As decisively as the idea of Western Europe as a self-reliant force continues to influence some of the PCI leadership, it is nevertheless becoming apparent that this view is gradually being replaced by one not too far removed from those of the Democratic Socialists in their election platform. This is true also with respect to Italy's links with NATO, which since 1974 the PCI has become more and more willing to accept. The party no longer treats the Atlantic Alliance merely as a necessary evil, in order to demonstrate its own ability to govern, and is no longer solely concerned with preserving the international balance of power to further détente, in the continuation of which it has a vital interest. It also accepts the alliance because it fears that any weakening of NATO, brought about by reductions in Italy's contribution to the defense effort, would automatically undermine Yugoslavia's position vis-à-vis the Soviet Union. All these factors have induced the PCI to give its active support to Italy's defense budgets in recent years.

It is true that, as Pierre Hassner rightly emphasizes,[32] this commitment to NATO on the part of the PCI does not necessarily cover strict *military policy* options. In this sector, the PCI, which tries to leave itself room to maneuver on all sides, advocates what might be called "pacifist Atlanticism," more as a consumer than a producer of security. Evasive answers to the question as to how the party would react in the event of a conflict between East and West make the PCI an unpredictable factor even today. However, precisely in the field of foreign relations, the outlook of the PCI has changed so quickly and so fundamentally in recent years that the declarations made by the Communists together with the other five parties of the "constitutional spectrum" in the autumn of 1977[33] in favor of Italy's ties to the West could sooner or later affect the security sector as well. Just as the PCI enabled former member of the EC Commission Altiero Spinelli to gain a set in Parliament on its party ticket in order to advertise its commitment to European integration, so it spotlighted its new attitude toward NATO by doing the same for Air Force General Nino Pasti, who had been responsible for the Nuclear Planning group at SHAPE (Supreme Headquarters Allied Powers Europe) from 1966 to 1968.

European Community and Eastern Europe

The PCI nowadays gives its unequivocal support to the integration of the EC, but with the express reservation that the integration process must not be directed against Eastern Europe but must be accompanied by political dialogue with the countries of Eastern Europe and by closer links with the Council for Mutual Economic Aid (CMEA). In other words, in the opinion of the PCI, the European Community, if it continues to grow closer together, must not lose sight of the pan–European dimension, including large–scale cooperation with the countries of Eastern Europe.

In this approach the PCI again reveals a certain move toward the positions of the Democratic Socialists. For this pan–European dimension is to be found in the positions of the French Socialists, for example, who have emphasized it by their leader Mitterrand's many trips to Eastern Europe. Most of all, however, the pan–European dimension forms an integral part of the European concept of the German Social Democrats, even though these had at first taken an extremely skeptical view of the EEC in general, regarding it as another obstacle to the reunification of Germany. Nowadays, support of West European integration is undisputed in the SPD, on the tacit understanding that it keeps up and intensifies the pan–European dialogue as an essential precondition to the development of better West German–East German relations. For the Federal Republic of Germany is—as the SPD–FDP–oriented journalist Peter Bender appropriately remarked, "the only Western state which [has] a national interest in an undivided Europe."[34]

This line pursued by the German Social Democrats, with its orientation toward Europe as a whole, a line which converges with those of the other Democratic Socialists, however diverse the motives of the various parties may be, is reflected in the election platform to which we have already made frequent reference. European unification, this platform states, is not directed against Eastern Europe. "The implementation of the final act of Helsinki" is for the Community "a decisive instrument toward improving bilateral and multilateral relations to the states of Eastern Europe." On the basis of this point of view, the Democratic Socialists not only advocate the cultivation of relations between the EC and CMEA on a larger scale but even go so far as cautiously to mention their willingness to review "initiatives designed to facilitate the establishment of pan-European institutions."

Conclusions and Prospects

An attempt such as the present one to look at developments within the Western European left as a whole and thereby to draw attention to certain points of convergence between Democratic Socialists and Eurocommunists affords the advantage that it brings to light movements and trends of a more general nature. At the same time, however, it involves certain dangers.

On the one hand this method might lead to the continuing *differences* between the concepts of the various parties being neglected. More importantly, however, this approach could result in a misleading perspective if it overlooks the possibility that similar positions held by various parties in some fields may be overshadowed and thus effectively rendered worthless by continuing *divergences* in matters of principle in other areas. In order to avoid misconceptions, it must be expressly pointed out that apparently similar positions may conceal completely different strategies. For this reason, until it becomes clearer with respect to the processes of transition within the various parties "how deep they will go and how much time they will take,"[35] there is little likelihood of the Western European left's establishing transnational links at a higher level than that of mere informational contacts.

This is particularly true with respect to the French Communists. Admittedly, they too nowadays look upon themselves, in deliberate delimitation from Moscow, as "democratic Socialists."[36] Since autumn 1977, however, it has become evident that the party leadership is neither able nor even willing to call the *Leninist identity* of the PCF into question, with respect neither to the formulation of a common position within the party nor to its strategy for social transformation or its policy of alliance. They continue to see the acquisition of power primarily as a *tactical* problem, one which presupposes that the Communists in effect play a leading role. If the PCF considers its leadership role to be in danger, it prefers to withdraw again to the shelter of its politico-ideological "bunker" and to treat its Socialist partner-competitor as its real opponent, as it did in former times.

It is typical of the transition of the Italian and Spanish Communists that they have not only refrained from supporting the PCF in its polemics on questions of principle against the PSF and against the Democratic Socialists, with the SPD at their head, but that they even condemned these attacks more or less openly. The PCF position was contrary to their strategic line of bringing about social change not by means of a radical break with the existing social system but rather through a series of individual reforms within that system, and of doing this in consensus with the majority of the population (that is, also with the expanding group of the "new salaried employees") and in a relationship of hard competition *and* loyal cooperation with its political partners.

It is evident, therefore, that some Eurocommunist parties have started to "reflect in a spirit of self-criticism on their present dogmatic positions, on the nature of state institutions in the capitalist system, on the question of the so-called "system boundary" between capitalism and socialism, and on the dialectical relationship between Socialist transformation and integration on the basis of an existing system as part of a strategy of reform."[37] There are also signs that the process of the intellectual and political emancipation of these parties has by no means come to an end. If it should prove true in the long term that "the nondogmatic,' leftist-Socialist trend within the Italian Communist party could gain dominant influence,"[38] then the possibility can no longer be excluded that at some time in the future similar or converging programmatic proposals may be jointly put forward by Democratic Socialists, progressive bourgeois forces, and Eurocommunists. In addition to the problems referred to above, the following issues may be important in the future: the austerity concept; the idea of a solidarity program for Southern Europe; détente; human rights problems; and, last but not least, the future of Yugoslavia.

The Austerity Concept

When it comes to the problem of surmounting the economic crisis which is affecting all the countries of Western Europe in one way or another, not even the left-wing parties, including the Italian and Spanish Communists, dispute the fact that austerity measures will have to be introduced if this problem is to be solved. The left wing will probably develop converging objectives in that they all look upon an austerity program not as consolidating the social status quo by means of a policy of unilateral sacrifices on the part of the labor force and of merely rationalizing and modernizing the existing system but as an opportunity for modifying the existing economic and social structures by introducing more programmed planning, worker participation, and democratic controls. In other words, common approaches could emerge from the fact that "linking positive crisis management and Socialist transformation strategies [is becoming] a problem of more and more urgent concern to the parties of democratic socialism and to the reformist Communist parties."[39]

Solidarity Program for Southern Europe

Both the Democratic Socialists and the Italian and Spanish Communists are committed advocates of the expansion of the EC to the South by means of the admission of the three Mediterranean countries, Spain, Portugal, and Greece. Of course, as much as they welcome this expansion for political reasons, they are well aware of the economic and social problems which this involves. It is against this background that the SPD's initiative in favor of an EC solidarity program for Southern Europe is important—a program with the aim of promoting "infrastructure projects and projects in trade and industry" and thus of making their "coalescence with the standard of development in Central and Northern Europe" easier for the Southern European countries.[40] Common approaches toward achieving these aims could emerge between Democratic Socialists and Eurocommunists, for, if the solidarity program is to be successful, conventional market mechanisms will have to be supplemented by a carefully planned and directed policy on economic structure and regional development and the various social groups—in particular the trade unions—will have to be mobilized in support of the program.

Détente and Human Rights

Further convergence appears possible with respect to how the future of the policy of détente is envisaged. In this context, the member countries of the EC should be able, by taking matters into their own hands and by entering into a "commitment to reciprocity,"[41] to so stabilize détente that it would survive even if the climate between the superpowers should deteriorate. This applies, for example, with respect to the continued implementation of civil and human rights. Since the mid-1970s there has been an intense discussion in progress in the West on the nature of the connection between the policy of détente and the human rights question. This discussion was not so much concerned with fundamental questions of principle, such as whether one or another of these goals might be in danger of not being realized, as with the *tactical* question as to how the two are *interrelated*.

One school of thought, the more conservative one, tends to make the implementation of human rights in Eastern Europe a *precondition* for the continued pursuit of the policy of détente and possibly even to use the latter as a lever with which to destabilize those systems. Another school of thought, to which along with numerous bourgeois parties the Democratic Socialists and the Eurocommunists subscribe, takes the opposite view and sees the continued pursuance of détente as the *precondition* for progress on the human rights question. But different as their détente concepts continue to be in other aspects, they distinctly converge in one point. Both think that any deterioration in the situation in Eastern Europe which reaches near-critical proportions and is accompanied by the prospect of sudden eruptions would ultimately lead only to Soviet repressive measures being stepped up and would not help the people living there. Just as they think little of a policy of a revolutionary break with existing society in Western Europe and follow a strategy of step-by-step reforms, so, too, in their policy toward Eastern Europe, they prefer to bank on an evolutionary process, albeit without lessening their politico-moral solidarity with Eastern European advocates of civil rights or relaxing their public support for their aims.

The Future of Yugoslavia

The future course of events in Yugoslavia is likely to be of key importance to the attitude of the Eurocommunists toward Europe and its non-Communist left. The problems which the future of Yugoslavia might entail have been the subject of intense discussion among the Italian and Spanish Communists, without any decisions as yet having been taken. On the one hand, it cannot be definitively precluded that closer links between Yugoslavia and the Warsaw Pact might induce the PCI to reverse its stance on NATO and thus give a new lease of life to neutralist tendencies or at least cause the party to reject any automatic obligation on the part of Italy to provide support in case of conflict. The party's present acceptance of Italy's membership of NATO, after all, rests to a great extent on Yugoslavia's nonaligned status and on the preservation of the present balance of power between the military blocs. On the other hand, it is quite conceivable that stronger pressure from Moscow on the Yugoslavs, not to mention Soviet intervention, could give rise to a situation in which the Eurocommunist parties would be driven even closer toward the West, that is, toward that of the Democratic Socialists. The PCI, in particular, which looks upon the nonaligned status of Yugoslavia as being of vital importance to Italy's national interests and upon the autonomous line followed by the League of Communists of Yugoslavia as being the mainstay of its own independent course, may be expected in such a case to seek more active involvement in NATO and to orient itself even more clearly toward the parties of the SI. This might also apply to the PCE, particularly since that Party's opposition to Spain joining NATO is essentially attributable to its determination not to give the Soviet Union any excuse for trying to integrate Yugoslavia into its own hegemonial system.

From the West's, and in particular from Western Europe's point of view, the transitions which the PCI and PCE have undergone and the resultant increase in those parties' potential for exerting political influence reveal not only adverse but also some beneficial aspects. For, problematic as it would still be from the point of view of military security and of political cooperation among the Nine, for example in the field of European political cooperation, were these parties to enter government, this would have welcome effects in the long term with respect to reforming the political and economic structures of the various countries by means of planning and participation and thereby stabilizing the West's southern flank in economic and social terms.

As the foreign policy spokesman of the Christian Democrats of Italy, Luigi Granelli, stressed, the difficulties in Europe would only become greater if the broad masses of the people, represented by parties including the Communist parties, did not have any opportunity to participate in building up a politically united, democratic, pluralist Europe. The process of the unification of Europe as the result of a profound economic, social, and institutional change must, in his opinion, "be borne by as wide a democratic cooperative effort as possible."[42]

Conversely, a Western Europe in the process of growing together should be strong and self-confident enough to be able to assimilate Eurocommunists, who are undergoing a process of transition. Even now, Granelli maintained, "the continued existence of democracy, the persuasive power of libertarian ideals, and the prospect of European unity" had already made their mark on the PCI and had caused the party to undertake a "profound strategic revision." One of the advantages to be gained from establishing such close links between Eurocommunists and Europe was, indeed, that this would incorporate additional safeguards against any future relapse into Leninist practices.[43]

Some of these issues are also important for an appraisal of the Democratic Socialists. For them, also, transition within Eurocommunist parties has a number of different aspects. As much as they welcome that transition in principle, its immediate effect is to present them with a challenge. In precise terms, the "gradually developing convergence in common political goals" makes it essential, in the words of the leader of the Italian Socialists, Bettino Craxi, to "articulate the differences between the two currents even more clearly in order to avoid unjustified leveling out and confusion."[44] François Mitterrand and Felipe González, both of whom are up against strong Communist parties, see the situation in a similar light.

For this reason, the Democratic Socialists will do their utmost to shift the balance of power within the left in their own favor, at the national and also at the Western European level. With this in mind, Willy Brandt made it clear than the Democratic Socialists would compete with the Communists in the directly elected European Parliament and that there could be no question of an alliance within that body.[45]

On the other hand, many Democratic Socialists also recognize the opportunity which further transition of the Eurocommunist parties could entail—the change that this might enable the democratic consensus in Europe to find a broader social basis and the opportunity for those forces which call for a Europe of Social Democracy to build up their influence in the long term. This is, especially from the point of view of the Latin European Socialist, *one* reason why there is no Social Democratic or Socialist party which nowadays continues to call for measures which would amount to (1) preventing the formation of a government incorporating members of Eurocommunist parties, provided that government was constituted by democratic means, or (2) presenting particular difficulties to or even "destabilizing" such a government.

On the other hand, this would depend upon the Communists' not working toward unilateral weakening of the Western Alliance and upon their acceptance of the basic values of Western democracy. These conditions are specified in these same terms, apparently with respect precisely to the possibility of Communist participation in government, in the April 1978 Copenhagen Declaration of the Heads of the Governments of the EC member countries.

The West German Social Democrats also subscribe to this position, though more for reasons of national than of social policy. The Federal Republic of Germany is extremely dependent upon its exports, is interested in stable political, economic, and social conditions in the countries with which it trades, and would itself suffer greatly from any attempt to destabilize those countries—a consideration, by the way, which is also important for the bourgeois parties in West Germany. It was not coincidence that German Chancellor Schmidt was impressed by the policy of the CGIL, which is closely associated with the PCI, "not to stand in the way of the government unnecessarily in its attempts to master the colossal economic and social problems [facing the country], while trade unions under other political influences in Italy are confronting the Italian government's attempts at stabilization with very much greater difficulties."[46]

See in this light, it is therefore conceivable that a West German government under Social Democratic leadership would, in the event of a Eurocommunist party's entering a government, play a mediatory and conciliatory role with the aim of preventing overreaction on the part of the West as well as any attempt by the Communists to break out of the basic consensus on political democracy, Western European integration, and the security links between the countries of the West.

On the whole, the Democratic Socialists nowadays take it for granted that the Eurocommunists, provided they are themselves willing, must be incorporated into the basic consensus on the construction and further development of Western Europe as an entity. The European level affords the greatest potential for accelerating the process of transition within the Eurocommunist parties. If, for example, the PCI had to deal not only with a relatively weak Socialist party (PSI) but also with a strong European Social Democracy, it is possible that any remaining pro-Soviet tendencies which that party still reveals might diminish and give way "in the course of the next five to ten years to a true European identity, effective autonomy from the Soviet Union, and the acceptance of democratic principles in theory and practice."[47] A PCI which had undergone this change could, continuing this line of reasoning, make such a contribution toward stabilizing the situation in Italy that the country could again become a constructive partner in the further integration of the EC and in its continued development toward social democracy.

Of course, such a scenario is accompanied by a number of uncertainties. It is by no means a coincidence that relations between Democratic Socialists and Eurocommunists are tending more strongly toward conflict precisely in a period in which these parties are (PCI) or have been (PCF) faced with the prospect of obtaining a share in government. This situation is unlikely to change in the immediate future, for such a prospect makes it essential to settle the question as to whether the course *and* the goals of these parties are the same, at least in their basic features, quite apart from the fact that both wings of the labor movement are competing for the same sector of the electorate.

Within the PSF, in particular, a rethinking process has been in progress, since the break-up of the Union of the Left in September 1977, on that party's relations with the PCF. Admittedly, it is hardly likely that the Socialists will orient themselves toward the bourgeois center, as has long been President Giscard d'Estaing's desire. On the other hand, the Socialists may in the future pay more attention to establishing their own profile and therefore may well steer clear of giving their alliance with the Communists such an intimate character as they have done up to now. For the PCF's conduct since the autumn of 1977 has shown that, despite all its verbal assurances, it has not yet undergone any fundamental change at all. If it feels its traditional Leninist identity threatened and considers itself forced into a minority position, it remains resolved to revert to attacking the PS as its real opponent and prefers to pursue a "strategy of defeat" rather than to run the risk of venturing upon the experiment of sharing in a government from a position which might mean, for example, sharing responsibility for austerity measures, and from a minority position.

In Italy and Spain, too, not to mention Portugal, relations between

Socialists and Communists are characterized at the moment more by conflicts than by cooperation. In Spain, this situation is due to a large extent to the PSOE's attempt to relegate the Communists to the sidelines and to establish itself as *the* big party of the left, an attempt which the PCE is trying to counter by setting its sights on a kind of "historic compromise" with Prime Minister Suárez's Democratic Center (UCD). The Italian Socialists (PSI) under their new party leader Craxi have embarked upon a policy of criticizing the PCI's central politico-ideological positions—in particular its acceptance of Leninism, its adherence to "democratic centralism" as the principle for decisions within the party, and the nature of its links to the CPSU. These altercations are more likely to be escalated than settled, not only because the PCI actually does continue to give occasion for critical questions but also because this forms an integral part of the PSI's attempt to shift the balance of power in the left to its own advantage and at the expense of the PCI. The Italian Socialists' endeavors to restructure the PSI, to make it more attractive to a wider section of the electorate, and generally to give it a new profile as the authentic and dynamic "Party of Progress and Reforms" (Craxi)—these endeavors, in the view of the leaders of the PSI, presuppose that the party's relationship to the Communists must be one of rivalry, if not one of conflict.

Consequently, despite signs of convergence in many fields, there is *no* closer transnational agreement between Democratic Socialists and Eurocommunists to be expected. This is particularly true with respect to the PCF, which gives the impression of reverting to its traditional policies and again regarding the Democratic Socialists at home and in Europe as its true opponents and which, for example in its attitude toward the state, in its strategy of social change, and in its policy toward the EC, is in the process of differentiating itself qualitatively from the Italian and Spanish *Communists.*

Nevertheless, the possibility cannot be excluded that, precisely in the process of West European unification, the common interests of the various currents in the Western European labor movement may in the long term prevail over the differences set forth above, one which in Italy and Spain are motivated more by tactical than by substantive considerations—that perhaps, after all, "the historic rift in the labor movement in Western Europe [could] one day be healed."[48] However, this would hardly come about within the perspective of Europe as a "Third Force" standing between the superpowers, as was the goal of Democratic Socialists and possibly also of Western European Communists in the years immediately following the war. For all "Europe, thanks most of all to Democratic Socialism and the labor movement, has developed its own conception of social democracy and of the principle of social justice."[49] Security problems and shared basic values nevertheless clearly indicate that, from the point of view of most of the significant parties of the left, the European Community can only develop its own identity in cooperation with the United States, in a partnership characterized not by subordination but by equality.

Furthermore, transnational cooperation among the parties of the left in Western Europe would probably not create compact fronts of mutually antagonistic bourgeois, Socialist, and Eurocommunist parties, but would rather give rise to multiple *lateral connections* among the various groups. For neither the Democratic Socialists nor the Italian and Spanish Eurocommunists, nor even the influential sections of the Christian Democratic and liberal-oriented bourgeois parties are interested in confrontation. In the long term, it is much more likely that configurations will arise in which parties of various ideological and political outlooks will cooperate to deal with certain specific problems. One possible such configuration could have the Democratic Socialists as its core, and embrace on the one hand the Italian (and later also the Spanish) Communists and on the other those bourgeois parties which, be it for Christian-Socialist or Socialist-Liberal motives, work toward step-by-step social reforms for the benefit of the working population.

Notes

1. The term "Democratic Socialists" will be used in the following to include those Social Democratic and Socialist parties of Western Europe which are members of the Socialist International or, in a more narrow sense, of the "Confederation of the Socialist Parties of the European Community." Within this broad category, the Socialists of Southern Europe differ from the Social Democrats of Northern and Central Europe in that, at least in their programs, they do not restrict themselves merely to reforming the existing social system but intend to change it by means of radical structural reforms.

2. Preface to Heinz Timmermann, ed., *Eurokommunismus: Fakten, Analysen, Interviews* (Frankfurt: Fischer, 1978), p. 13.

3. Cf. Richard Löwenthal (Paul Sering), *Jenseits des Kapitalismus.* Reprint of the first edition of 1947 (Bonn-Bad Godesberg: Dietz, 1977), pp. 247 ff., and his introduction to the reprint, p. xxxii.

4. Ibid., p. xxxiii.

5. Carrillo in his report presented to the II. National Conference of the PCE in September 1975, in *Manifiesto-Programa del PCE* (Paris: EBRO, 1975), p. 15.

6. "Les partis socialistes de l'Europe du Sud ne prétendent pas avoir de strategie commune," *Le Monde,* February 15-16, 1976.

7. Willy Brandt, "Socialismo in Europa," *Affari Esteri* 10: 37 (January 1978): 4.

8. Karsten D. Voigt, "Einheit in der Vielfalt—Pluralismus als Prinzip des sozialistischen Internationalismus," *Die Neue Gesellschaft* 22: 11 (November 1975): 943. Voigt is a member of the West German Bundestag and deputy leader of the foreign policy section of the SPD parliamentary group in the Bundestag.

9. The draft is printed in "Sozialdemokraten auf dem Weg nach Europa," *Vorwärts* 101: 24 (June 1977): i–viii.

10. Cf. Jean Ziegler, "Les équivoques de la socialdémocratie", *Le Monde diplomatique* 25: 1 (January 1978).

11. SPD-Parteitag, Hamburg, November 15–19, 1977, p. 42.

12. Felipe González in an interview with *Unité* 174 (October 1975): 4.

13. Speech at the Geneva Congress of the Socialist International, November 1976, *Frankfurter Allgemeine Zeitung,* November 27, 1976.

14. Preface to Timmermann, *Eurokommunismus...*, p. 13.

15. In a debate with Umberto Agnelli and Raymond Aron on the perspective of the European Community; see Barbara Spinelli, "Dove va questa Europa decadente," *La Repubblica,* May 10, 1978.

16. Cf. note 9.

17. Ibid, p. ii.

18. The speech is printed in Etienne Fajon, *L'union est un combat* (Paris: Edition Sociales, 1975), pp. 75–127.

19. Cf. for instance Manuel Azcárate in Timmermann, *Eurocommunismus...*, p. 200.

20. Ibid., p. ii.

21. Altiero Spinelli for the PCI in a speech before the European Parliament, *Das Parlament* 28: 19 (May 1978).

22. Ibid., p. ii.

23. *l'Unità,* May 16, 1976.

24. Cf. the chapter "Il PCI e le multinazionali" in Giacomo Luciani, *Il PCI e il capitalismo occidentale* (Milan: Longanesi Publishers, 1977), p. 59. A similar position is taken by the PCE: cf. Santiago Carrillo, *"Eurokommunismus" und Staat* (Hamburg/West Berlin: VSA Publishers, 1977), p. 115 ff.

25. Carrillo, *"Eurokommunismus" und Staat* p. 181.

26. "Contrary to the Interests of Peace and Socialism in Europe: Concerning the Book *Eurocommunism and the State* by Santiago Carrillo, General Secretary of the Communist Party of Spain," *New Times* 26 (June 1977): 9–13.

27. Sergio Segre, "L'esigenza di un nuovo internazionalismo," *Rinascita* 35: 14 (April 1978): 35.

28. Press Conference in Strasbourg, *Le Monde,* June 16, 1978.

29. Answer of Manuel Azcárate, in Timmermann, *Eurokommunismus...,* p. 198.

30. Speech to the Brussels Conference of the West European Communist Parties, *l'Unità,* January 27, 1974.

31. Giorgio Amendola, "L'Europa nel ciclone", *Rinascita* 30: 47 (November 1973): 1.

32. "The International Dimension." This analysis will be published as part of a book, *The Communist Parties of Southern Europe,* ed. by the Rome Istituto Affari Internazionali (in Italian) and the Bundesinstitut für ostwissenschaftliche und internationale Studien (in German) in 1979.

33. The Resolutions, approved by the Chamber and the Senate are in *Relazioni Internationali* 42: 44 (October 1977, extract) and 51 (December 1977).

34. Peter Bender, "Die Deutschen werden wieder deutscher," *Deutschland Archiv* 11: 5 (May 1978): 451ff.

35. "Da gibt es wirklich sehr Interessantes," interview with Willy Brandt, *Der Spiegel* 30: 5 (January 1976): 24.

36. Jean Kanapa, "Un débat naturel et sain," *France Nouvelle* 1614 (October 1976): 7.

37. Karsten D. Voigt, "Die Wurzeln des demokratischen Sozialismus heute," *Die Neue Gesellschaft* 24: 12 (December 1977): 1005.

38. "Willy Brandt views the shape of Europe, Eurocommunism," interview with the *International Herald Tribune,* May 15, 1976.

39. Karsten D. Voigt, "Die Wurzeln...."

40. Resolution of the Hamburg SPD-Congress, p. 40.

41. The German EC-Commissioner Haferkamp in a speech in February 1978 to the German Society for Foreign Policy: *Die Rolle der Gemeinschaft in den internationalen Beziehungen* (Bonn: Deutsche Gesellschaft für Auswärtige Politik, 1978), p. 9.

42. "Kein Europa ohne Kommunisten," *Vorwärts* 101: 20 (May 1977).

43. This line of reasoning was expressed clearly, for example, in a remark made by Prime Minister Andreotti to the effect that the Communists in Italy could assume governmental responsibility if they could be integrated into a Democratic-Socialist formation within the European Parliament (interview in *Le Monde,* March 2, 1977).

44. Interview with *Mondo Operaio,* reprinted in *Avanti,* October 27, 1976.

45. Cf. Parteivorstand der SPD, *Zum Verhältnis von Sozialdemokratie und Kommunismus,* epilogue by Willy Brandt (Bonn: Vorwärts, 1977), p.16.

46. "Da hat es sicher Fehler gegeben," interview with *Der Stern,* 30: 9 (February 1977): 70.

47. Contribution of the PSI politician G. Tamburrano, in L. Levi, S. Pistone, and D. Coombes, *L'influenza dell' elezione europea sul sistema dei partiti* (Turin: Fondazione Giovanni Agnelli, 1978), p. 41.

48. Ehmke, in Timmermann, *Eurokommunismus...*, p. 13.

49. "Sozialdemokraten auf dem Weg nach Europa," p. vi.

8

The Ties That Bind: West European Communism and the Communist States of East Europe

Joan Barth Urban

In mid-1978 the Italian Socialist party (PSI) launched against its Communist partners in Italy's parliamentary majority a polemical campaign whose central themes recalled the historic clashes between European socialism and communism some five or six decades earlier. In an essay published in the Italian news weekly *Espresso,* PSI leader Bettino Craxi denounced in thinly veiled terms the Italian Communist party's continuing commitment to Leninism, which Craxi equated with unqualified totalitarianism. About that same time the Socialist leadership also began to include allegiance to Moscow in its indictment of the PCI. The tenor of the PSI polemics underscored the depth of the chasm that still separated the Socialist and Communist parties of West Europe. It was reminiscent of the controversy that raged between the Portuguese Socialists and Communists during Lisbon's hot summer of 1975 and not dissimilar to the recriminations that erupted between the French Socialists and Communists after the defeat of the *union de la gauche* in the March 1978 National Assembly elections.

This latest round of Communist–Socialist tension at the domestic level had its international parallels and ramifications. The Italian Communists, confronted by the Socialist challenge, felt compelled to reaffirm their political affinity with the CPSU while denying that this in any way spelled subordination to or approval of Soviet–style socialism. By way of contrast, contacts between the Western Socialists and Moscow, always more diplomatic than ideological in nature, were on the wane. Soviet observers did not even attend the March 1978 Congress of the PSI (ironically, the one major Socialist party that had maintained an alliance with the Communists during the worst years of postwar Stalinism and cold war tensions). As for the French Socialists, PS leader François Mitterand had not visited Moscow since late April 1975. The timing of that trip was significant because it came directly on the heels of Soviet public endorsement, however hesitant and equivocal, of a democratic transitional stage on the path to socialism in the West, a policy that was represented in the French context by the programmatic goal of "advanced democracy" set forth by the *union de la gauche.* But developments in Portugal the following summer, combined with the subsequent deterioration of French Communist relations with the CPSU, effectively halted closer French Socialist ties with Moscow.

Only in the case of the Spanish Socialist Workers party (PSOE) did contacts with the Soviet Union intensify in the second half of the 1970s. In December 1977 PSOE leader Felipe González paid an official visit to Moscow, which was soon followed by a ten-day tour of the USSR by three of his party's executive committee members in August 1978. However, given the PSOE's status as the second-strongest political force in Spain and a likely contender for governmental power, these contacts could best be understood as diplomatic gestures rather than ideological or even political overtures. Indeed, the communiqués issued upon each occasion were notable for their observance of protocol rather than their conveyance of warmth or a mutuality of views. Historically no friend of Moscow, just about the only point the PSOE had in common with the CPSU was its opposition to Spain's adherence to NATO.

What is of immediate relevance for this chapter, then, is that generic anti-Communist attacks such as Craxi's *Espresso* polemic obscured the singular fact that relations between the West European *Communist* parties and the Soviet-oriented regimes of East Europe had begun to acquire during the 1970s some of the characteristics of the historic relationship between Social Democracy and Leninism. The schism within the European Marxist movement half a century earlier had been a rupture between ideological brothers whose shared vision of a future Socialist society was flawed by bitter controversy over the means to that end. For the Leninists of the Third Communist International the Socialists' commitment to democratic methods in the quest for social change spelled treason: their reformism would only shore up the capitalist order by dulling the revolutionary impulses of the common worker. For the Socialists the Leninists' use of dictatorial methods to preserve their power likewise spelled treason: party-controlled social development would never lead to the liberation of human potential envisioned by Karl Marx.

What Craxi and other Socialist critics neglected to note was that some of these same themes lay at the heart of the controversies that wracked the European Communist movement during the 1970s. However, historical analogies are never exact. And in this case there was one compelling difference which may explain the Socialists' oversight: the protagonists in the contemporary intra-Communist debate disclaimed any intention of repeating the organizational rupture of 1920. Their political differences and ideological polemics notwithstanding, they extolled the enduring nature of pan-European Communist ties.

To be sure, the Soviet leaders and their loyalist allies disparaged "Eurocommunism" with remarkably little restraint, as witnessed by the CPSU's controversial June 1977 attack on Spanish CP leader Santiago Carrillo in the Moscow weekly *New Times*. The CPSU's polemics against the Italian Communist leadership were more subtle yet no less barbed. Nevertheless, the Soviet leaders went to great lengths to paper over those differences in time for the sixtieth anniversary of the Great October Revolution in November 1977. Russian emissaries conferred with Carrillo in Madrid, assuring him of equal time to present his views if only he would attend the festivities. As a gesture of Soviet good will, in late October *Pravda* published a lengthy feature article by its editor-in-chief lauding the achievements of the Spanish CP and referring favorably to Carrillo. When Carrillo was actually prevented from speaking in the Great Hall of the Kremlin on November 2,[1] the Soviet leadership pleaded innocence (Carrillo, they claimed, had arrived too late for his speach to be translated into the seventeen languages required for the occasion) and proceeded to shower their attention upon PCI General-Secretary Enrico Berlinguer. Despite the influx of guests from some 100-odd countries, Brezhnev and the two Soviet leaders most directly responsible for relations with nonruling CPs, Mikhail Suslov and Boris Ponomarev, managed to find time the very next day to meet with Berlinguer for fifty minutes "in an atmosphere of cordiality and friendship." In view of the close personal and political ties between the Spanish and Italian CP leaders, the Kremlin's respectful treatment of Berlinguer must be interpreted as an attempt to minimize the negative impression conveyed by their clash with Carrillo.

Just as the CPSU leadership strove for a public image of pan-European Communist harmony, so too the Eurocommunist triad of major nonruling parties rejected the idea of a break with Moscow. Upon his return to Madrid on November 4, 1977, Carrillo declared that the Spanish Communists didn't want—nor did the Moscow incident represent—a rupture with the USSR, a theme which he repeated a week later at a joint press conference in Rome with Berlinguer. As for the PCI, Berlinguer and others had rejected the idea of a rupture any number of times, particularly at moments of high tension with the CPSU. Two such cases had already occured during 1977, first in the winter after the Italian CP's outspoken defense of the Czechoslovak "Charter 77" dissidents and then in July after the PCI's staunch rebuttal of the *New Times* attack on Carrillo. In a January 30, 1977, speech to an assembly of Communist workers in Milan, Berlinguer had hailed as immutable three PCI principles: the goal of socialism, the operational rule of democratic centralism, *and the maintenance of international Communist ties.* In an interview over Italian television the following month, Berlinguer once again insisted on the preservation of correct PCI relations with the CPSU. Similarly, after high-level PCI-CPSU talks in Moscow in early July 1977, following the *New Times* polemic, a member of the Italian delegation reiterated his party's opposition to a "rupture" with the CPSU, arguing that a break in interparty relations would not be in the interests of either the PCI or Italy.[2]

As will be discussed later, friction between the French Communist party and the Soviets developed at a different tempo and along different lines than in the case of the PCE and the PCI. The quality of personal links at the leadership levels varied accordingly. While the French representatives at the November 1977 Moscow celebration did not become involved in the Carrillo flap, PCF leader Georges Marchais chose not even to attend the festivities. Nevertheless, the head of the French delegation declared in the Kremlin that despite their differences "fraternal ties have always existed and continue to exist between the CPSU and the PCF."

This same pattern of outspoken criticism followed by professions of ongoing solidarity was to be repeated in mid-1978, especially in the case of the PCI. All three Eurocommunist parties heatedly denounced the Soviet trials and sentencing of dissidents Orlov, Shcharansky, and Ginzburg during the late spring and summer of 1978. The PCI's protests were accompanied by public signals of an interest in normalizing party ties with Peking, a particularly galling slap in Moscow's face given the CPSU's furious reaction to Chinese party chief Hua Guofeng's tour of Romania and Yugoslavia in August of that year. Yet at the same time a spate of statements appeared in the PCI press denying any intention whatsoever of a break with the CPSU. Morover, Berlinguer made a point of stressing his party's ideological affinity with the Soviet comrades in his speech to the annual festival of *l'Unità* in mid-September. And the very next month he journeyed to Moscow for top-level talks with the CPSU leaders, thereby underscoring the PCI's intention of observing proper norms of interparty conduct despite the ongoing PCI-CPSU differences. The Spanish CP didn't quite match the PCI's conciliatory mode of behavior. However, in late October 1978 it too indicated its readiness to remain on at least speaking terms with the Soviet bloc loyalists by receiving a delegation of the Bulgarian CP, previously one of the most trenchant critics of Eurocommunism. Only the French party stayed aloof, intensifying instead its ties with Titoist Yugoslavia, although by the spring of 1979 it too seemed bent on mending its fences with Moscow.

This almost defiant commitment to unity seems ironical when viewed against the backdrop of deepening controversies that has enveloped the world Communist movement since the 1960s. But the paradox does not end there. Beginning in the mid-1970s the Soviet leaders, intent on securing public manifestations of international Communist cohesion, repeatedly gave in to demands of the more autonomist Communist parties of West and East Europe. The independent-minded West European CPs, in turn, responded with ever more trenchant criticism of Soviet-style socialism— their avowals of enduring fraternal unity notwithstanding. In short, as will be argued in the following pages, the "correlation of forces" within the pan-European Communist movement was shifting in favor of what I shall call the loyal opposition, whose political center of gravity lay among the more innovative West European parties and their autonomist Romanian

(and Yugoslav)[a] allies but whose influence appeared gradually to be pene-
trating sectors of the loyalist Soviet-style regimes as well.

Echoes of 1920: Strategy and Organization in the
Pan-European Communist Movement

Divergent perceptions of party interest have always existed between Moscow
and one or another nonruling Communist party of Europe (and elsewhere),
even if only in latent form during the Stalin era. But from the mid-1950s
onward, and even more so after the Warsaw Pact invasion of Czechoslovakia in 1968, such differences became explicit on questions ranging from
the organizational structure of the international Communist movement to
the strategy of revolution and vision of socialism appropriate to the "countries of developed capitalism" (read West Europe). The controversies were
often couched in cumbersome and esoteric jargon. Yet the issues in dispute
boiled down to those that divided the Second and Third Internationals:
individual party autonomy versus a centralized international organization;
democratic versus dictatorial socialism; a legal electoral revolution versus
a minority power grab by manipulation and intimidation if not outright
armed force.
    Lenin's answer to Social Democratic insistence on party autonomy had
been the creation of the Comintern as a world revolutionary party organized
according to the same principle as the Bolshevik party: democratic centralism, or the absolute subordination of minorities to the majority will
expressed at multilateral CP conclaves. In point of fact the nonruling CPs,
financially and psychologically dependent on Moscow, were quickly subordinated to the Soviet minority within the Comintern bureaucracy. But
beginning with the post-Stalin era Khrushchev and his successors sought to
contain the movement's centrifugal tendencies by permitting wider latitude
to the practical implementation of the majoritarian face of democratic
centralism. The Soviet leaders gambled that even in a relatively open forum
they would be assured of solid majority support from the inconsequential
and/or dependent CPs that still predominated within the international
Communist movement as a whole. However, what all Communist opponents of Soviet control held in common was their insistence on *consensus*
rather than majority rule as the only viable basis for a joint international
Communist line. Thus the CPSU's attempt at centralism via majority rule

---

[a] Properly speaking, Yugoslavia should not be included in the loyal opposition. The Tito
regime is independent of the Soviet Union and nonaligned in its international politics. However, its ideological views incline it toward a special relationship with the autonomist forces in
the Communist movement, as evidenced by its role in the preparations for the June 1976 Berlin
Conference of Communist and Workers Parties.

foundered inter alia on the opposition of the Maoists at the 1960 World
Communist Conference in Moscow, the abstention of the PCI on major
portions of the final resolution of the 1969 World Communist Conference,
also held in the Soviet capital, and the emergence of a pan–European coalition of autonomist CPs during the preparations for the 1976 Conference of
European Communist and Workers Parties in East Berlin.[3] It is upon this
last turn of events that we shall focus our attention.

The Communist parties comprising the autonomist coalition varied
widely among themselves on strategic questions. The Romanians were
among the most orthodox when it came to matters pertaining to domestic
political and economic centralization. The Yugoslavs were orthodox on the
issue of exclusive Communist political hegemony yet innovative in their
policies of economic decentralization and international nonalignment. Most
pertinent to this discussion, however, were the Italian and Spanish Communist conceptions of socialism. For they set forth a vision of Socialist pluralism and regionalism the very articulation of which was tantamount to a
direct challenge to the domestic legitimacy of the single–party, Soviet–
oriented Communist systems of East Europe.

For both Latin European parties the Soviet–led invasion of Czechoslovakia in August 1968 acted as a catalyst in the evolution of their strategic
thinking. The PCI had a tradition of theoretical innovation and political
assertiveness vis–à–vis Moscow dating back to the mid–1920s.[4] Not surprisingly, therefore, it joined its impassioned defense of the Dubcek reform
movement with the postulation of an autonomous and pluralist alternative
to Soviet–style socialism. In his report to the party's Twelfth Congress in
February 1969 Luigi Longo, then PCI general–secretary, gave his official
blessing to the notion of a socialist society in which "a plurality of parties
and social organizations" would be "engaged in a free and democratic
dialectic of contrasting positions, something qualitatively different from the
experiences known till now." Such a conception of Socialist pluralism was
antithetical not only to political reality in the Soviet bloc but also to the
CPSU's "general laws for the construction of socialism," foremost among
which were the leading role of the Communist party and the blanket nationalization of the economy. These "general laws," first set forth by Mikhail
Suslov in December 1956 in the aftermath of the Hungarian Revolution,[5]
were thereafter touted by the CPSU ideolugues as binding on all CPs—
whatever their geographical locale or proximity to power. Yet at the June
1969 World CP Conference in Moscow Berlinguer, soon to become Longo's
successor as PCI head, questioned the very existence of any such "general
laws." At the same time he reiterated the PCI's support for "a pluralistic
and democratic political system" under socialism. And over the years the
concept of Socialist pluralism adumbrated in the wake of the Czechoslovak
crisis was gradually broadened to include the notions of civil rights, com-

petitive elections, and the secular, or nonideological, state generally associated with the Eurocommunist vision of socialism that evolved in the second half of the 1970s.

Under the guidance of Santiago Carrillo the Spanish Communist party seconded the PCI's programmatic support for a pluralist model of socialism. But the Spanish party was more forceful in its propagation of Socialist regionalism, that is, an entente of developed Socialist states in West Europe distinct and independent from the Soviet bloc of East Europe.[6] The concept of a regional mutuality of interests among CPs from similar national environments was not of course new to the Communist movement. It was popularized under the rubric of "polycentrism," the term coined by Palmiro Togliatti in his celebrated *Nuovi argomenti* interview of June 1956,[7] and concretized by the Chinese Communists in their jockeying for support within the international Communist movement in the 1960s, especially prior to the Cultural Revolution.[8] Still, it was the PCE leaders who argued that common regional interests pointed in the direction of a united Socialist Western Europe rather than merely a convergence of strategic views on Socialist revolution and construction. The reasons for their insistence on this point are still conjectural. In the early 1970s spokesmen such as PCE ideologist Manuel Azcárate accused the CPSU of sacrificing revolutionary change in West Europe to the interests of the Soviet state and the preservation of the pan-European status quo, that is, the division of Europe into American and Soviet spheres of influence. They thereby provided a theoretical rationale for according primacy to regional solidarity among the West European CPs. But the intensity of their commitment probably stemmed from outrage at the CPSU's barely concealed efforts to unseat the PCE's autonomist leadership in the 1969–72 period, combined with lingering resentment at Stalin's withdrawal of material support from the Spanish Republican forces from mid-1937 onward (as he edged toward a nonaggression pact with Hitler).

The CPSU took a differentiated approach to the deviationist postures of the Spanish and Italian CPs, betraying as it were a cautious respect for the political clout of the PCI. As noted above, Moscow actually gave its tacit backing to dissident groups within the leading organs of the PCE, factions that were later discredited and expelled by the Carrillo leadership. With regard to the PCI, however, the Soviets displayed their displeasure largely through esoteric polemics against Socialist pluralism, at times branding its proponents as imperialist agents and at other times merely deriding the misguided views of certain fraternal comrades in the West.[9] This two-pronged tack was especially apparent in a series of articles published in the CPSU agitprop bi-weekly *Partiinaia zhizn*, in early 1974. In the late February issue an unsigned commentary lambasted Azcárate for his views on Socialist regionalism and allegations regarding Soviet support for the European status quo. The very next issue carried an article by the prominent Soviet ideologue Aleksandr Sobolev (department head at the prestigious Institute of Marxism–Leninism and editor–in–chief of the journal published by the CPSU's Institute of the International Workers Movement) denouncing unnamed advocates of Socialist pluralism, that is, the PCI as well as the PCE. Moscow's June 1977 *New Times* denunciation of Carrillo's *"Eurocommunism" and the State* employed the same approach. Carrillo was the explicit target but he was castigated among other things for favoring the strengthening of NATO, a charge that was more probably (if not more accurately) aimed at the PCI. Indeed, only the PCI had publicly acquiesced in support for NATO, pending the dissolution of both military blocs.[10]

The question of how the PCI and PCE hoped to alter the status quo in favor of their vision of Socialist pluralism and regionalism would require an in–depth analysis of their respective domestic strategies: as such it can only be touched upon here. Suffice it to say that Khrushchev's endorsement at the Twentieth CPSU Congress of the possibility of a peaceful transition to socialism in the capitalist West—however equivocal that stance, given the Soviet leader's allusion to the 1948 Prague coup as a case in point—was taken to heart by the Italian, Spanish, and French CPs. All their natural peculiarities and nuances notwithstanding, they gave their unreserved backing to the strategy of a peaceful qua electoral revolution. It was the CPSU leaders who displayed misgivings over the implications of Khrushchev's initiative. Soviet theorists did not even seem to agree on whether a peaceful revolution in the West would be brought about by an "arithmetic" majority or a "political" majority, that is, by a vote of 51 percent of the electorate or by a minority of political activists infiltrating and manipulating the levers of state power in the interests of the working–class majority.

The more orthodox conception of minority–instigated revolutionary change was infused with new vitality as a result of the violent overthrow of Allende's *Unidad Popular* government in Chile in 1973 and the nearly victorious seizure of power by the Portuguese Communist party (PCP) in 1975. The sectarian proponents of revolution by a "political" rather than "arithmetic" majority again figured prominently in the pages of *Pravda* and the more specialized CPSU political journals. And even those Soviet publicists who stressed the potential for an electoral revolution and a democratic transitional stage were constrained by the formulation of "general laws of Socialist revolution" that began to appear in the Soviet press in the mid–1970s. Although first called for by Sobolev in early 1975, this new variant on the "general laws" of socialism was expounded mainly by Konstantin Zarodov, renowned for his August 1975 *Pravda* commentary disdaining proponents of revolution by an "arithmetic" majority (read PCI and PCF) and hailing the virtues of revolution by the "political majority" (read PCP). Two years later, again in a major *Pravda* feature, Zarodov spelled out as "general laws of Socialist *revolution*" directives that were almost indistinguishable from the CPSU's much-vaunted "general laws of Socialist construction." The leading role of the Communist party and the transformation of the economic base of society (read nationalization) were ineluctable preconditions for success. The only guideline peculiar to the revolutionary process as such was the requirement that Communists be prepared to utilize *all* methods of struggle. And that was hardly novel. What was significant in the Zarodov formulation was that even a ballot-box revolution by a numerical majority must be led by the CP vanguard. In the eyes of Moscow's more sectarian spokesmen the new alliance strategies of the West European CPs (*union de la gauche, compromesso storico*) were little more than tactical embellishments on the familiar theme of orthodox frontism. Once again the legacy of the Third International outweighed the pressures for *aggiornamento* in the relations between Moscow and the West European CPs.[11]

Origins and Outcome of the June 1976 Berlin Conference

The Helsinki Connection

Since the founding of the Soviet state the CPSU's approach to West European communism has been characterized by instrumentalism and ambivalence. On the one hand, the creation of the European CPs and their adherence to the Comintern in the early days helped to legitimize the Bolsheviks' seizure of power and rapid advance toward theoretical monism and single-party rule. In effect the nonruling CPs' allegiance to Moscow enhanced the CPSU's claim to represent the wave of the future. On the other hand, as revolutionary prospects receded during the 1920s the radical impulses that had fueled the formation of the world Communist movement became an embarrassment to the foreign-policy interests of "socialism in one country." Stalin's conversion of the Comintern into an instrument of Soviet *raison d'état* temporarily papered over but in no sense eliminated this historic tension between the CPSU's ideological interests and the USSR's foreign policy. And as we shall see, in the 1970s the contradiction between these two dimensions of Soviet international relations became almost as intense in the West European arena as it had proven to be in connection with Mao's China more than a decade earlier.

In a nutshell, the June 1976 Berlin Conference of European Communist and Workers Parties may be best understood as the direct, even inevitable, outgrowth of the Soviet Union's obsessive push for the Helsinki Conference on Security and Cooperation in Europe. If in Moscow's eyes the Helsinki agreement was designed to secure the status quo in *East* Europe, the Berlin conference was intended to reassure the western CPs and the world Communist movement as a whole that the CPSU opposed the status quo in *West* Europe. Détente and class struggle were to be viewed as compatible, at least in theory. What no one anticipated when the Soviet Union began to mobilize the European Communist movement in support of a pan–European collective security conference was that the Helsinki negotiations would develop in tandem with economic crisis in the West and political radicalization in Latin Europe. Discussions of revolutionary change thus moved from the abstract to the concrete. The Latin European CPs and their autonomist allies cooperated with the Soviet Union on Helsinki. But the price they exacted on the road to Berlin turned out to be an ideological can of worms for Moscow.

By way of historical background, the precursor of the Berlin meeting was the April 1967 conference of European CPs held in Karlový Varý, Czechoslovakia. At the time Moscow appeared once again to be successfully mobilizing the Communist movement behind a key Soviet foreign policy objective: the legitimation of the postwar division of Europe. The final document appealed for a "system of European collective security" that would acknowledge and guarantee the "existing situation" on the Continent with regard to the two Germanies and the postwar territorial arrangements in Central Europe.[12] True, its tone was virulently anti–American and anti–West German, and it was Moscow's militancy on this score that caused both Romania and Yugoslavia to boycott the conference—Yugoslavia because of its policy of nonalignment and Romania because of the restoration of diplomatic ties between Bucharest and Bonn some three months earlier. However, behind the antiwestern rhetoric of the Karlový Varý resolution lay concrete foreign policy proposals that Moscow has continued to advocate to this day: the withdrawal of all foreign troops and bases, the dissolution of both military blocs, recognition of the value of "neutrality" (not nonalignment), and international treaties banning the use of force and the proliferation of nuclear weapons. All of these measures would have the effect of shifting the East–West "correlation of forces" in Moscow's favor, and all were apparently supported by the West European CPs.

Some five years later the relationship between the superpowers had been altered beyond recognition. But so too had relations among the members of the European Communist movement. The shoring up of the Soviet hold over East Europe through the occupation of Czechoslovakia—in addition to the Soviet military build–up in general—enabled Moscow to proceed with détente. Nixon and Brezhnev initialed SALT I in May 1972. The thirty–five nation Helsinki consultations began the following November. But as we have seen, the Soviet march into Prague also called into question the ideological legitimacy of the Soviet system among important sectors of the European Communist movement, impelling at least the PCI and PCE to devise alternatives to the CPSU's "general laws" of socialism. And Moscow's preoccupation with East-West détente at a time of deepening economic crisis in the West raised further doubts concerning the CPSU's ideological integrity.

Signs abounded of a growing cleavage between Soviet *raison d'état* and the Latin European CPs' commitment to domestic social change. Spanish Communist allegations regarding the CPSU's preference for the pan-European status quo at the expense of revolutionary advance in the West, first voiced at the PCE's Eighth Congress in 1972, were forcefully reiterated at a Central Committee plenum in September 1973. That same month PCI chief Berlinguer proposed the strategy of the historic compromise, justifying it as a means of avoiding the political and social polarization that had led to counterrevolution in Chile. Initially viewed as a retreat from the Communist-supported new left radicalism of the late 1960s, the historic compromise represented in fact a strategy of cautious advance in the Italian context. The Berlinguer leadership sought quite literally to insert the PCI into the political status quo, thereby enabling it gradually to alter the Italian socioeconomic order.[13] With the overwhelming defeat of the Italian Christian Democrats in the divorce referendum of May 1974 and the onset of severe stagflation soon thereafter, PCI media and leadership pronouncements began to exude confidence in the imminence of political change. A similar situation prevailed in France. The March 1973 elections to the National Assembly signaled a return to the leftward momentum that had become apparent during the 1967 parliamentary elections (only to be quelled temporarily by the conservative backlash to the May 1968 upheaval). François Mitterrand's tally of 49.2 percent of the votes cast in the presidential election of May 1974 added to the sense of impending social transformation. The French Communists, exhilarated by the prospect of breaking out of their prolonged political isolation, scheduled an extraordinary party congress for October 1974 to plot out the steps that would presumably carry the *union de la gauche* to victory in the 1978 parliamentary contest, if not sooner.[14]

The political thrust of these separate initiatives was compounded by the January 1974 Brussels conference of *West* European CPs, ostensibly convened to devise joint measures for dealing with the mounting economic crisis. The CPSU's reaction to this regional gathering was symptomatic of its attitude toward West European radicalization in general: minimal and distorted coverage in the Soviet press. Significantly, *Problems of Peace and Socialism,* edited by the sectarian ideologue Konstantin Zarodov, did not see fit to publish the final Brussels communiqué—in contrast to the prominence it generally gave to international Communist documents. In fact the Brussels conference may well have been intended as a warning to Moscow that continued disregard for West European Communist concerns would further undermine not only the CPSU's ideological authority but the very unity of the pan-European Communist movement.

The upshot was Soviet acquiescence in the proposal for a second pan-European Communist conference, first suggested by the PCI in early 1973 after the inception of the Helsinki talks. CPSU spokesmen made it clear that such a gathering would be but the prelude to another world conference of CPs, as was the case with Karlový Varý in relation to the 1969 Moscow conference. Unlike Karlový Varý, however, ideological questions were to dominate the protracted negotiations for the Berlin Communist summit. At issue was not the Soviet Union's foreign policy of détente—with which all European CPs (except Albania) were in basic agreement—but the insistence on the part of the West European parties that détente be coupled with moves toward altering the status quo. Berlin was to be their reposte to Helsinki.

The Soviet Union could have no quarrel with the idea of social change as such. It was the content of that change that mattered. The crux of the polemics between Moscow and the Latin European CPs since 1968 had been their divergent visions of socialism and strategies of revolution. Not surprisingly, therefore, this was also to be the case during the lengthy preparations for the Berlin conference. And inevitably the debate over Socialist revolution and construction was to lead to a confrontation on the central issue of Moscow's authority within the European Communist movement and the validity of "proletarian internationalism" as an organizational norm within that movement.

The Eurocommunist Entente

From the outset of the preparatory talks,[15] the Soviet leadership was ambivalent and even defensive. It has been suggested that the CPSU endorsed the pan-European conference project in order to thwart the move toward West European regionalism and reassert Soviet influence over the nonruling CPs. Yet prominent CPSU leaders, including Brezhnev himself, never ceased voicing their preference for *world* Communist meetings (where Moscow would presumably command a larger "arithmetic" majority). And at the Budapest preparatory meeting in December 1974 Ponomarev warned of the dangers of "Eurocentrism."

Soviet misgivings could only have been exacerbated by the decision reached at the initial Warsaw consultative meeting in October 1974 to operate according to the procedural rules of consensus and public disclosure during the preparations for the Berlin conference. The Helsinki talks, it will be recalled, were conducted according to the consensus principle, partially at Yugoslav and Romanian insistence. The League of Communists of Yugoslavia (LCY) now stipulated as conditions for its participation in the Berlin summit not only the consensus rule but also each participant's right publicly to disclose its position on all matters relating to the conference proceedings.[16] Belgrade's views were announced by the LCY delegate at the preliminary consultations in Warsaw and simultaneously published in the Yugoslav press, thereby presenting the CPSU with a fait accompli. The Soviet leadership acquiesced, aware that the cooperation of the autonomist Italian, Spanish, and Romanian parties was contingent upon the LCY's presence. Yet the men in Moscow surely understood that decision-making by consensus and public disclosure would inhibit the imposition of CPSU views, even with majority support, on any document emanating from the Berlin conference.

Furthermore, it is reasonable to assume that the Soviet leaders were not only ambivalent toward the European CP summit but they were also defensive regarding the charges, explicit or otherwise, that their foreign policy was detrimental to the cause of revolution in the capitalist world. Ponomarev almost admitted as much in his speech to the October 1974 Warsaw meeting when he explained that the paramount importance of ending the cold war had perhaps led the CPSU to underestimate the extent and import of western radicalization during the 1960s. But Soviet defensiveness also took on a self-righteous and even admonitory tone: to wit, social radicalism *cum* economic crisis might well provoke a fascist reaction, as in the 1930s. Hence the continuing importance of the SALT and Helsinki negotiations.

During 1974 the Soviet position was probably complicated by differences of opinion within the leadership itself over the proper pace and mode of revolutionary change in the West.[17] Such differences could be discerned among the establishment intellectuals writing in the Soviet equivalent of think-tank journals. And the appearance of divergent viewpoints at that level presupposed either uncertainty or controversy in the upper echelons of the CPSU. The cleavages ran along two planes: cautious reformism versus militant activism and electoral majoritarianism versus orthodox political manipulation by a Leninist vanguard. As noted earlier, the latter dichotomy can still be seen in the Soviet press. However, the question of revolutionary tempo was resolved in a conservative direction by the winter of 1975. The CPSU could obviously not opt for the status quo, confronted as it was by the growing militancy of the West European CPs. Its solution to the dilemma of revolution versus détente was to endorse the strategy of a democratic transitional stage between capitalism and socialism, a formulation that was flexible enough to embrace the French, Italian, and even for a time the Portuguese Communist policies while at the same time cautioning against destabilizing revolutionary adventurism.

Both the Soviet conservatives and radical activists may well have supported the initiative for the Berlin conference, the former viewing it as a mechanism for restraining the Western CPs and the latter as a means of goading them on. But it was soon to become evident that the cautious conservatives had won the day in Moscow. The radical viewpoint no longer found an outlet in Soviet public affairs journals, while the CPSU displayed reticence toward the Portuguese crisis and preoccupation with normal state-to-state relations with Western powers even after the signing of the Helsinki agreement in August 1975. This posture soon drove the French Communist leadership to level against Moscow the same charges voiced by the Spanish party in the early 1970s: Soviet *raison d'état* inclined the CPSU toward acquiescence in the status quo rather than support for class struggle in the West.

This brings us back to the original linkage suggested between the Helsinki consultations and the pan–European CP summit. By compromising on the latter Moscow hoped to still criticism from within the Communist movement over the former. Accordingly, on the eve of the October 1974 Warsaw consultative meeting that laid the initial groundwork for the protracted Berlin negotiations, a formal CPSU–PCE communiqué was signed in Moscow, the gist of which was that steps toward détente should in no way impede social transformation in the West. The CPSU also agreed to refrain from interference in internal Spanish party affairs. The first such top-level CPSU–PCE meeting to be held since 1970, the Spanish delegation included Manuel Azcárate, the individual so recently singled out for censure in the Soviet journal *Partiinaia zhizn* because of his allegations of Soviet support for the status quo. His presence in the Soviet capital signaled that the CPSU leaders were prepared to reach an accomodation of some kind with the more alienated members of the West European Communist movement.

It may be conjectured that the PCI, formal cosponsor with the Polish party of the Berlin summit and early supporter of the conference project, played a part in the CPSU–PCE rapprochement. The Italian Communists had backed the Spanish party in its post-1968 clash with Moscow, regularly publishing PCE statements—including those of Azcárate—in the PCI press. The Italians had at the same time maintained correct if not cordial ties with the CPSU, notwithstanding the esoteric PCI–CPSU polemics over Socialist pluralism. Such conciliatory behavior was an integral part of the Italian party's tradition, as exemplified by its consistent opposition to Moscow's attempt to mobilize the international Communist movement against the Chinese Communists during the escalation of the Sino–Soviet dispute in the early and mid-1960s.[18]

It would be appropriate, then, that the Italian party should play the role of mediator in the clash that developed between the Soviet-bloc loyalists and West European dissident CPs in the mid-1970s. This was even more the case since, as noted earlier, the historic compromise represented something of a paradox, that is, a forward strategy within the context of the Italian political status quo. Not only precedurally but strategically the PCI bridged the chasm between the defiant Spaniards and restive French, on the one hand, and the conservative Soviets on the other.

With the PCE–CPSU rapprochement of mid–October 1974 and the subsequent agreement on the consensus rule at the Warsaw consultative meeting, a tenuous compromise was reached that permitted the beginning of the twenty months of bargaining that led to the Berlin conference in late June 1976. The tortuous intricacies of the sixteen–odd meetings of drafting groups and editorial commissions, not to mention the many bilateral consultations, required to achieve consensus on a final conference document have been masterfully recounted by Kevin Devlin. What is important to underscore here is the impact on that process wrought by the French Communist *volte-face* of mid–1975. In November 1975 the PCF publicly aligned itself with the PCI and the PCE on questions of revolutionary strategy, thereby giving rise to the tripartite entente that was soon to receive the label of Eurocommunism. But at the root of the growing PCF–CPSU controversy lay the question of revolutionary tempo: namely, the degree to which Moscow's cordial relationship with the French government ran counter to the interests of French communism.

PCF–CPSU tension over the nature of Franco–Soviet interstate relations had probably been simmering for some time.[19] Moscow's eagerness to pander to the powers–that–be in the Élysée was evident ever since De Gaulle's rupture with NATO in the mid–1960s. But only in the 1970s, under the twin prods of economic crisis and leftist electoral gains, did the contradiction between Soviet *raison d'état* and PCF militancy come to the surface. For despite the seeming radicalization of French politics, Moscow did not alter its line. The first open sign of dissension came in May 1974 when the Soviet ambassador to Paris paid a visit to then presidential candidate (and Finance Minister) Giscard d'Estaing between the first and second rounds of the closely contested presidential election, thereby provoking a protest in the PCF daily *L'Humanité* against such a public display of favoritism. Thereafter, during the PCF's Extraordinary Twenty–first Congress in October 1974, convened just after the Warsaw consultative meeting for the purpose of further mobilizing the French left, *Pravda* waxed enthusiastic over the fiftieth anniversary of Franco–Soviet diplomatic relations. While devoting some attention to the PCF congress, the CPSU daily compressed Marchais's critique of President Giscard d'Estaing's pro–NATO foreign policy into one terse sentence. By the same token, *Pravda's* coverage of Brezhnev's trip to Paris the following December for the annual Franco–Soviet state summit was extensive and glowing. Then in March 1975—on the heels of the conservative victory over the radical militants within the CPSU—French Premier Jacques Chirac was warmly received in Moscow.

A signal of French Communist displeasure at this attitude of business as usual came in mid–May 1975 when the PCF issued a statement asserting that the crux of the dispute in the snarled Berlin talks lay between those who favored détente *cum* revolutionary struggle and those who would "go easy on imperialism, for the sake of diplomatic considerations or domestic opportunities." This was among other things a jibe at the CPSU for its preoccupation with Helsinki and the improvement of governmental ties with the western powers at a time of heightened prospects for radical change in France as well as in Portugal.

But it was President Giscard's visit to Moscow October 13–18, 1975, that marked the decisive turning point in PCF–CPSU relations. By way of backdrop, one of the Berlin conference working groups had just concluded a meeting on October 9–10. On October 10 the PCF Politburo drafted a communiqué announcing its sharp opposition to the political status quo, defined as Giscard's pro–Atlantic orientation as well as his domestic conservatism. The statement also chided Brezhnev for not publicly repudiating a purported appeal to him by Premier Chirac the previous March to help restrain the PCF's militancy. Although the communiqué was dated October 10, it was not published in *L'Humanité* until October 13, the day of Giscard's arrival in Moscow. The very same issue of the PCF daily carried an interview with Jean Kanapa, the PCF's international affairs spokesman, on the recent meeting of the Berlin conference editorial group. While conceding that any document emanating from the projected CP summit should focus on détente, Kanapa stipulated that this in no way precluded the PCF from pursuing "our revolutionary struggle in France for the burning needs of the working people, against the Giscardian power of the monopolies, for democracy and socialism." He was, in short, saying yes to détente but no to the status quo back home.

It seems clear that both the Politburo communiqué and the Kanapa interview were timed to coincide with Giscard's visit to Moscow, thereby throwing down the gauntlet to the CPSU. On October 15, *Pravda* carried an abridged version of the communiqué, omitting the personal attacks on Giscard and Brezhnev. That same day Brezhnev unexpectedly cancelled a scheduled meeting with Giscard, to the consternation of western newsmen who assumed (once again) that the general secretary was on his deathbed. As Brezhnev reappeared in sound health the very next day, it seems more than probable that on October 15 he was simply back at the CPSU Secretariat trying to cope with this latest challenge to Soviet authority.

The PCF's attempt to arouse Moscow to a more militant ideological stance was to no avail. The Brezhnev–Giscard talks ended with their usual fanfare and the signing of a series of Franco–Soviet technical agreements. On October 25 *L'Humanité* resumed the offensive with an article condemning Soviet imprisonment of dissident mathematician Leonid Pliushch in a mental institution. *Pravda* replied the next day with a long, unsigned commentary hailing Franco–Soviet state relations. Then came the electrifying PCF–PCI declaration of common strategic principles that heralded the French party's adherence to the emergent Eurocommunist grouping. Its publication on November 18 coincided with yet another in the ongoing series of Berlin preparatory meetings, this one notable for the unexpected intransigence displayed by a CPSU delegation that included among its members Konstantin Zarodov.

A high point in PCF–CPSU tensions came during the Soviet party's Twenty-fifth Congress when Brezhnev, in spite of the earlier PCF protests, not only declared that Franco–Soviet *state* relations and views on a number of foreign policy questions had grown closer, but also claimed that "this has met with widespread support from the French people and the majority of political parties in France." Marchais, who had made a point of not attending the CPSU congress, quickly informed the world that the PCF was not one of those parties! On February 26, the day after Brezhnev's report appeared in *Pravda, L'Humanité* retorted with verbatim excerpts from the PCF leader's scorching attack on Giscard's foreign policy at the Twenty-second PCF Congress held earlier that same month.

The winter and spring of 1976 were marked by escalating polemics between the CPSU on the one hand and the PCI on the other.[20] (The PCE was preoccupied with the evolving post–Franco political scene in Spain.) Soviet publicists now focused on the norms that should govern relations among Communist parties. They insistently demanded the observance of "proletarian internationalism," defined by them as recognition of the international responsibilities of each party and the primacy of inter–CP unity. And they stipulated as a major criterion of proletarian internationalism the avoidance of anti–Soviet criticism on the part of fraternal CPs. The French rejoined that proletarian internationalism entailed reciprocity, that is, that Moscow should practice what it preached. The Italians called for an entirely new form of internationalism, one that assigned priority to *national* party interests while also embracing solidarity among *all* progressive forces, Communist, Socialist, and Catholic alike. At the same time, the PCF stepped up its criticism of Soviet repression of domestic dissidents. The PCI did likewise, although its spokesmen characteristically accentuated the positive, insisting that Soviet economic and social development had reached the point where the free confrontation of dissenting ideas was not only inevitable but would be beneficial. The mutual sparring became quite nasty when Suslov, at a meeting of the Soviet Academy of Sciences in mid-March, equated "regional" and "national" versions of Marxism with opportunism. Leading PCF and PCI spokesmen promptly rebuked him by name in their party dailies. Meanwhile, on each side of the polemical barricades, lesser party personalities were subjected to more invidious accusations.

The truth of the matter, however, was that the fate of the Berlin conference already lay in the hands of the autonomists. Should the CPSU not concede to their demands, the conference would simply not take place. Should the conference not take place, Moscow would have to shoulder the blame. Once the traditionally pro–Soviet PCF had thrown in its lot with the defiant Spaniards and maverick Italians, the CPSU would have difficulty persuading even the loyalist CPs that the twenty months of negotiations had foundered on the objections of a small band of recalcitrant dissidents. The CPSU had too much at stake ideologically to risk either the onus for, or the fact of, a breakdown in the conference talks. Not only would the mounting charges that the Soviet Union was a status quo–oriented super-power be bolstered; the CPSU's domestic legitimacy as the vanguard of the world Communist movement would also be further undermined.

The Soviet Quandary

The European Communist conference finally took place in East Berlin on June 29-30, 1976. With the proceedings open to the public, western news media focused on the unprecedented diversity of views expressed in the speeches of the twenty-nine participating CP leaders, including Marshal Tito—present at an international Communist meeting for the first time since the Soviet-Yugoslav break of 1948. Neither the pro–Soviet loyalists nor the East European autonomists and West European pluralists broke substantially new ground in the presentation of their respective party positions. But the articulation at a common forum of the widely disparate visions of socialism and norms of interparty relations that had evolved during the preceding half decade was a momentous development in the annals of the Communist movement.

Equally significant was the content of the Berlin conference document that finally emerged with the consent, however reluctant, of all participants.[21] The Berlin declaration elaborated upon those foreign policy proposals of the 1967 Karlový Varý statement that had not yet been achieved while avoiding the earlier document's fulminations against U.S. aggressiveness and West German militarism. (Was this the result of the CPSU's support for détente or the ever more perceptible PCI and PCE, as well as Romanian and Yugoslav, even-handed approach to Moscow and Washington?) In contrast to the Karlový Varý statement, however, the Berlin document stressed not the need to guarantee the pan–European territorial status quo (which presumably had been achieved at Helsinki) but the need to *alter the West European political and social status quo* in favor of socialism. And it did so without prescribing in any way the manner in which such a change should be affected. Gone were the Soviet dictums on "general laws" and "proletarian internationalism" that had featured so prominently in the concluding statement of the 1969 World Conference of Communist and Workers parties. [22] In their place were the autonomist formulations regarding "different paths" to socialism, "internationalist solidarity" among CPs and all other forces working for social progress, the legitimacy of "nonalignment," and acknowledgment that criticism of communism was not tantamount to anticommunism. Perhaps most portentous was the injunction to observe in practice the Helsinki principles of "respect for the rights of man and fundamental liberties, including the liberty of thought, conscience, religion or creed ...." In the international Communist context the autonomist coalition had succeeded in putting together a genuinely revolutionary document. Fortunately for Moscow, the contents of the final Berlin statement were merely prescriptive rather than binding upon the conference participants.

The CPSU's first reaction to the proceedings and outcome of the Berlin conference was defensive and domestically oriented. Readers of *Pravda* would not have suspected the range of views espoused by the European CPs. The most controversial portions of the Carrillo, Berlinguer, and Marchais speeches were simply deleted from the *Pravda* summaries. For example, Carrillo drew an analogy between the Communist movement and early Christianity, only to proclaim that "we are beginning to lose the characteristics of a church," including what he called the mysticism of predestination. Berlinguer emphasized the importance of regional CP ties, "on the West European level" as well as "on the all-European level," alluding favorably to the concept of Eurocommunism. Marchais stressed the depth of the capitalist crisis yet debunked the notion that the imperialists could resolve it by recourse to war or fascism, thus rebutting a standard Soviet (and PCI!) argument against undue revolutionary militancy in the West. Indeed, he insisted that the PCF would not permit steps in behalf of peaceful coexistence to inhibit in any way its struggle for socialism. All these themes were expunged from the CPSU daily, as were all critical innuendos against the Socialist systems in East Europe. In the same vein, statements made in support of Socialist pluralism by Carrillo and the suddenly rather eloquent Marchais were also omitted. Curiously, Berlinguer's advocacy of libertarian socialism appeared intact, perhaps because he had said much the same thing at the Twenty-fifth CPSU Congress the previous March. But the Soviet overseers of ideological probity evidently had no intention of informing the Soviet public that the French and Spanish CPs had joined forces with the PCI on this question. Distortion by censorship was compounded by outright falsification: *Pravda's* editorial commentaries on the Berlin summit repeatedly lauded it as a victory for "proletarian internationalism," the "general laws," and the growing unity of the international Communist movement.

Then in the autumn of 1976 the CPSU shifted from the defensive to the offensive, initiating a campaign against Eurocommunism that resembled in manner and substance the post-1968 campaign against pluralism. Much as in the early 1970s, Soviet criticisms were echoed and often magnified by loyalist CP spokesmen, with the Czechs replacing the East Germans as the most vitriolic antagonists of the Eurocommunist deviation. Similarly, the attacks were made on two levels; one treason, the other revisionism. At times the Euro-communists were accused of anti-Sovietism and collusion with imperialism because of their divisive impact on the European Communist movement. At other times they were merely censured for denying the validity of the CPSU's "general laws," or ridiculed for touting as theoretical verities propositions that had never been tested in practice. Authoritative Soviet commentators and political media (for example *Kommunist* and *Pravda*) took the latter, more moderate tack. The former, more extreme charges were voiced in lesser Soviet journals of limited domestic circulation (for example, *New Times*) or by the more sectarian CPSU allies (for example, Bulgarian CP chief Todor Zhivkov and the prominent Czech leader Vasil Bílak). Again, the Soviet leadership proved reluctant to reveal to its own citizens the widening breach in the purportedly ever more unified movement.

As in the antipluralism drive, there was also an escalation from generalized polemics to attacks on specific individuals and parties. From late 1976 through the first half of 1977 the Soviet loyalists stuck to broad-gauged diatribes. Then in June 1977 Moscow launched the *New Times* attack on Carrillo, castigating him for what amounted in Soviet eyes to treasonous conduct, that is, aid to NATO by way of his support for West European regionalism and "conscious anti-Sovietism." These themes were reiterated to varying degrees by the loyalist CPs of East Europe. By autumn 1977 sideswipes against the PCI also began to appear in *Pravda*. In a major feature in the CPSU daily on September 1, the day before top-level talks between Suslov and PCI Secretariat member Gian Carlo Pajetta were to take place, the leader of the pro-Moscow Greek CP attacked the "revisionists'" theory of Eurocommunism precisely for its denial of "the basic general laws of Socialist revolution." On October 1 an unsigned TASS report in *Pravda* noted with "surprise" the participation in "anti-Soviet" seminars and symposia by members of the PCI, "whose leadership has not once denounced the campaigns against the Soviet Union and other Socialist countries." In effect Moscow seemed to be stepping up its own criticism of the PCI for the twin sins of revisionism and anti-Sovietism. As we have seen, the CPSU managed to put on a facade of harmony for the sixtieth anniversary celebration of the October Revolution in early November. But immediately thereafter Soviet polemics against Eurocommunism resumed, while the PCI-PCE entente was further cemented during Carrillo's visit to Rome.

The question that must be addressed is why the CPSU returned to a posture of confrontation with the West European CPs *after* Berlin. The pre-Berlin polemics can be interpreted as part of the jockeying for position that accompanied the final stages of bargaining on the conference document. But with the conclusion of the summit and the subsequent concealment of the CPSU's concessions from the Soviet people, what was there to be gained from a confrontation that would only further publicize the cleavages in the European Communist movement? Indeed, the frequent Soviet-inspired attacks on "Eurocommunism" fairly invited western media to concentrate on the phenomenon of West European CP regional ties and their convergent views at a time when the major parties involved were actually focusing their attention more on domestic concerns than interparty issues and contacts. The PCI was busy enhancing the quasi-governmental status accruing from its electoral gains of June 1976. The PCF was bent upon advancing its position within the *union de la gauche* as well as among French voters in the upcoming municipal elections of March 1977. The PCE was preoccupied with obtaining legal status in the kaleidoscopic context of post-Franco Spain. True, the March 1977 Madrid meeting of Carrillo, Berlinguer, and Marchais signified that the concept of Eurocommunism as an affinity of strategic views was alive and well, a point that was to be reaffirmed at the bilateral PCI-PCE summit the following November. But the participants refrained from responding collectively to the Soviet polemics (just as they refrained from a joint condemnation of Soviet-bloc repression). To their sectarian CP critics they turned, as it were, the other cheek.

One may, therefore, surmise that a major impetus for the intensifying polemics against Eurocommunism came from developments within the Soviet bloc itself. Dissident activism in support of human rights was growing in Czechoslovakia and Poland, and to a lesser degree in the Soviet Union and GDR. The loyalist ideologues evidently sought to discredit one of the wellsprings of that activism, the Eurocommunist vision of socialism, by stigmatizing it as revisionism if not outright subversion.

Yet the CPSU and its allies were caught in a bind. They justified their single-party rule at home on the basis of their claim to knowledge of universal laws of historical development. The ongoing allegiance of the international Communist movement to the legacy of the October Revolution provided a major buttress to that claim. Increasingly, however, Moscow and its loyalist allies were confronted with the systemic challenge from the most substantial remaining component of that movement, the major nonruling western CPs. The CPSU could not condone the pluralist alternative to Soviet-style socialism but neither could it break with its proponents without undermining the ideological matrix of its own domestic power. Thus limited in its options, it confined itself to largely esoteric polemics aimed at party cadres close to home as much as those in the West European CPs. Probably much to its chagrin it was discovering that Soviet superpower status was of little consequence as the correlation of ideological force and appeal within the pan-European Communist movement began to shift in favor of the Eurocommunists.

The Loyal Opposition: Constraints and Opportunities

If the Soviet-bloc parties were bound to the West European CPs by the exigencies of domestic power and legitimacy, the Western Communists' opposition to a rupture with Moscow was rooted as much in ideological commitment as in political expediency. One must bear in mind that the members of the PCI, PCF, and PCE are Communists by choice, not circumstance—in contrast to so many of their East European comrades. And while the appeals of communism have changed over time, the international dimension of that commitment has remained a constant attribute.

From the 1930s into the 1960s West European Communist criticism of "existing socialism" was minimal and "proletarian internationalism" was the accepted standard of interparty relations. The contradiction between the promise and practice of socialism in the East was either rationalized away as imperialist propaganda or relegated to the inner recesses of the individual Communist's consciousness. During the mid-1930s Moscow's support for the Spanish Republican forces and the antifascist cause in general, especially when contrasted with the inaction of the western democracies, inured many party stalwarts to the extent and import of Stalin's Great Purge. By the same token, the postwar conservative restoration in France and Italy (in terms of political orientation and neoliberal economic policies) not only dashed the hopes for sociopolitical transformation harbored by the militants who had flocked to the Communist banner during the Resistance years. It also lent a positive cast to the emerging people's democracies in East Europe. Even during the Khrushchev era the revelations of Stalin's crimes were apparently counterbalanced by the trends toward consumerism and reduced political regimentation in the East. Similarly, the surge in French, Italian, and Spanish economic growth rates was vitiated in the minds of the western Communist activist by the wide disparities in income distribution.

It was the shock of the Soviet invasion of Czechoslovakia that impelled West European CPs to articulate alternative visions of socialism and to launch systematic critiques of the Soviet model. This process of critical rethinking was further galvanized by pragmatic considerations as ever wider sectors of the western electorates became disenchanted with the domestic status quo, especially in the face of mounting economic crisis. Still, the West European CPs rejected the prospect held out by some political analysts of electoral gains at the expense of international Communist ties. As we shall see below, they began instead to acquire the characteristics of a loyal opposition within the pan-European Communist movement.

The tenacity of the West European Communists' internationalism may be explained in a number of ways. Three major reasons come to mind, involving questions of ideological affinity, historical identity, and political calculation. First of all, considerable ideological agreement continued to exist among the West and East European CPs not only with regard to the obvious issue of militant, Third World "liberationism" but also with regard to the economic structure of a Socialist society. Despite the polemical exchanges of the 1970s, PCI leaders from Berlinguer on down repeatedly endorsed the "fundamental directions" of Soviet economic policy, claiming that it represented the interests of the working class. For Italy they projected a mixed economy under socialism but for the USSR they merely sought more extended participation in economic decision-making. In a more striking example of convergent views, PCF leader Georges Marchais voiced allegiance to the "general law" of "common ownership of the principal means of production and exchange" even at the French party's Twenty-second Congress in February 1976—notwithstanding the intensifying polemics with the CPSU and the party's decision at that same congress to discard the slogan of the "dictatorship of the proletariat." The PCF's later rupture with the French Socialists over the question of how far to nationalize French industry in the event of an electoral victory by the *union de la gauche* should thus have come as no surprise. As for the Spanish party, in *"Eurocommunism" and the State* Carrillo deplored not so much the economic structure of Soviet society as the absence of democratic control over the public sector and within the workshop.

A second consideration that bound the Eurocommunists to the CPSU was the simple fact of their historical identity. A new generation of leaders may have been coming to power. But the men, now in their fifties, were nurtured in their twenties on the ideals of international solidarity, Soviet ideological prowess, and the historic breakthrough of the October Revolution. And the surviving members of the Comintern generation were at one time intimately linked to Moscow by a web of personal and bureaucratic ties. Carrillo remarked revealingly in his speech to the Berlin conference, "Today we have grown up." But adults rarely disavow their parents, however critical of their upbringing they may be in retrospect. Not only that, but it would be rather absurd for the West European CPs to break with the Soviet Union of the 1970s when they failed to do so in the 1930s or late 1940s. How could their leaderships explain such inconsistency to themselves, let alone their followers? Finally, unlike the Chinese and Yugoslav Communists, whose historical legitimacy was rooted in their lonely partisan struggles, the legitimizing matrix of the major West European CPs could be traced to events and time-frames that inextricably linked them to the CPSU. The PCI leaders proclaimed themselves disciples of Gramsci and Togliatti. Yet both men were hailed in turn as onetime guardians of Comintern interests (Gramsci in the mid-1920s and Togliatti in the mid-1930s). The PCF acquired its mass base during the Popular Front era of the 1930s, a time when its Stalinist credentials were beyond reproach. The PCE emerged as a significant political movement only during the Spanish Civil War, when it was perforce subordinated directly to Soviet power.

This brings us to the third question of political calculation. A rupture with the CPSU, at least by the PCI or PCF, with their entrenched party structures, would be likely to provoke a schism in that party itself, encouraged all the while by the Soviets. The rank-and-file members who flocked to the Soviet booths at local festivals of *l'Unità* and *l'Humanité*, who delighted in cut-rate excursions to Moscow and Leningrad, would be incensed and bewildered. To be sure, pro-Soviet sentiments seemed to be on the wane. Nevertheless, an undetermined number of older militants still harbored the ideological image of the "peoples' democracies" inculcated during the cold war years and reinforced by their firsthand experience with the unemployment statistics and the staggering disparities in income distribution that prevailed in Mediterranean Europe during the early postwar years and continued in evidence into the 1970s. Thus for the party leaderships to break with Moscow would mean to risk an undetermined degree of damage to the internal cohesion of their cadres. And they would also lose that aura of transcendent internationalism that must account for some of their devoted following.

There is another more speculative yet also more grave aspect to the political importance of ongoing West European Communist ties with Moscow, namely, their possible linkage to the Soviet Union's policy of détente. The PCE and PCF may have criticized Moscow in the mid-1970s for excessive preoccupation with harmonious East-West relations. But given the deterioration of Soviet-American détente in the late 1970s, such criticism appeared somewhat fatuous. Indeed, it seemed not inconceivable that the CPSU would react to a pronounced tilt to the West by, say, the PCI in a manner not dissimilar to Mao's reaction to Khrushchev's overtures to the West in the late 1950s: namely, a hard-line militant foreign policy. Since it was under conditions of East-West détente that the western CPs had enhanced their domestic stature, a return to cold war hostility would be Moscow's most deadly riposte to an interpary schism. This is not to say that the CPSU would consciously wave over the heads of its western comrades a damoclean threat of renewed cold war tensions. However, heightened conflict with the Eurocommunists, especially in the context of a western CP rapprochement with Peking, could exacerbate the Soviet leadership's latent tendencies toward a siege mentality and self-imposed isolation.

Whatever the case, in the late 1970s the major western parties proved intent on maintaining correct interparty ties with Moscow while simultaneously asserting with ever greater concreteness their particular views on issues pertaining to the European Communist movement. The PCF confined itself largely to the defense of absolute autonomy for all CPs, ruling and nonruling, in their ideological and policy choices. For the PCI and PCE, however, their more insistent advocacy of socialism in liberty entailed the spillover effect of harsher criticism of the absence of liberty in the Socialist systems of East Europe.[23] Both tactical expediency and theoretical coherence dictated such a linkage. Since the Italian and Spanish Communists argued that a pluralist form of socialism was possible and necessary in West Europe precisely because of the high level of economic development in that region, they could scarcely avoid defending similar political principles for the countries of "developed socialism" in the Soviet bloc. Carrillo was blunt on the subject, calling for the transformation of the USSR into a democratic workers' state. True to form, the PCI leaders were more subtle and conciliatory. The most effective contribution the Eurocommunists could make to "the renewal of existing Socialist societies," they claimed, would be the completion of the revolutionary process in the capitalist metropoles, the achievement of Socialist pluralism in their own societies. Thereafter they would influence developments in the East by force of example, as it were. At the September 1977 national festival of *l'Unità,* this position was eloquently spelled out by Secretariat member Paolo Bufalini—and echoed by Berlinguer himself in his closing speech to the gathering a week later. It was subsequently to become a recurrent theme in PCI policy statements touching on international relations.

However, the Eurocommunist leaders did not limit themselves to statements of abstract principle in their efforts to influence the Soviet-style systems. They also cultivated close ties with those regimes that shared one or another aspect of their programmatic goals—while criticizing those that did not. This differentiated approach helps to explain the autonomist coalition that evolved on the road to the Berlin conference between the internally rigid Romanian CP, on the one hand, and the Eurocommunist triad on the other. Their mutual interest in CP independence as well as their inception of frequent interparty contacts dates back to 1967, the year that Romania broke with the Soviet foreign policy line by establishing diplomatic relations with Bonn and maintaining them with Israel after the June War. The West European CPs' selective treatment of the East European ruling parties according to the criterion of programmatic affinity also accounts for the cordial relations between the PCE and PCI, on the one hand, and the League of Communists of Yugoslavia (LCY) on the other.

Steps toward a PCI-LCY entente were begun by Togliatti back in 1956 and resumed during the early and mid-1960s, with the Italian party playing a moderating role in the renewed Soviet-Yugoslav party clash of the late 1950s. In early October 1977 a PCI-LCY communiqué, published after a visit by Berlinguer to Belgrade, underscored the two parties' agreement on the importance of the Berlin conference document, the positive value of "nonalignment," and the need to respect "in practice" the principle of autonomy in the face of "negative tendencies still present in the international Communist movement" (a slur at the Soviet attack on Carrillo). Small wonder that *Pravda* ignored both the visit and the communiqué. As for the rationale behind the PCI-LCY entente, the Titoist posture on autonomy needs no elaboration. The Yugoslavs also endorse Socialist pluralism in principle, ascribing their own insistence on exclusive CP control at home to the danger that multi-partyism might intersect with and exacerbate the ethnic tensions that plague their land. Thus they were staunch supporters of the West European CPs' pluralist orientation, including the bid for closer ties with Socialist and democratic forces in general. The LCY outdid even the PCI in its ardent defense of Carrillo and the PCE after the *New Times* incident.

Perhaps the most significant and at the same time sensitive area of pan-European CP ties involved the PCI's relations with the party leaderships of Poland and Hungary.[24] With regard to such ties, the PCF was relatively detached because of the primacy it accorded to autonomy, while the PCE was effectively precluded because of its blatant "anti-Sovietism." Moreover, geopolitical considerations were conducive to a more West European orientation on the part of the Spanish party. By the same token, geopolitics went far in explaining the Italian party's preoccupation with pan-European as well as West European interparty contacts. But as far as the PCI's relations with Poland and Hungary were concerned, there was an additional factor to consider. In both countries the top CP elite appeared to be divided between an orthodox conservative wing and an innovative moderate wing. It may be surmised that the PCI's intensification of multiple-level interparty contacts with Warsaw and Budapest was designed to enhance the political leverage of the more innovative leadership groupings in those countries, including CP chiefs Edward Gierek and János Kádár.

The PCI took an ambivalent posture toward the crisis that erupted in Poland after the June 1976 worker's riots sparked by sharp hikes in the price of basic food products. On the one hand, the Italian party press carried full and apparently objective reports on the riots, the resulting arrests, and the subsequent activities of the Polish dissident Worker's Defense Committee in support of those arrested. The PCI refrained from direct editorial censure of the regime's conduct, all the while intimating its disapproval by juxtaposing the dissidents' allegations of police brutality and violations of legality to the official party denials of such conduct. On the other hand, the Italians maintained high-level party contacts with Warsaw in 1977 and published authoritative commentaries on the Polish scene that coincided with the views of the Polish Communist innovators on such themes as the need for more decentralized decision-making and consultation with public opinion groups, including nonparty intellectuals and the Roman Catholic Church. When the arrested workers and their allies among the dissident intelligentsia were finally granted amnesty and released from prison, the PCI warmly commended the regime's conduct, singling out Gierek for particular praise. There is no way of gauging the extent to which the PCI's attitude may have influenced the course or outcome of the Polish crisis. Nevertheless, its show of support for conciliation rather than confrontation on the issue of internal dissidence was indicative of its overall posture toward developments in the Soviet bloc: encouragement to the forces of moderation without undue provocation to the more sectarian elements in the party leaderships.

PCI-Hungarian relations became ever more cordial during 1977, as if the Hungarian party leadership had been encouraged by the outcome of the Berlin conference to assume a more independent posture on European Communist matters. Open political dissidence didn't appear to be a domestic issue in Hungary. There were, however, differences within the party leadership regarding economic policy. In the immediate aftermath of the Polish food-price riots, *l'Unità* carried several reports on a somewhat similar rise in Hungarian food prices. Not only did the PCI daily comment favorably on the smooth manner in which the Budapest regime had implemented these unpleasant measures. But in doing so it also alluded to an inner party controversy over the size of the peasants' private plots, indicating firm PCI agreement with the resolution of that controversy in favor of the peasants.

The Hungarian experiment in market socialism was understandably of great interest to the PCI, given its own program of a mixed economy in a future socialist Italy. This was to be made clear during October 1977 summit talks between Berlinguer and Kádár which included, according to the official communiqué, a discussion of "political economy." The meeting itself was doubtless facilitated by Kádár's favorable comments on Eurocommunism during visits to West Europe (Austria, Italy, and West Germany) in late 1976 and the first half of 1977, precisely at the time of the escalation in Soviet, Bulgarian, and Czechoslovak polemics against Eurocommunism. More importantly, the reports on the bilateral meeting as well as the contents of the ensuing communiqué indicated growing rapport between the two parties. And as Berlinguer commented during an interview on Hungarian television, the positive state of Italian-Hungarian CP relations was a good thing not just for their two countries but for the international Communist movement as a whole. Evidently the CPSU did not view this budding pan-European Communist entente in the same light. *Pravda* omitted from its report of the official communiqué the following sensitive points: the discussion of economic questions, the call for more frequent exchanges of experiences and ideas between the two parties, and the statement that the talks took place "in an atmosphere of fraternal cordiality and in a spirit of solidarity and reciprocal understanding." Soviet discomfort notwithstanding, Hungarian-PCI lower-level contacts multiplied during the course of 1978.

While the Eurocommunists were friendly with the nonaligned and innovative Yugoslavs, cooperative with the independent-minded Romanians, and outgoing toward the more moderate Soviet-oriented regimes, they were openly critical of political repression in the USSR, Czechoslovakia, and to a lesser extent the GDR. There were, to be sure, gradations in the intensity of their positions. As a rule, the PCE's critiques tended to be systemic, the PCI's systematic, and the PCF's selective and fairly superficial. For instance in *"Eurocommunism" and the State* and elsewhere, Carrillo questioned whether the Soviet system could even be considered Socialist, given the absence of political liberty. PCI leaders and commentators, on the other hand, readily conceded the Socialist nature of the USSR's economic base while suggesting, usually in a friendly manner, the need to democratize its political superstructure, and rather consistently criticizing domestic Soviet regimentation and repression. The French Communists interspersed occasional blunt denunciations of CPSU violations of democratic principles with generally bland and positive coverage of internal Soviet developments in *L'Humanité*. Only in mid-1978 did the French party initiate a more systematic critique of Soviet reality in its daily press. But it is too early to say whether this marked a fundamental shift in PCF policy or a tactical adjustment to the internal party recriminations triggered by the March 1978 defeat of the *union de la gauche*.[25] (Marchais's kind words for the USSR at the PCF's Twenty-third Congress in May 1979 would indicate that the latter is more likely.)

The three parties' reaction to the emergence of the "Charter 77" movement in Czechoslovakia clearly reflected the variegated posture noted above. The PCE published the document[b] in its entirety. The PCI press merely summarized the document but immediately came to the defense of its signatories in its editorial commentaries and daily coverage, expressing outrage at their persecution by the Prague regime. The PCF was relatively

---

[b]The "Charter 77" document appealed to the Prague regime to respect the rights guaranteed to its citizens by the Czech constitution and international human rights covenants.

mild and conspicuously belated in condemning the repressive actions against the "Charter 77" dissidents.[26]

When Carrillo, Berlinguer, and Marchais met in Madrid in March 1977, they declined to make any critical references to the Soviet-bloc systems in their joint communiqué. This may have been partly due to the substantive differences in their evaluations of those regimes. But it was surely also due to their conviction that collective denunciations by the West European CPs would invite collective rebuttals from the East European party-states. Such a confrontation, in turn, would make more difficult the promotion of bilateral East-West CP ties on matters of mutual interest. Indeed, collective denunciations could develop a dynamic of their own, leading to a polarized, "two-camp" mentality or even to an outright schism. For all the reasons noted earlier, the West European CP leaders wished to avoid such a denouement.

However, criticism of political reality in the eastern half of Europe could not be avoided. When, for example, Soviet dissidents Orlov, Shcharansky, and Ginzburg—initially detained in early 1977—were tried and sentenced in mid-1978, the French, Italian, and Spanish CPs were impelled by programmatic dictates and electoral exigencies to denounce Moscow's conduct. Each did so on its own account. Yet their separate denunciations came close to provoking the collective rebuttal they had hoped to avoid. In mid-December 1978 a surrogate world Communist conference was held in Sofia under the auspices of the Bulgarian CP and the Soviet-sponsored journal *Problems of Peace and Socialism*. It was ostensibly convened to discuss theoretical questions relating to the construction of socialism. But it turned into a polemical broadside, the cutting edge of which was aimed at those Communists who criticized the workings of "existing socialism," that is, the political order in the Soviet bloc.[27] As the delegate from the Paraguayan CP put it, "anti-Sovietism" had become "the main danger" to the solidarity of the world Communist movement.

On this score as on many others the Peking regime was lambasted. More notable, however, was the chorus of reproaches leveled against "Eurocommunism." Explicit attacks by the Czech leader Vasil Bilak and half a dozen nonruling CP delegates (those from Norway, Luxemburg, Israel, Canada, Jordan, and Turkey) were accompanied by veiled innuendos on the part of numerous other CP spokesmen. The PCI and Romanian (also the British) delegates stood firm, taking issue with the Soviet leaders on a wide range of questions. The French and Spanish CPs stuck to straightforward expositions of their respective domestic programs. The Yugoslavs, who had never been associated with the Soviet-dominated *Problems of Peace and Socialism*, were not present. In the end the dissonant voice were all but lost amid the repeated refrains that criticism of communism was tantamount to anticommunism. Moscow had gone far in reversing one of the major gains of the 1976 Berlin Conference.

In February 1979 the pan–European coalition of autonomist CPs that had evolved during the negotiations for the Berlin Conference appeared further weakened by divergent reactions to the outbreak of the Sino–Vietnamese border war. In many respects the Italian, French, and Spanish Communist parties paralleled Moscow in their denunciation of Peking. There were of course variations in their positions. The Spanish party prided itself on having condemned the Vietnamese invasion of Cambodia the previous December just as it now condemned the Chinese invasion of Vietnam. The French party defended the Vietnamese move into Cambodia but attacked China's "premeditated aggression" against Vietnam. The Italian party tilted toward Hanoi on the Cambodian affair and expressed "open disapproval" of China's incursion into Vietnam. By way of contrast, the Romanian and Yugoslav parties assumed a posture of strict neutrality, simply calling for the withdrawal of all foreign troops, the Chinese from Vietnam and the Vietnamese from Cambodia.

The seeming alignment of the PCI and PCF behind Moscow on the Southeast Asian conflict was preceded by a PCI shift to a harder line on China in mid–October 1978, following a summit meeting between Berlinguer and Brezhnev. During the summer months signs of Italian Communist interest in a rapprochement with Peking had multiplied. (The PCE had discussions with the Chinese party in the early 1970s while the PCF remained the most intransigent of the three Latin CPs with regard to the Peking regime.) In a press conference on the eve of his departure for Moscow, Berlinguer had reiterated his party's receptivity to the restoration of ties with the Chinese Communist party (CCP). Significantly, however, Berlinguer's trip to Moscow, which included stops in Paris and Belgrade, coincided precisely with Chinese Foreign Minister Huang Hua's state visit to Italy, the first such top–level governmental meeting since the establishment of diplomatic relations between Peking and Rome in 1970. Contact between the two men was thus precluded. Moreover, the PCI–CPSU communiqué issued on October 10 included a joint condemnation of anti–détente moves by "certain imperialist, militarist, and reactionary circles." In the contemporary Soviet lexicon the term "militarist" denoted the Chinese. Finally, as if to underscore the turnabout, in a press conference upon his return to Rome Berlinguer indicated that "for now" the PCI would not normalize relations with the CCP.

In no other respect did the Berlinguer trip to Moscow result in a change in PCI policy. The October 10 communiqué underscored the urgency of proceeding with détente and reiterated a major Soviet concession at the 1976 Berlin Conference: the legitimacy of disagreements among CPs. In his above–mentioned press conference after the Moscow summit Berlinguer

spelled out as continuing areas of PCI–CPSU disagreement their conceptions of socialism, attitudes toward political dissent, and *positions on
China*. It may thus be inferred that Moscow had sought a much more direct
condemnation of Peking thant the veiled allusion included in the communiqué.

By the same token, the CPSU remained adamant in its support for
"proletarian internationalism" and antipathy toward Eurocommunism. To
be sure, its spokesmen had become a bit more sophisticated in advancing
their arguments. In the pages of *Pravda* during the weeks following the
PCI–CPSU summit, only Soviet surrogates such as the inconsequential parties of Luxemburg, Uruguay, the FRG, and the United States expressed
unqualified support for "proletarian internationalism." A seasoned CPSU
ideologue like Vitalii Korionov referred instead to "internationalist solidarity" and ridiculed the idea that the Soviet party was trying to impose
"recipes" (read general laws) on other CPs, insisting rather that it would
"win minds and hearts by force of its example." Nevertheless, on the eve of
the sixty-first anniversary of the October Revolution Vadim Zagladin, first
deputy chief of the CPSU's international section, publicly stigmatized the
idea of "Eurocommunism" as an attempt to set the western CPs against the
CPSU. He also dismissed as "a dangerous delusion" the notion that the
bourgeoisie would peacefully renounce power in the event of a Communist
electoral victory, citing the fate of the Allende regime in Chile as a case in
point.[28] The next day, November 7, 1978, Zagladin's views were roundly
trounced in *l'Unità*. The ongoing cleavage between the CPSU and the western CPs was further underscored by the anti-Eurocommunist overtones of
the Sofia conference a month later.

Why, then, did the Italian, French, and Spanish CPs part company
with their Romanian and Yugoslav allies on the issue of the Sino-Vietnam-
ese border war? A partial answer may lie in the fact that the western parties' association with Moscow was largely free of the *nationalist* frictions
that encumbered Soviet–East European relations. In the case of Romania
and Yugoslavia the reality of inter*state* hostilities had exploded the myth of
international Communist camaraderie and gone far in undermining ideological and historical ties with the CPSU. Indeed, the Romanian and Yugoslav leaderships' visceral insistence on sovereign independence and equality
vis-à-vis Moscow constituted the fundamental link between themselves and
Peking. Its practical corollary was scrupulous respect for the autonomy of
every Communist party. Bucharest and Belgrade deplored in principle the
Southeast Asian hostilities but refrained from passing critical judgment on
the belligerents.

By way of contrast, the postwar experience of the West European CPs
inclined them toward anti-Americanism rather than anti-Sovietism. And in
France and Spain this sentiment was reinforced by similar feelings on the

part of a large portion of the non–Communist population. As a result, their policy toward China during the winter of 1978–79 may have been colored by the Chinese leadership's growing alignment with the United States. Even more to the point, support for the Hanoi regime had been for years a touchstone of ideological probity for the western CPs. It had stood as a symbol of their commitment to Third World liberationism. And the Vietnamese party had reciprocated with unqualified acclaim for such western advances as the PCI's electoral gains of June 1976. In short, historically conditioned attitudes helped to explain the West European Communist parties' prompt condemnation of Peking's incursion into Vietnam.

For the Italian Communists there was a further consideration: the preservation of East–West détente took precedence over rigid adherence to the principle of CP autonomy. The emergence of détente had been an essential precondition for the PCIs political advances in recent years. And its claim to a share of domestic power was threatened by any deterioration of Soviet–American relations and by the specter of a return to cold war polarization at the domestic as well as the international level. There were of course many reasons for the growing strains between Moscow and Washington during the second half of the 1970s. Peking's unabashed anti–détentiste posture, its attempt to rally the West to an anti–Soviet crusade (the mirror–image of its efforts to rally Moscow to an anti–imperialist crusade some two decades earlier), was one cause among many. Nevertheless, PCI leaders feared that Chinese conduct with regard to arms purchases from the West as well as border frictions with Vietnam might further exacerbate Soviet–American tensions. It may even be conjectured that the CPSU exploited that fear to pressure the Italian party into closer alignment on the China question during Berlinguer's trip to Moscow. Whatever the case, the PCI viewed China's invasion of Vietnam as a potentially destabilizing force in the European arena as well as in East Asia.

In sum, the western Communist parties' posture on the Southeast Asian imbroglio was dictated by all the considerations of ideological affinity, historical conditioning, and political calculation that in general continued to link them to the CPSU.

From the vantage point of mid–1979 the loyal opposition within the pan–European Communist movement was thus heterogeneous in its composition and goals. Alone each component had but limited clout. Together, however, they still constituted a not inconsiderable political force. Whether pluralist or merely autonomist by East European standards, they provided one another with backing and leverage vis-à-vis the orthodox conservatives that dominated the CPSU and its closest allies. Such support extended also to the discredited innovators within these latter countries, including the members of the Dubček reform movement and the Soviet Union's "loyalist" dissidents such as Roy Medvedev. This multi-faceted and amorphous coalition had been responsible for the final document of the 1976 Berlin Conference and certainly deserved partial credit for the CPSU's vacillation toward Carrillo. It may even have contributed to the relative moderation of the Polish and Hungarian regimes. Despite the setbacks suffered during the winter of 1978–79, there seemed no reason not to anticipate from it additional evidence of genuine clout in the future.

Notes

1. This incident is described and analyzed by Eusebio M. Mujal-Léon in "The Spanish Left: Present Realities and Future Prospects," chapter 4 of this volume.
2. For a detailed exploration of CPSU-PCI relations during the 1970s, see my paper, "Moscow and the PCI: Kto Kogo?" presented to the American Political Science Association Annual Meeting, Washington, D.C., September 1–4, 1977.
3. Kevin Devlin exhaustively analyzed the antecedents and preparations for the 1976 Berlin conference in "The Interparty Drama," *Problems of Communism* (Washington, D.C.) XXIV: 4 (July–August 1975): 18–34, and "The Challenge of Eurocommunism," XXVI: 1 (January–February 1977): 1–20. For a general analysis of the earlier world conferences see William E. Griffith, "The Diplomacy of Eurocommunism," in Rudolf L. Tökés, ed., *Eurocommunism and Détente* (New York: New York Univ. Press, 1978), pp. 385–436.
4. For the PCI's strategic and organizational views in the 1920s see my "Italian Communism and the 'Opportunism of Conciliation,'" *Studies in Comparative Communism* (Los Angeles) VI: 4 (Winter 1973): 362–396.
5. Zbigniew Brzezinski, *The Soviet Bloc,* second revised edition (Cambridge: Harvard Univ. Press, 1967).
6. The PCE's regional orientation is analyzed in Eusebio M. Mujal-León, "The Domestic and International Evolution of the Spanish Communist Party," in Tökés, *Eurocommunism and Détente,* pp. 204–270.
7. It should be noted that for Togliatti the term polycentrism denoted not only regional convergences among Communist parties but the broader idea of political convergences among multiple Socialist-oriented forces. It is this second connotation that underlies the PCI's present insistence on cooperation among Communists, Socialists, and reform-oriented Catholic groups both in Italy and on a European scale.
8. The key studies of China's role in the international Communist movement during this period remain William E. Griffith's *The Sino-Soviet*

Rift and his *Sino-Soviet Relations, 1964-1965* (Cambridge: The MIT Press, 1964 and 1967, respectively).

9. See note 2 above.

10. Robert D. Putnam, "Italian Foreign Policy: The Emergent Consensus," in Howard R. Penniman, ed., *Italy at the Polls* (Washington, D.C.: American Enterprise Institute for Public Policy Research, 1977). See also Putnam's "Interdependence and the Italian Communists," *International Organization* XXXII: 2 (Spring 1978): 301-349.

11. For Soviet attitudes toward the West European CPs, see Robert Legvold, "The Soviet Union and West European Communism," in Tökés, *Eurocommunism and Détente* pp. 314-384; Richard Löwenthal, "Moscow and the 'Eurocommunists,'" *Problems of Communism* XXVII: 4 (July-August 1978): 38-49; Claudio Terzi, "L'URSS e l'eurocomunismo," *Il Mulino* (Bologna) XXVII: 257 (May-June 1978): 391-407; and my "Contemporary Soviet Perspectives on Revolution in the West," *Orbis* (Philadelphia), XIX:4 (Winter 1976): 1359-1402.

12. The English text appeared in *World Marxist Review* X: 6 (June 1967): 4-8.

13. For sensitive analyses of the PCI's domestic strategy, see Stephen Hellman, "The Longest Campaign: Communist Party Strategy and the Elections of 1976," in Penniman, *Italy at the Polls;* and Peter Lange, "Notes on the PCI and Possible Outcomes of Italy's Crisis," unpublished paper.

14. The French presidential elections of 1974 are exhaustively treated in Howard R. Penniman, ed., *France at the Polls* (Washington, D.C.: The American Enterprise Institute for Public Policy Research, 1975). For the PCF's orientation during this period see Ronald Tiersky, "French Communism in 1976," *Problems of Communism* XXV: 1 (January-February 1976): 20-47.

15. For discussions of the protracted preparations for the Berlin Conference, see note 3 above.

16. The Yugoslav conditions were stated by a LCY delegate to the Warsaw meeting, Aleksandar Grličkov, on October 17, 1974 and publicized that same day by the Belgrade press agency Tanjug.

17. I explore these differences in the *Orbis* article cited in note 11 above.

18. See note 4 above and Donald L.M. Blackmer, *Unity in Diversity: Italian Communism and the Communist World* (Cambridge: The MIT Press, 1968).

19. For an illuminating discussion of the evolution of PCF-CPSU relations see Ronald Tiersky, "French Communism, Eurocommunism, and Soviet Power," in Tökés, *Eurocommunism and Détente.*

20. For details see my APSA paper cited in note 2 above.

21. The English text appeared in *New Times* (Moscow) 28 (July 1976): 17–32.

22. The English text appeared in *World Marxist Review* XII: 7 (July 1969): 3–25.

23. In addition to their running press commentaries, see Santiago Carrillo, *"Eurocomunismo" y Estado* (Barcelona: Editorial Critica, 1977), as well as two recent PCI collective volumes: Sergio Bertolissi, ed., *Momenti e problemi della storia dell'URSS* (Rome: Editori Riuniti-Istituto Gramsci, 1978) and Pietro Valenza, ed., *I Paesi Socialisti nell'analisi dei comunisti italiani* (Rome: Newton Compton Editori, 1978).

24. This subject is treated by Charles Gati, "The 'Europeanization' of Communism?" *Foreign Affairs,* April 1977, pp. 539–553; my chapter, "The Impact of Eurocommunism on the Socialist Community," in Andrew Gyorgy and James A. Kuhlman, eds., *Innovation in Communist Systems* (Boulder, Colo.: Westview Press, 1978); and Rudolf L. Tökés, "Eastern Europe in the 1970s: Détente, Dissent, and Eurocommunism," in his *Eurocommunism and Détente,* pp. 437–511.

25. Dissident PCF historian Jean Elleinstein deplored *L'Humanité's* "prettification" of Soviet reality in a series of articles in *Le Monde,* April 13–15, 1978. The PCF daily subsequently carried extensive condemnations of the Soviet trials of Orlov, Shcharansky, and Ginzburg during the spring and summer of 1978. Then, on September 4, 1978, *L'Humanité* published a PCF Politburo endorsement of a harsh indictment of the Soviet system written by five Communist intellectuals. See Francois Cohen et al., *L'URSS et nous* (Paris: Editions socials, 1978).

26. See note 2 above.

27. For abridged texts of the conference speeches, see the North American edition of *Problems of Peace and Socialism: World Marxist Review* (Toronto) 22: 2–4 (February, March, April 1979): 3–27, 3–107, and 3–73, respectively. At the Sofia conference Michele Rossi, PCI delegate as well as editorial board member, denounced the journal's involvement in the organization of the conference. He also argued that *Problems of Peace and Socialism* "should be nothing but a journal,...a rostrum for the exchange of opinion and experience," threatening the Italian party's withdrawal from the journal's editorial board should this not be the case. The decision to publish the highly polemical proceedings may well have been Moscow's riposte to Rossi's specific criticisms as well as to the PCI's posture of overall defiance.

28. *Pravda,* November 6, 1978, pp. 4–5.

9 The Problem of Western Policy toward the West European Communists

Richard Löwenthal

Introduction: Defining the Subject

The general theme of this volume is the state of the West European "left" and the problems posed by its evolution. However, the West European Socialists and Social Democrats are themselves a conscious part of the western community, except for such sections as may at different times and places come under Communist influence. There are therefore no problems of western (foreign) policy toward the Socialist left. Foreign policy problems only arise for those western countries that have no significant Communist party at home—above all for the United States, Britain, and West Germany—in dealing with the influence of strong Communist parties in other western countries.

The most acute form such problems may take, and have taken in recent years, are Communist bids for power, or at least for government participation, in a West European country. A less acute but still significant type of problem might arise if Communists outside the government succeeded, by effective cooperation with other neutralist or nationalist forces, in creating what amounted to a "veto group" against the participation of their country in West European or Atlantic cooperation.

The only serious Communist bid for power in a West European country in recent years occurred in Portugal in 1974–1975, in the wake of the overthrow of the right-wing dictatorship by a revolutionary military junta including strong pro-Communist influence. As this attempt has failed and the danger no longer exists, it will not be discussed in this chapter. By contrast, serious efforts for government participation have been undertaken by the "Eurocommunist" parties of France and Italy, and the Italian attempt has achieved partial success and may yet be crowned with full success. The French attempt has failed for the time being, but the French Communists have the continued potential of an anti-Atlantic and anti-European veto group in cooperation with the Gaullists.

It should also at least be mentioned that the official Greek Communist party led by Florakis, which is not Eurocommunist but unconditionally loyal to Moscow, has at least some prospect of eventually forming a similar veto group with the "Panhellenic Socialist Party" of A. Papandreou (which is not affiliated with the Socialist International) and smaller groups.

Assumptions Concerning the Nature and Policy of the
"Eurocommunist" Parties

Any discussion of western policy toward those West European Communist parties that may acquire government influence in a foreseeable time must rest on an analysis of the roots and the degree of their "Eurocommunist" transformation. As that analysis has been assigned to other contributions, it cannot be undertaken in detail in the present chapter. Instead, a summary of the results of such an analysis as the present writer would see them will be presented so as to clarify the assumptions underlying his views on western policy.

I believe that the "Eurocommunist" transformation of a number of Communist parties in a number of advanced industrial countries, including those of Italy, France, and Spain as well as Japan, is due to three main causes:

1. The prolonged existence of Communist mass parties in a number of modern, increasingly prosperous countries, in persistently nonrevolutionary situations and—except until recently in Spain—in democratic conditions has produced a growing integration of the masses of Communist members and followers into non–Communist societies. This has presented the Communist parties with the choice of either becoming an increasingly effective participant in the process of democratic decision of these countries by accepting its rules and overcoming their isolation, or losing their mass following and becoming sterile sects.

2. The gradual weakening of the international authority of the Soviet Union and the CPSU, first by the long-term effects of the crisis of de-Stalinization and then by the Sino-Soviet schism, has enabled Communist parties outside the Soviet bloc under able and ambitious leaders to acquire increasing ideological and strategic autonomy. The fruit of that autonomy has been, in a number of cases, the rejection of the model of the Soviet and East European regimes for advanced countries with democratic traditions, as well as a number of particular criticisms of specific actions and policies of those regimes.

3. While the growth of East-West 'détente' in the course of the past decade has enabled the Communists in some western countries to overcome their traditional isolation as the "party of the enemy" in the cold war and to find partners for tactical cooperation, the economic crisis of inflation plus recession has in the last few years strengthened the general attraction of the left opposition in countries with conservative governments, enabling the Communist parties to benefit in different degrees from country to country.

The formal commitment of the "Eurocommunist" parties to the rejection of single-party rule and the acceptance of pluralistic democracy with all civil rights, notably the right of opposition to a government including

Communists and to its overthrow in free elections, must be seen in the light of those three causes: it has become acceptable or even desirable to the majority of Communist followers and cadres due to their increasing integration in their existing social and political system; it has become possible despite the resistance of Soviet ideological spokesmen due to the decline of Soviet authority; it has become urgent as a precondition for winning allies for "progressive" government coalitions.

On this basis, I make the following assumptions about the present policy goals of the West European Communist parties and their possible collision with western interests:

1. No West European Communist party at present has either serious prospects or indeed, since the Portuguese Communist defeat of 1975, serious intentions of "taking power" by the "peaceful road" on the model of postwar Eastern Europe, let alone by a violent road.

2. Several West European Communist parties have seriously endeavored for some years to join coalition governments by means of mass mobilization and electoral propaganda combined with interparty diplomacy, in the hope of occupying important positions in the state apparatus and influencing both domestic and foreign policy.

3. In a situation in which democratic institutions were only emerging, as in Spain, or appeared to be in increasing danger, as in Italy, the consistent attitude of the Italian and Spanish Communist parties has been a responsible concern for the creation and stability of democracy as the best condition for their activity. On the other hand, not only have the Moscow-oriented Portuguese Communists tried to prevent the establishment of parliamentary democracy, but the "Eurocommunist" French CP has taken an attitude of irresponsible demogoguery, regardless of the consequences for democracy.

4. While the "Eurocommunist" parties are no longer under effective Soviet control, they retain an important sense of fundamental solidarity with the Soviet Union as "the country of the October Revolution" or "the first Socialist country." This does not make them accept Soviet leadership in their own affairs and does not prevent them from criticizing the Soviet and East European regimes on specific issues, including such vital and sensitive issues as the 1968 intervention of the Warsaw Pact in Czechoslovakia; individual "Eurocommunists" have even gone so far as to doubt the Socialist character of the Soviet Union. But it remains important, in degrees varying from country to country, for the direction of their influence on the foreign and defense policies of their governments if they should join them.

5. All "Eurocommunist" parties, even those who have otherwise moved farthest from Leninist doctrine, still cling to Lenin's formula of "democratic centralism" in principle, while practicing it with different degrees of rigidity or flexibility: the PCE has moved farthest from the

Leninist model, the PCF hardly at all. This continues to enable the leaders
to impose sudden tactical changes, again in different degrees.

Western Policy Options

The key questions posed for western policy by the approach of some West
European Communist parties to government participation are, first,
whether the "outside" western powers—those without a substantial internal Communist problem—should try to prevent Communist government
entry in other western countries, and if so, by what means; and second, how
they should react if Communist government participation in one or more
western countries actually comes about. A third relevant question is what
the outside powers can do to prevent the rise of national "veto groups"
opposed to a common western policy, consisting of Communists with neutralist or nationalist allies, even outside the government.

The Western Interest

It is not a matter of course that Communist government participation in any
western country is, in present circumstances, necessarily more harmful to
the common interest of the West than any realistically conceivable alternative. For two years after the end of World War II Communists sat in the
governments of all the liberated countries of Western Europe, including the
provisional governments in the western states of occupied Germany
appointed by the Americans, British, and French; in every case, they left
office when this was demanded by the elected parliamentary majority. In
Italy, the Communists took an active part in drafting the democratic constitution that is still in force, and they keep reminding the other parties of it to
this day. More recently, a period of Communist government participation
in Iceland caused some difficulties for the country's role in the NATO organization, but passed without serious harm—which any attempt at outside
interference with the forming of that coalition might well have brought
about. On the other hand, Communist government participation in post-
revolutionary Portugal plainly constituted for a time a serious danger both
to the democratic evolution of that country and to its membership in the
western alliance, and common western interest clearly justified the effort of
the West Europeans both to offer to Portugal a European alternative and to
support the democratic rivals of the Communists.

Evidently, the western attitude to a possible Communist entry into a
West European coalition government should depend on its likely effect on
both the country's democratic stability and its foreign and defense policies.

In the case of France, the French Communists' strongly anti-Atlantic, anti-European, anti-American, and anti-German outlook augured ill for France's foreign and defense policy, even on the (probable) assumption that the Communists would not or could not insist on the direct control of either of the ministries involved. Though the French Communists had declared that they would not demand the abandonment of the Atlantic Alliance, their opposition to any practical move of interallied cooperation that could be interpreted as a step back toward integration was certain, and their demand for a defense concept directed *tous azimuts,* against the United States and the Federal Republic of Germany as well as against Russia, promised serious problems. Similarly, they had only reluctantly accepted the European Community as an accomplished fact, had opposed direct elections to the European Parliament, and remained determined to oppose any further progress toward European integration.

But French Communist government participation had, in the last six months before the 1978 elections, also become increasingly problematic from the viewpoint of democratic stability—not because the PCF had any plans for the revolutionary overthrow of democracy, but because its sudden tactical switches and uninhibited demagoguery showed no sense of responsibility for the working of the democratic system. The attempt to raise the range of industries to be nationalized and of wage increases to be granted beyond what had originally been agreed to in the "Common Program" with their Socialist partners showed complete unconcern with the risks of sharpening the economic crisis or with the danger of extreme political tension if such a program was carried out by a narrow majority—the very danger that had caused the Italian Communists to advocate a "historic compromise" for ensuring a broad majority. Their repeated sudden transition from political cooperation with the Socialists to bitter attacks on them as "traitors" justified the worst fears for their behavior in a government coalition with them. On all those grounds, French Communist membership in such a coalition was clearly undesirable from a general western—as indeed from a French—point of view.

In the case of Italy, the negative impact of Communist government participation on western foreign policy and defense interests would be much more limited. Not only have the Italian Communists explicitly stated their willingness to leave the foreign and defense ministries to other parties; they have long been active supporters of the European Community, and are committed to the view that the Community's—and Italy's—foreign policy should be "neither anti-American nor anti-Soviet." Their statement that Italy should not leave NATO "as long as Europe remains divided between opposing military blocs" has not been explained as a tactical concession to their prospective coalition partners, but based on the argument that security and peace in Europe demand a balance between the eastern and western forces as long as their conflict continues; and that argument has been made more convincing by references to the Warsaw Pact intervention in Czechoslovakia, which the Italian Communists have never forgiven, and to the need for protecting the independence of Yugoslavia, with whose leaders the Italian Communists have long maintained a close understanding. However, while their European policy can in no way be described as antiwestern, but at worst as semi-neutralist, their sympathies in conflicts within the Third World, notably in the Middle East and in Africa, are wholly on the Soviet side, except for minor reservations at the time of the Soviet switch from Somalia to Ethiopia. Moreover, they have taken an active part in the Soviet-orchestrated campaign against the "neutron bomb." It may thus be argued that Communist government participation in Italy might create problems if Italian NATO bases were to be used in an extra-European conflict, though in the absence of Communist control of the defense ministry those problems would not necessarily be larger than if a massive campaign against such use of the bases were conducted by a nongoverning Communist party.

On the other hand, it may be argued with considerable plausibility that direct government participation by a Communist party genuinely committed to the stability of Italian democratic institutions would be healthier for those institutions thatn an indefinite prolongation of the agony of a succession of governments lacking a solid majority. The advantage of greater democratic stability might even outweigh the limited dangers in the foreign and defense field.

Apart from France and Italy, there are no other cases in which Communist government participation seems likely in the foreseeable future.

The Tools for Western Influence from Outside

The means open to the "outside" western powers for influencing the decision on Communist government participation in the "critical" countries are economic cooperation, advice, and pressure, including the threat of various "destabilizing" measures.

Economic support for the "critical" countries in their struggle against inflation and recession is clearly useful and necessary independent of any effect on the position of the Communists. But to the extent that it is successful, it may also, by diminishing the causes of mass discontent, diminish the pressure for including the Communists in the government. It is strongly to be recommended, within the limits of the "outside" countries' capacity to help, and on terms calculated to insure economic recovery without excessive social hardship.

Advice should be addressed to the potential coalition partners of the Communists, and should come rather from western public opinion in general and from the foreign ideological friends of those potential partners in particular (Socialists to Socialists, Christian Democrats to Christian Democrats) than from foreign governments: advice on the internal affairs of a country given publicly by foreign governments is not received as advice but resented as pressure. Advice from the right sources should normally concentrate on the institutional safeguards to be ensured by the partners of the Communists, such as the need to keep them from the control of such key positions as the premiership, foreign affairs, defense, and the police. In cases of strikingly irresponsible Communist behavior on the threshold of entry into the government, as recently in France, the advice should also stress the lessons of such behavior for the Communists' would-be partners.

Pressure could range from general government statements, describing the entry of Communists into western governments as unacceptable, to explicit threats of withdrawing economic cooperation from such governments and to propagandist encouragement of a flight of capital; in theory it could even extend to support for antidemocratic coups to prevent such a government or to the threat of direct military intervention from outside. Obviously, the last-named threats or measures would be incompatible with the democratic principles to which the members of the western alliance are committed and would risk greatly weakening the external authority and credibility and even the internal cohesion of the states engaging in such a policy of direct or indirect intervention in the internal affairs of their allies. But even purely economic pressure or demonstrative official statements opposing Communist government entry regardless of its terms would tend to be counterproductive in the sense of promoting a nationalist solidarization with the Communists and an antiwestern radicalization of their prospective allies. It is characteristic that following a statement of the U.S. administration early in 1978 that warned against Communist government participation in Western Europe, some of the very same Italian Christian Democratic spokesmen who had privately asked for such a warning protested against it publicly, under the counter-pressure of Italian public opinion, in the name of national sovereignty. Generally speaking, the appearance of external pressure would thus tend to anticipate and promote the very effects of Communist government participation that it is supposed to prevent—a sharpening of conflicts between the "critical" and the "outside" countries. It is my considered opinion that it should be strictly avoided.

The Practice of Some "Outside" Governments

In general, the economically stronger western governments, notably of the United States and West Germany, have been willing to support the economy of the "critical" countries, above all Italy, on nondiscriminatory terms and have tried to restrain the flight of capital from them as much as was in their power. The means of support have been either direct loans or the approval of loans by the International Monetary Fund. It is true that while those loans were not tied to political conditions in the sense of a veto against Communist government participation, they had in the nature of the situation to be linked with economic conditions to ensure rational use of the funds involved; in particular, budgetary measures and a restraint in wage increases had to be demanded as safeguards against an accelerating inflation. Inevitably, such economic conditions could be, and were, interpreted by important sections of public opinion in the receiving country as the pressure of foreign capital on the living conditions of the Italian workers. Nevertheless, the Italian Communists and the Communist-controlled trade unions have to some extent cooperated in making their enforcement possible, as they understood that the conditions were not directed against them but were needed to achieve the economic stabilization required for the survival of Italian democracy.

Political advice opposed to Italian Communist government entry has been emphatically given to the Italian Christian Democrats by the German and to some extent by other Christian Democratic parties. The Italian party has pretended to accept the advice but has in fact agreed to several transitional steps incorporating the Communists into the government majority, short of giving them seats in the cabinet. The episode seems to have contributed to the development of divergent trends among the Christian Democrats of Europe, where the German and some other parties are increasingly cooperating with the British Conservatives and the French Gaullists while the Italian and Belgian parties do not.

The German Social Democrats have carefully refrained from criticizing the French Socialists for their electoral alliance with the Communists—though they clearly viewed it with mixed feelings—or from advising them against Communist government participation. It may be presumed, however, that in personal contacts they have expressed their views about the safeguards to be taken in such a coalition.

As for government statements, the British government has been very reticent. The former British Foreign Secretary, David Owen, has, in a carefully balanced speech on the phenomenon of Eurocommunism, recognized important changes in the policy statements of the parties concerned, but expressed the view that the evidence of their durability is still insufficient for trusting them. But he has refrained from emphatic warnings in the name of his government.

The U.S. administration, on the other hand, has been both outspoken and inconsistent. Under President Ford, the warnings of Secretary of State Henry Kissinger against Communist government entry anywhere in Western

Europe were nothing short of alarmist, and he has repeated them no less emphatically when out of office. The Carter administration started with the publicly announced intention to regard the question of Communist government entry by democratic procedures as an internal affair of the countries concerned, but early in 1978 the president issued a new public warning against such entry. As far as is known, this was not due to a reconsideration of the merits of such a policy by the president and his principal advisors, but due on one side to American domestic pressures and on the other to the promptings of leading Italian Christian Democrats transmitted by the U.S. ambassador in Rome, Richard Gardner. The domestic pressures were due to the wave of anti-Communist emotions created in American public opinion by Soviet-Cuban activities in Angola and at the Horn of Africa; more specifically, they came from the "moderate" wing of the Republican opposition around Kissinger and Ford, whose support Carter then urgently needed for the ratification of his Panama treaties, from the rigidity of the anticommunism adopted by the AFL-CIO, and from the intellectual "New Right."

Finally, the Federal German Chancellor, Helmut Schmidt, was quoted after the 1976 western summit meeting in Puerto Rico as stating that the assembled western statesmen had agreed on their attitude to the danger of Communist government participation in Western Europe. The report was officially denied by him, and it is likely that a discussion had taken place but no formal decision been reached. Since then, there have been no German government statements on the matter. There is reason to believe that the German government was greatly relieved when the imminence of French Communist government participation disappeared after the elections of March 1978. On the other hand, the belief now appears to be widely shared in the Bonn federal government (though not in its foreign ministry) that the advantages of Italian Communist government entry for Italy's democratic stability might outweigh the risks of a limited Communist influence on Italian foreign policy.

None of the "outside" governments has played with encouraging antidemocratic opposition in the event of legal Communist government entry in Italy or France, nor have any entertained the idea of military intervention in such a case.

Policy toward Communists in Government

So far, no Communists have entered the government of any major western country, though the Italian Communists have recently made important advances on the road to such an entry. If such an event takes place, the options open to the "outside" western governments remain basically the same as before, and so would the main arguments. But there may be in that case a more continuous range of options from unconditional economic cooperation through various forms of conditional cooperation to destabilizing pressure.

Willing and generous cooperation with a government including Communists might counteract the risk or its "antiwestern" radicalization by improving economic conditions, strengthening the influence of the Communists' "moderate" partners, and promoting the further integration of the responsible Communist leaders and the majority of their followers into the western democratic system. As this integration proceeds and the government concerned is economically successful, an increase of tensions between the representatives of such a type of "Eurocommunism" and the Soviet leaders is also likely.

However, unconditional cooperation regardless of the economic and other behavior of the governments concerned is not realistically possible for democratic governments responsible to their own electorate: they must ensure that any economic support is used to reasonably good effect, and that it does not benefit a government basically hostile to the common western cause.

Deliberate destabilizing pressure against a coalition government including Communists is likely to prove even more dangerous to western interests than threats and pressure before the Communist entry: it would be felt as expressing hostility not only to the Communists but to their partners in government and drive them together into an explosive mixture of both nationalist and social radicalization. In the end, there would be a serious likelihood that the western country or countries concerned would be lost to the western cause and indeed turn against it and lead increasingly to the Soviet side in world affairs.

The real problem for the "outside" western powers will therefore be to find the right methods of practicing conditional cooperation. They must urge rational economic behavior by the countries to be supported, not in a spirit of doctrinal prejudice and petty chicanery, but in order to ensure a good chance for the people concerned to come to enjoy the fruits of willing and generous support. Any economic conditions should be obviously relevant to the chances of recovery and free from the stigma of ideological prejudice.

Political conditions should not be explicit at all, but implicit in the fact that the cooperation is offered to a friendly, democratic country. In other words, the only political reasons for withdrawing it should be a drastic impairment of basic democratic liberties, which is unlikely in the conditions envisaged, or an unmistakable turn to an actively antiwestern course in foreign affairs. Support should not be suspended because of isolated differences over particular issues, but only because of a reasoned conviction that the country in question is already lost to the West.

Summary

A situation in which independent, "Eurocommunist" parties may come to enter western governments is equally unprecedented and fraught with risk for the "outside" western powers and for the Soviet bloc. The side which shows greater caution and flexibility in reacting to the new situation is the one most likely ultimately to profit from it.

Index

CSCE (Conference on Security and
Cooperation in Europe), 3, 163,
211–212, 214–215
CSI (Conferencia Socialista Iberica), 91
Calamandrei (Italian senator), 150
Cambodia, 4
Canary Islands, 161–162
Carlos Comin, Alfonso, 88
Carrillo, Santiago, 9, 84, 96–98, 99,
103–104, 171, 186, 204, 205, 209,
210, 221–231 *passim,* 237
Cartels, 109–117 *passim*
Carter administration, 249
Castellano, Pablo, 89, 105
Catholic Action (Spain), 85
Catholic People's party (PPI), 23
Center for Economic Studies (CESPE),
116
Center for Socialist Study and Research
(CERES), 10, 59–60, 130–131, 156
Centrist governments, 52, 67, 68, 144,
156
Centro de Investigaciones Sociológicas,
100
Ceutra, Morocco, 161
"Charter 77," 205, 230–231
Chevénement, Jean-P., 120, 130–131
Chile, 210, 213
China, 4, 206, 209, 216, 225, 231,
232–233, 236, 242
Chirac, Jacques, 68, 217
Christian Democratic Union/Christian
Socialist Union alliance, 4–5
Citroën, 128
Coal mining, 115
Coalición Cemocrática, 101
Colombo, E., 38
Cominform (Communist Information
Bureau), 19, 27, 167, 170
Comintern, 167, 207, 211
Comisiones Obreras, 85–86, 84, 95–96,
98–99, 100
Common Market. *See* European
Economic Community
Communist Information Bureau
(Cominform), 19, 27, 167, 170
Communist International, 50, 51

Compensation agreements, 119, 120
Concorde, 118, 128
Confederation of Socialist Parties of the
EC, 167, 176
Conference of European Communist
and Workers Parties (East Berlin,
1976), 10, 63, 208, 214–221 *passim*
Conference on Security and
Cooperation in Europe, 3, 163,
211–212, 214–215
Conscription, 159
Consensus principle, 214–215, 217
Convergencia Socialista de Madrid, 91
Copenhagen Declaration (1978), 195
Council for Mutual Economic Aid, 120,
189, 190
Craxi, Bettino, 35, 36, 37, 194, 197, 203
Creusot, 128
Cuba, 186, 249
Czechoslovakia, 170, 222, 223;
dissidents, 29, 205, 230–231; Soviet
invasion, 3, 6, 19, 28, 29–30, 63, 97,
171, 208, 212, 224

DC. *See* Italian Christian Democratic
party
DP (Democrazía Proletaria), 28
Dankert (Dutch socialist), 153
De Gasperi, Alcide, 18, 19, 20, 147
De Gaulle, Charles, 7, 52, 55, 57–58, 60,
64, 143, 145, 155, 156, 158, 217
De Martino, Francesco, 35
Delors, Jacques, 121
Democracy: centralism vs. pluralism,
178, 207–211, 242, 243; economic vs.
political, 169, 179–180
Democracy by alternation, 23
Democratic Socialist party (PSDI,
Italy), 20, 25, 32, 33, 34, 39
Democratic Socialists: and EC,
167–198 *passim;* and Eastern
Europe, 189–190, 193; economic
policy, 183–184; and NATO,
187–188; and PCI, 186–187; and
political democracy, 179–180; and
US, 187
Democrazía Proletaria, 28

About the Contributors

Wolfgang Berner is a senior member of the Bundesinstitut für ostwissenschaftliche und internationale Studien, Cologne. He is the editor of the institute's yearly handbook on Soviet affairs and the author of numerous articles.

Richard Löwenthal is emeritus professor of political science of the Berlin Free University. Among his many books and articles is *Model or Ally? The Communist Powers and the Developing Countries* (New York: Oxford University Press, 1976).

Eusebio Mujal-León received the Ph.D. in political science from the Massachusetts Institute of Technology and is assistant professor of political science at Georgetown University. He has published several articles on the Spanish and Portuguese Communist parties.

Giuseppe Sacco is professor of economics at the University of Florence, senior research associate of the Istituto Affari Internazionale, Rome, and formerly was associated with the OECD.

Stefano Silvestri is senior research associate of the Istituto Affari Internazionale, Rome. He is the author of numerous articles on defense and Italian affairs.

Ronald Tiersky is assistant professor of political science at Amherst College. His most recent book is *French Communism, 1920–1972* (New York: Columbia Univ. Press, 1974).

Heinz Timmermann is a research associate of the Bundesinstitut für ostwissenschaftliche und internationale Studien, Cologne. He is the editor of *Eurokommunismus: Fakten, Analysen, Interviews* and the author of numerous articles.

Joan Barth Urban is associate professor of politics at the Catholic University of America. She is the author of several articles on the relations between the Soviet Union and the West European Communist parties.

About the Editor

William E. Griffith is Ford Professor of Political Science at the Massachusetts Institute of Technology and adjunct professor of diplomatic history at The Fletcher School of Law and Diplomacy, Tufts University. His most recent book is *The Ostpolitik of the Federal Republic of Germany* (Cambridge, Mass.: The MIT Press, 1978).